The Unrecognised Peril:
Threats to Environmental Security

The Unrecognised Peril:
Threats to Environmental Security

Editor

S. Utham Kumar Jamadhagni

Associate Professor
Dept of Defence and Strategic Studies
University of Madras
Chennai (India)

Vij Books India Pvt Ltd

New Delhi (India)

Published by

Vij Books India Pvt Ltd
(Publishers, Distributors & Importers)
2/19, Ansari Road
Delhi – 110 002
Phones: 91-11-43596460, 91-11-47340674
Fax: 91-11-47340674
e-mail: vijbooks@rediffmail.com
we b: www.vijbooks.com

Contents

Preface

The traditional and non-traditional security issues of the region of South Asia are of continuing research interest. However, the current scenario of burgeoning population, the mandrake of terrorism and religious fundamentalism and widespread environmental damage, draws the problem of non-traditional security to the forefront. The security paradigm no longer revolves around the military understanding of security. Its scope has expanded to necessarily include other areas such as human security, environmental security, economic security, food security, societal security and also maritime security.

The region of South Asia poses many challenges not restricted to housing the world's poorest, experiencing fast paced economic growth while simultaneously pushing many more under the poverty line. The acute need for more and more resources to meet the bare necessities of life, has led to severe pressure on the environment. Over exploitation of natural sources of existence and anthropogenic intervention in nature's normal cycles has resulted in large-scale pollution. This not only affects humans themselves, but also permanently scars the environment. The irreparable damage is now snowballing into worrisome conditions of climate change and global warming. Political systems are undergoing constant flux in this region compounded with societal upheaval due to drastic changes in economic and political status of various groups. All these changes warrant examination.

This book is an attempt to define the contours of South Asia using the lines of non-traditional security. Each of the above mentioned security areas would be dealt with chapter wise. In the early chapters the book provides a brief introduction of the concept of security, the primacy of human security in today's world, and the place of environmental security in the human security rubric. The twin problems of effect of war on environment and climate change have been dealt with elaborately in three chapters of the book. Next the book highlights the major environmental challenges that South Asia as a region faces with specific problems associated with each country. Moving on to focus on India the rest of the chapters deal both with the bigger picture and particular issues that pose serious challenges to environmental security in India. This includes the threat to marine biodiversity through pollution and other threats; fishing and its effects; internal water security; energy security and even nuclear threat.

My thanks are due to my wife CS Anuradha who has helped with the editing. I am grateful for the constant encouragement of my colleagues Prof. Gopalji Malviya and Dr. A Thennarasu at the Department of Defence and Strategic Studies, University of Madras, without which this book could not have seen the light of day.

- S Utham Kumar Jamadhagni

Contributors

1. Yagama Reddy is a former Director of Centre for Southeast Asian and Pacific Studies, Sri Venkateshwara University, Tirupati. He is a geographer and an environmental studies scholar. He has written many books and contributed a number of articles in leading journals in his area of expertise.

2. Adluri Subrahmanyam Raju is Associate Professor at the Madanjeet Singh Centre for South Asian Studies, Pondicherry University. He has many books to his credit.

3. Col P.K.Gautam (Retd) is an Institute for Defence Studies and Analysis (IDSA) Research Fellow. His main area of research interest is Environmental security. He has held the DRDO, D.S.Kothari Chair on Environment Security at the USI of India from 2002-2003.

4. Ajay Lele is an Institute for Defence Studies and Analysis (IDSA) Research Fellow. His areas of expertise include Weapons of Mass Destructions with major emphasis on Biological Weapons, Space and National Security and Non Military Threats.

5. Sudhir K. Singh is Assistant Professor, Department of Political Science, Dayal Singh College, New Delhi. He has edited many books and regularly conducts topical seminars on a variety of subjects.

6. Lalitha Ramadurai is Program Officer at Parampara an NGO in Chennai and is researching for her doctoral degree in environmental science.

7. R.Sudhakar is Assistant Professor, Department of National Security Studies, Central University of Jammu.

8. Mathew George is Deputy Director, Project on Human Security, Centre for South Asian Studies, Pondicherry University.

9. Ramakrishnan Ramani is a Freelance Researcher of Security Studies.

10. O. Nirmala is a UGC Senior Research Fellow at the Department of Defence and Strategic Studies, University of Madras.

11. Udhaya Kumar is Project Fellow in a UGC Major Research Project at the Department of Defence and Strategic Studies, University of Madras.

12. C.S.Anuradha is a former faculty member, Department of Politics and International Studies, Pondicherry University and a Fulbright scholar. Currently, she is an independent researcher based in Chennai.

I

Introduction

Conceptual Understanding of the Security Paradigm

The security paradigm has moved from the traditional understanding of the state remaining the principle unit of enquiry and its military capabilities shaping its survival to wider connotation. The fall of the Soviet Union and with it, the loss of a well-defined enemy; the resurgence of East European nationalism, which highlighted the importance of domestic factors to security and the opposite trend of pan-state processes, such as globalization, revealed the poverty of traditional security in its inability not in the multiplicity of threats, but the "inadequacy" of its "responses to such threats"[1]. However, this has changed recently and the meaning of security has now widened to include economic, environment and societal dimensions in addition to the military aspect. The referent object of security has shifted from the state to individuals[2].

Richard Ullman in a 1983 paper titled 'Redefining Security'[3] argued that military security 'conveys a profoundly false image of reality... it causes states to concentrate on military threats and to ignore other, and perhaps, even more harmful dangers. Thus, it reduces their total security. Second, it contributes to a pervasive militarisation of international relations that in the long run can only increase global insecurity.'[4] Such work emphasised the need to recast security in a different light so as to involve issues such

---

1   Bill McSweeney, *Security, identity and Interests: A sociology of International relations* (Cambridge University Press), p.4

2   For a discussion of referent objects of security see Karin Fierke, *Critical Approaches to International Security*, Polity press, Cambridge UK, 2007 pp 44-46.

3   Richard Ullman, 'Redefining Security', *International Security*, Vol.8, No.1 (1983) pp.129-53.

4   Ibid., p.129.

as population growth and resource scarcity. Joseph Nye and Sean Lynn-Jones, reporting on a conference on the future of security studies held at Harvard in 1987, pointed to the weaknesses of traditional security studies.[5] However, the landmark scholarship in this regard made by Barry Buzan and the 'Copenhagen school' widened the security agenda to add political, economic and societal security sectors to the existing military "sense" of security. Buzan's work *People, State and Fear* has been hailed as the most comprehensive theoretical analysis of the concept of security in international relations literature. While revisions, objections and debates have carried on with regard to the 'Copenhagen School'[6] it is to be acknowledged that the work has been nothing short of innovativeness. This expanded agenda for security is what is termed non-traditional security.

Subsequently, another term known as "securitisation"[7] which refers to a two-stage process of making an issue as a security issue has been introduced. Here the state has to articulate the issue as an existential threat. However, it also requires a population that accepts the state's interpretation of events and recognises that extraordinary measures must be implemented. Thus, the redefinition of 'security' is not just a discursive act, but carries political import that can simply be perceived as the state's idea to increase its power vis-à-vis its people. At present, security concerns a holistic evaluation of the subject in question and has come to be referred to as 'comprehensive security'.[8]

Non-Traditional Security

There needs to be an understanding of the meaning of "non-traditional security" to identify issues that rise to the level of security concern. For this we must first comprehend what is security. In defining what constitutes "security", five sets of questions need to be asked. First, what values are being threatened? Second, what is threatening those values? Third, what

5 Joseph Nye and Sean Lynn-Jones, 'International Security Studies: A Report of a Conference on the State of the Field', *International Security*, Vol.12, No.4 (1988), pp.5-27.

6 For a detailed account of the various objections and counter claims see, Smith, Steve 'The increasing insecurity of security studies: Conceptualizing security in the last twenty years', *Contemporary Security Policy*, Vol.20 No.3 (1999), pp.83-87

7 Ibid., pp.85

8 Kurt Radke and Raymond Feddema eds., *Comprehensive Security in Asia*, Brill Academic Publishers, 2000 discusses the concept from a regional point of view.

means are available to counter the threat? Fourth, who is expected to provide protection or security against the threat? Fifth, and finally, who will pay the cost of the protection/security? Issues become "securitised" when a threat exists or is believed to exist against some fundamental values that are held by some actor, be it an individual, a group, a community, a nation, a group of nations, or an international community. Those fundamental values vary depending on the subject. From the perspective of national security policy makers, the national sovereignty, territorial integrity and political independence of a state are the fundamental values they are charged to protect and threats to those values are viewed as threats to national security. These threats may emanate from within the society, for example, an open challenge to the legitimacy of the government in power, or a civil strife, a civil war, or other developments that threaten the society the policy makers are expected to provide. Inability to meet such challenges itself may be seen as a national security threat; therefore, a weak state is deemed inadequate in meeting the challenges of national security. Challenges to national security are mostly seen as emanating from outside the national society. Of particular concern are the challenges posed by the use of force or threat of the use of force by another state against the sovereignty, territorial integrity, and political independence of a state. This is the traditional view of national security, as most elaborately developed within the realist approach to international relations.

Thus, the realist focuses primarily on military threats against the state from external sources. Though domestic developments may be sufficiently threatening to the viability or stability of the state, the realist is concerned with external threats alone. The realist also tends to emphasise military response, or non-military coercive countermeasures, for example political and economic sanctions, against the sources of such threats.

In contrast, the liberal's security concerns move beyond the realist construct of external threats and looks at other types of values and threats as well. The principal values that attract the liberal include human rights, individual and communal identity, individuals' spiritual growth, the material well-being of individuals and communities, social and cultural viability of ethnic and national groups, individual and public health, environmental protection and sustainable development.

The realist–liberal dichotomy is not the only differentiation between traditional and non-traditional security. One may employ some time frame to distinguish between "traditional" and "non-traditional" security concerns. A society may consider as "traditional" those issues that have existed for some time and around which it has formed certain views and expectations. "Non-traditional" security issues emerge when some members of the society view more recent concerns as threatening their fundamental values. Other members of the society may not share the same degree of concern over those issues, or may in fact oppose elevating those issues to the level of security.

The traditional versus non-traditional differentiation in terms of the realist versus liberal views of international relations helps us avoid the problem of inconsistent time frames used in different societies in defining security problems. It helps to highlight another important aspect of the security discourse. The issue has to do with the respective roles of the state and society in providing for the security of its citizens. A closely related issue has to do with the values that need to be protected from variously viewed threats. Of particular relevance here is the distinction between national security and human security.

The Dimensions of Security

In the wake of the measured success in the climate change talks of 2011 to work towards a legal framework to address the issue of carbon emissions that would be "applicable to all countries"[9] including major emitters, effect of environment on overall security needs to be looked at with renewed interest. The Post Cold War world saw the expansion of the concept of security beyond the confines of traditional security. Security as a concept has preceded the formation of states and is a primordial condition. As territorial possession became a prime determinant of political life, security or saving or securing what one possesses has been paramount. While traditionally the effective monopoly on the use or licensing of violence within a territory lay with the state and the change to this condition through external invasion or internal rebellion affected national security, the post Second World War world has seen more threats emanating from within the states than external. The concept of security has now moved from this

---

9   Delegates at climate talks agree to extend efforts of Kyoto Protocol, *CNN*, December 11, 2011 http://edition.cnn.com/2011/12/11/world/south-africa-climate-pact/index.html

narrow confine and has yet to attain a consensus. The altered paradigm has found little agreement as much of scholarly literature on the subject clearly highlights the ambiguity (Arnold Wolfers)[10], narrowness (Buzan)[11], inadequacy (Hugh Mcdonald)[12], deficiency (Ken Booth)[13] and dilemmas (Mohammed Ayoob)[14], inherent in the understanding of national security.

Arnold Wolfers talks of security only as "an ambiguous symbol" that "may not have a precise meaning at all"[15]. Though he introduced the many dimensional complexities of the concept, his interpretation of security as a militarised element is criticised as being extremely narrow and hollow. Arguing that there is an intrinsic link between individual, national and international security, Buzan calls for a holistic perspective that brings out this bondage. According to him, national security per se is a narrow concept that invites serious distortions of perspective. Buzan, for example, believes that instead of viewing security as a derivative of power it has to be elevated to the rank on par with power and peace. When we confront difficulties in understanding the concept of security, how do we go about defining what national security is? As Buzan puts it the national security problem could be approached through the concepts of security, power and peace[16]. For realists who believe in security and power it is traditional security that is important. For liberals, it is peace and cooperation.

Stephen Walt defines security as "the study of the threat, use and control of military force"[17]. Mohammed Ayoob provides an interesting definition,

---

10 Arnold Wolfers, 'National Security as an Ambiguous Symbol' in *Discord and Collaboration* (Baltimore, Johns Hopkins University Press, 1962) pp 147-166.

11 Barry Buzan, 'People, States and Fear', (New Delhi, Transasia Publications, 1987), p 3-4 .

12 Hugh Macdonald, 'The Place of Strategy and the Idea of Security', *Millennium*, 10:3(1981) pp 229-239

13 Ken Booth, *Strategy and Ethnocentrism* (London, Croom Helm, 1979) pp191.

14 Mohammed Ayoob, 'Defining Security: A Subaltern Realist Perspective' in Navnita Chadha Behera edited *State, People and Security – The South Asian Context* (New Delhi, Har-Anand Publications Pvt Ltd, 2002, p.67.

15 Arnold Wolfers, "National Security as an Ambiguous Symbol," in *Discord and Collaboration*, ed. Arnold Wolfers, 147–165 (Baltimore: Johns Hopkins Press, 1964)

16 Buzan, Barry, *Peoples, States and Fears: An Agenda for International Security Studies in the Post-Cold War Era*, 2nd edition. (Boulder CO, Lynne Rienner Publishers, 1991)

17 Stephen M. Walt, 'The Renaissance of Security Studies', *International Security Studies Quarterly*, Vol.35, no.2, 1991, pp.211-39.

"Security or insecurity is defined in relation to vulnerabilities, both internal and external, those threaten to, or have the potential to, bring down or significantly weaken state structures, both territorial and institutional, and regimes"[18]. Ken Booth's definition of security as a destination through the root of emancipation lacks the methodological rigour. "Emancipation means freeing people from those constraints that stop them carrying out what freely they would choose to do, of which war, poverty, oppression, and poor education are a few. Security and emancipation are in fact two sides of the same coin. It is emancipation, not power and order, in both theory and practice that leads to stable security"[19].

The nature of war itself has undergone a change and low intensity wars and internal strife occupy centre stage. Also the very concept of security has undergone a rethink. Now the emphasis is more on the safety of the individual and the concept of 'human security' has come into vogue. However from the policy point of view this expansive goal is unwieldy. Thus many authors have expressed concern over the effort at making a definition of security "all-inclusive" as it would lose its utility "as an analytical tool"[20]. Though traditional understanding of national security needs revision this should address only the means by which security is achieved and not its end of protection of the local monopoly of violence.

The need for shifting of focus of national security from military matters is imminent. However, the extent to which such change can move is a contested field. Over expansion of the term would make it impractical because it would only create an additional term for traditional security, which no longer holds sway. Any attempt to retain status quo or not widen the term of reference at all, will bring up the danger of marginalising security studies especially in times when traditional security issues are seen to be losing salience.

National Security - Then and Now

In its traditional meaning national security was aimed at defending territorial integrity and ensuring state survival. Thus, protecting borders,

18 Mohammed Ayoob, *The Third World Security Predicament: State Making, Regional Conflict and the International system*, (Boulder, Lynne Reinner Publishers, 1995), p.5.

19 Ken Booth, 'Security and Emancipation', *Review of International Studies*, Tokyo, no.17, pp.316-26.

20 Mohammed Ayoob, "The Security Problematic of the Third World," *World Politics* 43:2 (Jan. 1991), p. 259

fighting wars and deterring aggressors – purely military functions – were the approaches to defending a nation's security. The fall of the Soviet empire not only signified the end of cold war but also redrew the contours of securing and security. No longer were a few hundred nuclear weapons or other mass destruction machinery enough to ensure the safety or welfare of a nation. Rather, they highlighted the various facets of national life that need to be closely looked at in order to provide a holistic view of security.

With the end of the Cold War the polarization of security issues towards ideological conflict or geopolitical interests of the superpowers changed. The threats from these quarters were replaced by civil unrest, internal conflict, localised wars and other people- related issues. In the absence of a stabilizing force or intervening one, security issues became more complex. Thus internal security rather than external threats determined national security. Secondly, in an era of globalisation and interdependence, events occurring abroad affected a nation in hitherto unknown ways and military might was incapable of stemming this effect. In essence, concepts that make a state and its relation with its entities and other international constituents have undergone enormous changes.

A nation's security now depends not only on the threat it faces from the military point of view but other challenges that if left unchecked might affect the very essence of the nation and its people. Even in a purely strategic sense the nature of threat has transformed. No longer is the enemy known. Contrast this with the earlier case wherein another country's armed forces were clearly the military source of threat. The spectre of terrorism has obliterated the identity of the 'enemy'.

Also, the threats are not confined to geographical boundaries and cross-border and transnational problems are the order of the day. They emanate from non-state actors such as insurgents and terrorists, trans-national criminals, narcotics smugglers, counterfeiters, etc. These having increased, there is now a realisation that techniques and tradecraft, which served us fairly adequately against predictable state adversaries, may not be adequate against often unpredictable non-state actors, and that new analytical tools are required to meet the new threats. The old concept of threat analysis has been supplemented by risk analysis and vulnerability analysis. Lucid analysis – whether of threats, risks or vulnerabilities – is the starting point of effective national security policy-making, implementation and co-ordination.

Not only threats but also the nature of responses to threats have transformed. Overwhelming military power has proved ineffective even in dealing with low intensity conflicts. Diplomacy and other tactics are often resorted to. Interdependence characterises economic and more often security activities. The nature of threats warrants cooperation among nations in the case of surveillance, information gathering and actual execution. Joint operations are enriched by earlier individual experiences and bring to bear reinforcement and greater resources to curb non-conventional threats.

The issue

While the non-traditional matters have overshadowed the traditional component of national security, it has yet to lose its relevance. The various developments in the fields of strategic affairs like Revolution in Military Affairs (RMA) in the form of combat method and machinery; the changing concepts of war that have moved war from battle theatres to cities and towns; the dominance of limited war – circumscribed in time, space or objective; the theory of deterrence; the threat of WMDs and finally the menace of terrorism that has achieved sophisticated patterns of operation while using relatively simple ammunition indicate that force is still relevant in a nation's security agenda.

Non-traditional/comprehensive

The recently added non traditional aspects of security be it political, economic, environmental (national and international), energy, securitisation of disease HIV/AIDS, health security/food security, governance/civil society shifted the protagonist from nation states to individuals inhabiting this earth. However several contradictions in the roles, actions and effects of one upon the other have made their inclusion anything but smooth. Also, the Westphalian concept of national security as meaning the security of a nation would not fit the needs of a nation of nations like India. Thus the questions of who and what are being secured becomes whose nation needs to be secured? Multiethnic and cultural societies and their security warrant a relook at the ontological bases of security studies.

To the poser of how it is to be secured? The answer now seems to be cooperation not confrontation can achieve security. The new age concepts of CS4 as I call them collective, common, comprehensive and cooperative security all sprang from the above. Inclusion of all the above mentioned, defeats the purpose of the concept as an analytical tool. It might end with identifying all problems as aspects of national security.

One of the first ideas that came to be discussed was comprehensive security. Then, security aspects were divided into traditional and non traditional where the conventional military based hard core meaning was infused into the traditional garb and the others clubbed as non traditional. However the problem with this understanding was that it opened the flood gates so to say. Now all aspects of human life that were considered worthy were encompassed in this framework. Nothing remained out of the purview of security. If this is the case, then security would become an all-embracing, all-inclusive idea that presents itself unwieldy to rigorous analysis and theorization.

The nature of war itself has undergone a change and low intensity wars and internal strife occupy centre stage. Also the very concept of security has undergone a rethink. Now the emphasis is more on the safety of the individual and the concept of 'human security' has come into vogue. However from the policy point of view this expansive goal is unwieldy. Thus many authors have expressed concern over the effort at making a definition of security "all-inclusive" as it would lose its utility "as an analytical tool". Though traditional understanding of national security needs revision this should address only the means by which security is achieved and not its end of protection of the local monopoly of violence.

In its traditional meaning national security was aimed at defending territorial integrity and ensuring state survival. Thus protecting borders, fighting wars and deterring aggressors – purely military functions – were the approaches to defending a nation's security. With the end of cold war the polarization of security issues towards ideological conflict or geopolitical interests of the superpowers changed. The threats from these quarters were replaced by civil unrest, internal conflict, localised wars and other people- related issues. In the absence of a stabilizing force or intervening one, security issues became more complex. Thus internal security rather than external threats determined national security[21]. Secondly, in an era of globalisation and interdependence, events occurring abroad affected

---

21 Evans, Gareth 1994. Cooperative Security and Intra-State Conflict, *Foreign Policy*, No. 96 (Fall), p.3.

a nation in hitherto unknown ways and military might was incapable of stemming this effect. In essence, concepts that make a state and its relation with its entities and other international constituents have undergone enormous changes[22]. A nation's security now depends not only on the threat it faces from the military point of view but other challenges that if left unchecked might affect the very essence of the nation and its people. Even in a purely strategic sense the nature of threat has transformed. No longer is the enemy known. Contrast this with the earlier case wherein another country's armed forces were clearly the military source of threat. The spectre of terrorism has obliterated the identity of the 'enemy'.

Human Security

Most understandings of human security trace it to the 1994 Human Development Report of the United Nations Development Program (UNDP). "The concept of security", the report argues has for too long been interpreted narrowly: as security of territory from external aggression, or as protection of national interests in foreign policy or as global security threat of nuclear holocaust. Forgotten were the legitimate concerns of ordinary people who sought security in their daily lives."[23]

Security cannot just assume the state centric connotation but also include the assurance of basic human well being as defined by access to basic amenities and a dignity of life that is bereft of want, violence and fear. Despite the possession of enormous military capability states are constrained in many cases to use that force, to restore order or bring peace and ensure safety of its citizens.

Threats to the security of the individual and group even in a circumscribed physical sense arise from ethnic, religious, cultural and other differences that are simply not confined to geographical borders. Since threats are not local, the panacea to these threats namely the use of power and force also cannot be local or state bound. Hence the meaning of security has been widened.

---

22 Goran Hyden, Livelihoods And Security In Africa: Contending Perspectives In The New Global Order, *African Studies Quarterly* Vol1, Issue 1, 1997 gives a comprehensive understanding of the stand of various schools on the security concept. http://www.africa.ufl.edu/asq/v1/1/1.htm

23 UNDP Report as cited in Roland Paris, 'Human Security: Paradigm Shift or Hot Air?', *International Security,* 26, 2 (Fall 2001), p. 89

While the different interpretations of human security are not necessarily incompatible, they do create ground for controversy and suspicion. Reconciling the different meanings of, and approaches to, human security is thus crucial to any meaningful effort to integrate the concept as a national security component. Human security is a concept that focuses on the strengthening of human-centered efforts from the perspective of protecting the lives, livelihoods, and dignity of individual human beings and realizing the abundant potential inherent in each individual.

The eternal debate of the state versus the individual characterises the political dimension of security. While the relation between the state and its principal constituent – the individual has varied through history from discord in Hitler's Germany to harmony in a welfare state; the type of state structure has been a vital determinant of the nature of this relation. Not only strong but also weak states pose a problem. With no control or legitimacy of authority or power there is a perpetual struggle over the control of state apparatus and the tendency to secede. Interestingly this has come to assume the most common form of violent conflict the world over. The constant testing of democracy as the ideal political tool for organizing societies has had differing degrees of success.

Environmental Security

The threat that environment can affect the security of a nation or many nations, is gaining currency. It is fuelled by the fear that not only catastrophic, cataclysmic events but also regular global processes can seriously endanger the health, productivity and well-being of the entire planet. While stretching environmental problems to form a component of national security is termed far-fetched by many, it is to be acknowledged that resource exploitation; demand and the rates of depletion can give rise to conflicts[24]. The reverse could also occur in that conflict in the form of war resulting in large-scale destruction of natural resources triggering a vicious cycle of retribution and revenge.

India on the threshold of higher growth and development needs to examine its progress in all these fields. More than half of India's forests have been depleted. The Himalayan glaciers are melting and this would mean

---

24 A well-researched field of study is the conflict over water. Vandana Siva's *Water wars: Privatization, Pollution and Profit,* (Cambridge, South End Press, 2002) pp176 provides an interesting angle to the issue.

flooding of the plains[25]. On the other hand water scarcity is leading to the expansion of the Thar Desert. Pollution and other anthropogenic factors are deeply affecting the natural resources and their availability for posterity. Rapid urbanization, unplanned expansion of human settlement and the exploding population soon to make India the most populous country in the world have pitted man against beast in competition for food and land. Illegal hunting and poaching activities have led to dwindling of a number of rare species pushing many towards extinction and seriously affecting the environment. Over exploitation of precious commodity like water has driven rural-urban migration, water scarcity and is also leading to conflict situations within and across borders. Destructive natural phenomena like tsunami, floods, cyclones and hurricanes have wreaked havoc costing life and property.

Interfering in the natural cycles by the introduction of synthetic and harmful materials like chemicals and waste has permanently damaged natural resources like rivers, oceans and other water bodies and even cultivable land. The direct dumping of untreated waste into water bodies results in contamination; the spread of diseases and epidemics, thus risking vast populations. These can eventually trigger unrest. Unsustainable development activities like the building of huge dams and other infrastructure displaces millions, renders prime forest land unusable and adds to the cost of development. Global climate change effects such as rise in temperatures and sea levels could affect crop yields, disrupting the supply chain and causing major distress.

The mutual dependence of the people of the world on a single common planetary biosphere means that the environmental decline of one country or region is a problem for the entire community of nations. Thus it can be seen that "a growing number of people are now being vulnerable to trans-boundary environmental degradation".[26] The problem has attained global proportions due to the continuous, deep and mostly harmful interaction of man with nature. The effect is more pronounced for countries that have weak administrations, skewed resource distribution and widespread poverty. Scarcity of resources, damage to soil fertility

---

25 Chen Zhiyong Himalayan glaciers 'melting fast' *China Daily*, 24 March 2005, http://www.chinadaily.com.cn/english/doc/2005-03/24/content_427609.htm

26 Ashok Swain, Environmental Migration and Conflict Dynamics : Focus on developing regions, *Third world quarterly* Vol. 17, no.5, 1996, pp.959-973.

directly affecting crop protection, over exploitation of available meagre resources leading to pollution, destruction of resources are the principal concerns of environmental degradation. The possibility of social unrest that could result in conflict situations both within a country and among countries causes its link to national security as a concept. The fear is that environmental degradation can vitiate an already fragile balance that is being tested by economic and demographic pressures.

Defining Environmental Security

The recently added non traditional aspects of security be it political, economic, environmental (national and international), energy, securitisation of disease HIV/AIDS, health security/food security, governance/civil society shifted the protagonist from nation states to individuals inhabiting this earth. However several contradictions in the roles, actions and effects of one upon the other have made their inclusion anything but smooth[27]. In the case of environment security, individuals, states and the entire international community are all factors and hence the linkages have to be examined in depth and understood before remedial measures are designed.

Lothar Brock defines environmental security as the avoidance of negative linkages between the environment and human activities. For him, this includes the avoidance of warfare, war over natural resources and also environmental degradation, which he defines as a form of war.[28] Environmental security gains importance from the fact that environmental causes not only fuel conflicts but in many cases could be the principal reason behind it. In other words, they can act as multipliers that aggravate core causes of conflict or act as a catalytic in creating conflict.[29] Degradation or the significant decline in the quantity and quality of available resources is mainly occurring due to human intervention. The actual natural process of renewing resources is a slow and balanced one. Anthropogenic interaction has hampered this process leading to scarcity and is feared to head towards

---

27 Philippe Bourbeau discusses one issue namely migration in his Migration and Security: Securitization theory and its refinement, http://www.iir.ubc.ca/isac2006/Bourbeau%20 ISA%202006%20Paper.pdf

28 Narottam Gaan, Sudhansubala Das, *Recrudescence of Violence in Indian North-East States: Roots in Environmental Scarcity, Induced Migration from Bangladesh*, Gyan publishing house 2004, p.120

29 Ibid., p.4

complete and irreversible destruction of some of the most precious resources known to man. Another factor that aggravates the degradation issue is the population growth. We are now 6 billion-strong worldwide and the already shrinking resource pie now needs to be sliced thinner for every person. The complication here is that the resource is unequally distributed. With the available meagre resources getting concentrated in the hands of a few, the problem of scarcity for the deprived is accentuated.

Unequal resource access and population growth could "cause migrations to regions that are ecologically fragile."[30] Termed 'ecological marginalization' this process puts enormous burden on the depleted land areas, increasing the hardships of an impoverished people. In due course this could pave way for rebellion and even conflict. The movement of population to escape the effects of environmental change or disaster is now on the rise and one UN estimate even indicates that by 2050, 150 million people may be displaced due to climate-related events[31]. Such sudden and unregulated shift in population could destabilise the state internally, aggravate trans-border conflicts and create tension between the migrant and settled groups. Historically there are examples of drastic climatic changes causing conflicts and even resulting in the rise or fall of civilizations. Cold temperatures drove the Huns to the Roman Empire and climate change could have ended the Chinese Tang Dynasty as well as the Mayan civilization. Similar climatic changes could trigger widespread unrest and destabilization. Thus, climate change should figure in worst-case scenario-building just as terrorism, infectious disease and conventional challenges to military security have already made to the contingency planning drawing board.[32]

The problem for developing economies like India is that while on the one hand they have to pursue the path of development rigorously, the environmental concerns cannot be ignored on the other. The choice is further complicated for democracies that have an active civil society and

---

30 For a detailed analysis see, Thomas Homer-Dixon, Environmental Scarcities and Violent Conflict: Evidence from cases, *International Security*, Vol. 19, No. I (Summer 1994), pp. 5-40

31 Climate Change and Displacement: Identifying Gaps and Responses Expert Roundtable, Bellagio Conference Centre, 22-26 February 2011, http://www.unhcr.org/4d1c92bb9.pdf

32 Alan Dupont, The Strategic Implications of Climate Change, *Survival*,Vol.50, No.3, p.44 http://faculty.maxwell.syr.edu/rdenever/USNatSecandForeignPol/Dupont,%20Strategic%20Implication%20of%20Climate%20Change.pdf

an independent judiciary where every developmental and infrastructural project comes under public scrutiny and might have to face severe criticism and pressures to abandon or modify plans of 'developing' specific areas or propose new schemes for improving the general living standards of a country.

Chapterisation

In these the succeeding chapters elaborate on one facet of non-traditional security namely, environmental security, while the final chapter attempts to emphasise the need to employ the best methods to address the issues dealt with in the book. The book aims to deal with the specific issue of environmental degradation through over use and exploitation of land, water and other resources in the region of South Asia in a broader manner and dwell on India's concerns in particular. The **third** chapter outlines the concept of human security and how vital environmental security is to this. The chapter also emphasises the need to examine the human dimension of environmental security. It highlights the role India can play as a leader in recognizing and forging partnerships to address environmental security issues that would come to affect the entire world. Unilateral efforts of countries can only yield short-term gains. However, the cooperative approach alone can put efforts in a proper perspective. The **fourth** chapter lays down the broad outline of the problems relating to environmental security that affect South Asia in general and India in particular. Among the most important issues that dog the under developed and over populated South Asian region is that of environmental security. With "security" assuming a wider paradigm, the state of the environment and the effect of depletion, degradation and destruction over its various components like air, water, land would give a fair idea of the current situation and future needs. Explaining briefly about the various concerns in the region namely, land degradation, water scarcity, air pollution, urbanization, marine ecological destruction, deforestation and loss of biodiversity, the chapter makes a case for increased cooperation among stakeholders including other countries in tandem with state attempts to deal with environmental security.

The **fifth** chapter seeks underline the threat to national security due to environmental degradation. The author traces the theoretical evolution connecting environment to security and more importantly highlights the problems of the declining quality of land, water and air due to overuse and pollution in India and how these and other issues could directly impact India's national security. The chapter not only discusses the existing problems but future possible challenges like climate change and global warming that could affect the whole of South Asia making India a refugee receiving state which could pose threats to national security.

Taking a deeper look into the subject of climate change and security the **sixth** chapter takes up India as a case study and provides statistical data to support the view that effects of climate change on resource availability, distribution, and overall economic health of India interacting with other factors like poverty, population, health issues and poor governance could lead to political instability, failed states and even wars. Interestingly, the chapter also points out that almost all the states face similar challenges be it in the form of effects due to deforestation, damage to water resources, the problem of demand and supply due to the increase in population and role that poverty plays in accentuating the above said difficulties.

The **seventh** chapter draws insights from current historical research to establish the link of climate change with war in China and some other regions. It highlights that the looming adverse impact of climate change combined with resource scarcities could create a situation where conditions for war may get pronounced in South Asia. However, scientific evidence assures us that it is possible to have policies for peaceful resolution of future conflict situations. It is suggested that regional policies on the Himalayan Ecosystem, international rivers, food security, migration, climate related disasters would facilitate peace and emphasises the need for further historic research on the subject. It argues against the militarization of environmental security.

The **eighth** chapter looks at the role of war affecting our environment. The chapter offers a brief narrative about how over the years various military campaigns have adversely impacted environment and then discusses international efforts undertaken to limit these damages and what could be done in future. Detailing the impact of the various wars around the world from the First World War, Gulf Wars and even the Sri Lankan conflict, the chapter indicates the extent of pollution, ecological destruction, deforestation and loss of biodiversity. It suggests that the issue of environment must form part of war planning.

The **ninth** chapter focuses on the problems of Indian fishermen in the Palk straits and Kutch. Damage to coral reefs the fish factories of the seas and the widespread marine pollution affect the availability of fish. Fishermen all over South Asia cross maritime borders regularly in search of fertile fishing grounds bringing them in confrontation with navies of neighbouring states. The chapter calls for drawing up a common maritime law that could deal with much of these issues. Another area of critical significance is the Tibetan plateau – the site of most of the area's major river systems. The Chinese occupation of this pristine region is not just a political issue but more seriously one of environmental security. This is the topic of the **tenth** chapter.

Pollution of the marine environment poses increased threat to a country as large as India with a vast coastline and concomitant problems to grapple. The increasing urbanization is making the seas the largest waste dump with all untreated waste directly being dumped here. Industries also pollute the marine environment. The **eleventh** chapter highlights how polluting our marine environment is posing a threat to India's security as a whole. Continuing with the focus on water resources the **twelfth** chapter examines the Cauvery river water dispute from the national security angle. It cautions that future water disputes might achieve unprecedented forms emphasizing the need to 'securitise' environment.

The **thirteenth** chapter looks at the environmental degradation of marine ecosystems with particular reference to Gulf of Mannar. The **fourteenth** chapter highlights the danger posed by the movement of nuclear powered submarines and ships in the Indian Ocean and the lack of Indian preparedness for any contingency in this area. The **conclusion** sums up the preceding chapters. The suggestions regarding the status of the environment and its effect on war and vice-versa are enlisted and the chapter also makes a case for the inclusion or even the primacy that needs to be accorded to environmental security in the National Security calculus.

II

Human Security

Utham Kumar Jamadhagni

Meaning

The narrow interpretation of security for long as security of territory from external aggression, or as protection of national interests in foreign policy or as global security from the threat of a nuclear holocaust is now moot. It has been related more to nation-states than to people. The superpowers were locked in an ideological struggle–fighting a cold war all over the world. The developing nations, having won their independence only recently, were sensitive to any real or perceived threats to their fragile national identities. Forgotten were the legitimate concerns of ordinary people who sought security in their daily lives. For many of them, security symbolised protection from the threat of disease, hunger, unemployment, crime, social conflict, political repression and environmental hazards. With the dark shadows of the cold war receding, one can now see that many conflicts are within nations rather than between nations.

The redrawn contours of our understanding of security, widens it to encompass several of areas of concern to the individual and the community. The nature of threats that states face at present, highlight the need for transnational mechanisms. The concepts that help understanding, comprehending and analysing international system are under constant flux due to the changes in the security environment, strategic balance and world order. One such concept that has come to define or least encompass several if not all areas of the international system is **human security**.

For most people, a feeling of insecurity arises more from worries about daily life than from the dread of a cataclysmic world event. Will they and their families have enough to eat? Will they lose their jobs? Will their streets and neighbourhoods be safe from crime? Will they be tortured by a repressive state? Will they become a victim of violence because of their gender? Will their religion or ethnic origin target them for persecution? In the transition period from one epoch to another, it is only natural that existing concepts and paradigms are reviewed and reconsidered.

After the end of the Cold War, a great many suggestions were made for how to amend and widen the concept(s) of security. Upon reviewing and screening them, there is one concept in addition to that of state security that appears relevant and important for the long term: that of **human security**, building on the distinction between the security of states and the security of people. As such, human security has been presented variously as a means of reducing the human costs of violent conflict, as a strategy to enable governments to address basic human needs and offset the inequities of globalization, and as a framework for providing social safety nets to people impoverished and marginalised by sudden and severe economic crises[1]. Championed by Canada and elaborated upon in the bilateral Canadian-Norwegian Lysøen process, this concept is gaining ground in international security discourse[2].

Concept Genesis

Most understandings of human security trace it to the 1994 Human Development Report of the United Nations Development Program (UNDP). "The concept of security", the report argues has for too long been interpreted narrowly: as security of territory from external aggression, or as protection of national interests in foreign policy or as global security threat of nuclear holocaust... Forgotten were the legitimate concerns of ordinary people who sought security in their daily lives."[3] But the origin of the notion is rooted in debates about the meaning of security that predated the end of the Cold War. One important source of human security was the debate over the disarmament-development nexus that took place in various UN forums in response to the Cold War arms race.

---

1   Amitav Acharya, Debating Human Security: East versus West, www.hsph.harvard.edu/hpcr/events/hsworkshop/acharya.pdf

2   Sverre Logaard Human Security: Concept and Operationalization www.hsph.harvard.edu/hpcr/events/workshop/lodgaard.pdf

3   UNDP Report as cited in Roland Paris, 'Human Security: Paradigm Shift or Hot Air?', *International Security,* 26, 2 (Fall 2001), p. 89

An important multilateral meeting that focused on human security was a UN sponsored International Conference on the Relationship between Disarmament and Development, held in July 15-Aug. 2 1986 in Paris. A media preview of the meeting appearing in Toronto's Financial Post described it as "an opportunity to enlarge world understanding that human security demands more resources for development and fewer for arms."[4] Preceding the conference was a three-year study by 27 experts "from every area of the world", headed by Inga Thorsson of Sweden, which concluded: "The world has a choice. It can continue to pursue the arms race, or it can move with deliberate speed toward a more sustainable economic and political order. It cannot do both . . . the arms race and development are in a competitive relationship." [5]

The fact that this was a UN meeting based on a report authored by a world-wide panel and which took up a cause already advocated by the developing countries through forums such as the Non-Aligned Movement is significant in considering the current human security debate. Indeed, the concept of human security was also invoked in a Xinhua News Agency Report of a World Disarmament Conference held in Beijing in June 1988 at which the President of the Conference, Zhou Peiyuan, who was also president of the Chinese People's Association for Peace and Disarmament, "stressed the peaceful utilization of new scientific inventions for mankind, but not for military purposes", and stressed "growing concern from the international community for disarmament, which is connected with world peace and human security."[6]

While the disarmament–development nexus served as one of the bases for the human security concept, the concept was also used in conjunction with developing multilateral capabilities to deal with non-military threats. A 1987 report by a 23-member panel, chaired by former U.S. Attorney-General Elliot Richardson, and including former World Bank president Robert McNamara, former West German Chancellor Helmut Schmidt, former U.S. Secretary of State Cyrus Vance and former Nigerian President Olusegun Obasanjo, proposed a "global watch" council under UN auspices

---

4   Douglas Roche, 'Balance out of kilter in arms/society needs', *The Financial Post* (Toronto), 18 January1986, p.8.

5   ibid.,

6   'Beijing hosts disarmament conference', *The Xinhua General Overseas News Service*, 14 June 1988

[20]

which could serve as "a small political centre for high-level consultations on urgent matters of human security and welfare." According to this report, while the UN Security Council dealt with direct military threats to world order, the global watch council consisting of up to 25 member states could deal with non-military threats, which would include world debt repayments, environmental hazards, natural disasters, disease, drug trafficking, urban growth, refugees and special Third World problems such as capital flight.[7]

The work of several independent commissions, such as the Brandt Commission, the Bruntland Commission and later the Commission on Global Governance, helped shift the focus of security analysis from national and state security to security for the people[8]. This was followed by a growing recognition of non-military threats in global security debates. The UNDP approach to human development represented a synthesis between these earlier representations of human security.

The United Nations lent recognition to this concept by announcing the setting up of a commission on Human Security. The Commission on Human Security (CHS) established in January 2001, co-chaired by former United Nations High Commissioner for Refugees Sadako Ogata and Professor Amartya Sen, Master of Trinity College, Cambridge. Among the 12 key internationally prominent members comprising the Commission was Special Representative of UN Secretary-General for Afghanistan Lakhdar Brahimi. The goals of the Commission are to develop the concept of human security and make recommendations that will serve as a guideline for concrete action to be taken by the international community.[9] By the efforts of countries like Japan, a United nations trust fund has been formed. The Trust Fund for Human Security, a fund established within the UN has grown to become the largest UN trust fund. The Fund assists projects by international institutions that engage in global-scale issues from a human security perspective.

---

7   Gordon Barthos, 'U.N. urged to set up council to deal with crises', *The Toronto Star*, 30 September 1987, p.A28

8   Kanti Bajpai, Human security: Concept and measurement

9   For a detailed run-up and progress of the CHS see www.humansecurity-chs.org/index.html

Current Understanding of Human Security

Security, shedding its military colours has now come to mean the assurance of basic human well being as defined by access to basic amenities and a dignity of life that is bereft of want, violence and fear. States with their limited authority are not in many cases able to use force, by way of coercion or violence to restore order or bring peace and ensure safety of its citizens. Threats to the security of the individual and group arise from ethnic, religious, cultural and other differences that are simply not confined to geographical borders. Since threats are not local, the panacea to these threats namely the use of power and force also cannot be local or state centric. Hence the meaning of security has been widened. By this we mean security of groups and individuals, and not states as earlier, which caters to the freedom from want and freedom from fear.

While the different interpretations of human security are not necessarily incompatible, they do create ground for controversy and suspicion. Reconciling the different meanings of, and approaches to, human security is thus crucial to any meaningful effort to operationalise the concept and make it into a potent instrument of just and secure world. Human security is a concept that focuses on the strengthening of human-centred efforts from the perspective of protecting the lives, livelihoods, and dignity of individual human beings and realizing the abundant potential inherent in each individual. The international community currently faces a range of threats, including terrorism, poverty, environmental degradation, conflict, land mines, refugee problems, drugs, and infectious diseases such as HIV/AIDS. The terrorist attacks of September 11, 2001 reminded the international community that it needs to pay attention to the risk that factors such as conflict and poverty would create hotbeds of terrorism. The international community must make active efforts to remove the various threats that endanger the lives of individuals, as well as to combat terrorism.[10]

Dealing effectively with the growing diversity and complexity of the various threats to the post–Cold War international community will require the cooperation of all actors in that community, including not only governments but also international organizations and civil society

---

10 Main efforts by the international Community http:// www.mofa.go.jp/policy/human_ secu.html

including non-governmental organizations (NGOs), in order to create and sustain a society in which every individual can realise his or her potential.

Human Security Contour

A consideration of the basic concept of human security must focus on four of its essential characteristics:

- Human security is a universal concern. It is relevant to people everywhere, in rich nations and poor. There are many threats that are common to all people–such as unemployment, drugs, crime, pollution and human rights violations. Their intensity may differ from one part of the world to another, but all these threats to human security are real and growing.

- The components of human security are interdependent. When the security of people is endangered anywhere in the world, all nations are likely to get involved. Famine, disease, pollution, drug trafficking, terrorism, ethnic disputes and social disintegration are no longer isolated events, confined within national borders. Their consequences travel the globe.

- Human security is easier to ensure through early prevention than later intervention. It is less costly to meet these threats upstream than downstream. For example, the direct and indirect cost of HIV/AIDS (human immunodeficiency virus/acquired immune deficiency syndrome) was roughly $240 billion during the 1980s. Even a few billion dollars invested in primary health care and family planning education could have helped contain the spread of this deadly disease.

- Human security is people-centred. It is concerned with how people live and breathe in a society, how freely they exercise their many choices, how much access they have to market and social opportunities–and whether they live in conflict or in peace[11].

Defining Human Security

Several analysts have attempted rigorous definitions of human security. But like other fundamental concepts, such as human freedom, human

---

11 New Dimensions of Human Security www.hsph.harvard.edu/hpcr/events/workshop/ new-dimension.pdf

security is more easily identified through its absence than its presence. And most people instinctively understand what security means. Nevertheless, it may be useful to have a more explicit definition. Human security can be said to have two main aspects. It means, first, safety from such chronic threats as hunger, disease and repression. And second, it means protection from sudden and hurtful disruptions in the patterns of daily life–whether in homes, in jobs or in communities. Such threats can exist at all levels of national income and development. The loss of human security can be a slow, silent process–or an abrupt, loud emergency. It can be human-made–due to wrong policy choices. It can stem from the forces of nature. Or it can be a combination of both–as is often the case when environmental degradation leads to a natural disaster, followed by human tragedy.

In defining security, it is important that human security not be equated with Human development. Human development is a broader concept–defined in previous Human Development Reports as a process of widening the range of people's choices. Human security means that people can exercise these choices safely and freely–and that they can be relatively confident that the opportunities they have today are not totally lost tomorrow. There is, of course, a link between human security and human development: progress in one area enhances the chances of progress in the other. But failure in one area also heightens the risk of failure in the other, and history is replete with examples. Failed or limited human development leads to a backlog of human deprivation–poverty, hunger, disease or persisting disparities between ethnic communities or between regions. This backlog in access to power and economic opportunities can lead to violence.

When people perceive threats to their immediate security, they often become less tolerant, as the anti-foreigner feelings and violence in Europe show. Or, where people see the basis of their livelihood erode–such as their access to water–political conflict can ensue, as in parts of Central Asia and the Arab states. Oppression and perceptions of injustice can also lead to violent protest against authoritarianism, as in Myanmar and Zaire, where people despair for drastic change.

Ensuring human security does not mean taking away from people the responsibility and opportunity for mastering their lives. To the contrary, when people are insecure, they become a burden on society. The concept of human security stresses that people should be able to take care of themselves: all people should have the opportunity to meet their most essential needs and to earn their own living. This will set them free and help ensure that they can make a full contribution to development–their own development and that of their communities, their countries and the world. Human security is a critical ingredient of participatory development.

Human security is therefore not a defensive concept–the way territorial or military security is. Instead, human security is an integrative concept. It acknowledges the universalism of life. It is embedded in a notion of solidarity among people. It cannot be brought about through force, with armies standing against armies. It can happen only if we agree that development must involve all people.

Need for Human Security

The Cold War subordinated national and international affairs to the logic of bloc politics. When the dictates of superpower rivalry were removed, the interests of governments and peoples came more clearly to the fore. Complex conflicts came into the open, and intra-state wars were waged with great ferocity. In this situation, the classical definition of security no longer sufficed. To retain its relevance to questions of war and peace, a companion concept to that of state security had to be introduced to cover the security of people as well. Defence could no longer be limited to the defence of state borders. It was also a matter of defending international rules, norms and standards in support of human beings at risk. Accordingly, there was a distinct tendency to restrict the sovereignty of states and enhance the salience of international norms. Governments guilty of gross violations of such norms should not be able to hide behind the claim to sovereignty.

State security and human security are interlinked, however. On a positive note, state security is a means of providing human security – or so it should be - whereas a high degree of human security may shed legitimacy on governments, regimes and states. On a negative note, outwardly aggressive and inwardly repressive regimes can be major sources of human insecurity. The security of people may be undermined by other states supporting oppressive regimes. Failed states – states that can no longer provide effective governance – invariably fail in human security.

In other words: to maintain its legitimacy, the state has to comply with an expanding body of international law – expanding because of a multiplication of legal instruments and stretched interpretations of existing ones. At the United Nations, the Security Council has extended the meaning of "international peace and security" – originally phrased with a view to conflicts between states – to cover conflicts that are predominantly domestic, on the ground that most of them have some international ramification or other. On this basis, a variety of peace operations have been set in motion. They peaked in 1994, when more than 80,000 people were deployed in UN operations. They came to a low in 1998 when only 14,000 were involved. By 1 May 2000, with the peace operations in East Timor and Sierra Leone ongoing, the number had once again increased to 35,000. While their predictability and efficiency obviously leave much to be desired, peace operations remain prominent on the international security agenda.

Collective security actions in the name of human security must have a basis in international law. They are triggered by gross violations of international treaties, most importantly the UN Charter, the Universal Declaration of Human Rights, the Geneva Conventions (humanitarian law) and the Convention and Protocol relating to the status of refugees (refugee law). This is a necessary condition for international action, but not a sufficient one: collective decisions also depend on a convergence of national interests, which is harder to obtain. Obviously, there are normative bases and dire needs for many more collective security initiatives than those that are actually taken. The sum of these factors – the constraints on state sovereignty, the mobilization of international civil society in defence of international norms, and the sharing of power between state and non-state actors in a globalizing world – nevertheless leaves a clear message: the state is no longer able to monopolise the concept and practice of security. Issues of security and defence go beyond the state system. The security of people has entered the political agenda and here, a wide range of actors are involved. A multitude of non-governmental organizations play a role in early warning, preventive action and post-conflict reconstruction, and many of them assist civilians also while war is being waged.

We have therefore passed the point when scholars and politicians could legitimately discuss whether the concept of security ought to stay within the state paradigm. Today, the conceptual challenge is to shape a security paradigm that captures the need to reach out in defence of people as well as states, and that can orchestrate and steer our endeavours in both directions. The meaning of human security is synonymous with that of "the security of people", and "societal security" is incorporated into it. While building on previous conceptualizations, this has the advantage of deflating a field of conceptual discourse that has become overcrowded. A time dimension must be added: an OECD study of security sector reform uses "a sense of security" to indicate an expectation of human security for the time ahead, strong enough and long enough for socio-economic development, development aid projects, foreign investments, nation-building and other collective endeavours to take place.

The rule of law, public order and peaceful management of conflicts provide protection against physical torture, arbitrary arrest and detention; crime and street violence; rape and other domestic violence directed at women; child abuse; mishandling of refugees; and, last not least, armed conflict between factions/groups. This is what policies of human security should try to achieve. Should war nevertheless be waged, a number of "remnants" may cause fear of physical violence long after the war has ended. Glaring examples are landmines and detained war criminals. Similarly with other physical excesses: they leave behind a feeling of insecurity that can only be erased over time by a convincing record of non-violence. To foster a "sense of security" for the long term may therefore be a tedious process. Even when limiting the concept to freedom from fear of physical violence, the human security agenda is obviously a long one. Many agree that freedom from fear of physical violence constitutes the core of human security. Fewer agree that the concept should be limited to that. For instance, there are those who emphasise that for most people of the world, hunger, disease and environmental contamination represent graver security concerns than physical violence. They hold that the concept should include freedom from structural as well as direct violence. Astrid Suhrke has suggested that "vulnerability" could be the defining characteristic, homing in on three categories of extremely vulnerable people: victims of war and internal conflict; those who live close to the subsistence level and thus are structurally positioned at the edge of socio-economic disaster; and victims of natural disaster. In support of this approach, it is claimed that the condition of abject poverty or powerlessness is not qualitatively different from vulnerability to physical violence during conflict.

Human security has been presented variously as a means of reducing the human costs of violent conflict, as a strategy to enable governments to address basic human needs and offset the inequities of globalization, and as a framework for providing social safety nets to people impoverished and marginalised by sudden and severe economic crises.[12] Major changes in international affairs have led to security considerations along two tracks, namely, state centric and human centric, where previously, there had been one. In the post-Cold War world, a new security concept was needed to capture the realities of physical violence. It was needed both for analytical purposes and to develop more adequate policies. In the political arena this is well known: once in a while, new concepts are introduced not merely as tools of analysis, but also in an effort to draw more attention to specific political concerns. Scholarly contributions are needed to shape the analytical tools while for politicians; the mobilizing function is of the essence.

However, for concepts to have a political impact, they must be defined in a reasonably clear and consensual manner. The definition offered above is a strictly limited one. We have shown that even so, the practical political agenda becomes quite substantial. In any case, if some broader definition gains ground, this is the core around which the concept would have to be developed. In the final analysis, human security is not a concern with weapons–it is a concern with human life and dignity. The idea of human security, though simple, is likely to revolutionise society in the 21st century.[13] In a variety of forms human security has united a coalition of states, international agencies and NGOs (as a rallying cry); achieved particular goals as a political campaign like negotiation of land mines convention. However as a novel security concept human security is feared to be vague verging upon meaninglessness. Thus human security can at the least be used as a label for a broad category of research[14].

The future of human security studies could include an annual human security audit that would develop a record of the safety and freedom of individuals all over the world together with threat countering capabilities[15].

---

12 Amitav Acharya, Debating human Security: East versus West, www.hsph.harvard.edu/hpcr/events/hsworkshop/acharya.pdf

13 New Dimensions of Human Security www.hsph.harvard.edu/hpcr/events/workshop/new-dimension.pdf

14 For a detailed discussion on the concept of human security see Roland Paris op. cit.,

15 As suggested by Kanti Bajpai in his article 'Beyond Comprehensive Security: Human Security', in *Comprehensive Security: Perspectives from India's regions*, Seminar proceeding (Delhi Policy Group, August 2001), pp 22-25.

Whatever be the impact of Human security on the security studies discourse it is certain that the concept is here to stay if not as a rallying point but at least as a topic of contention.

Chart 1: Four Images of Security

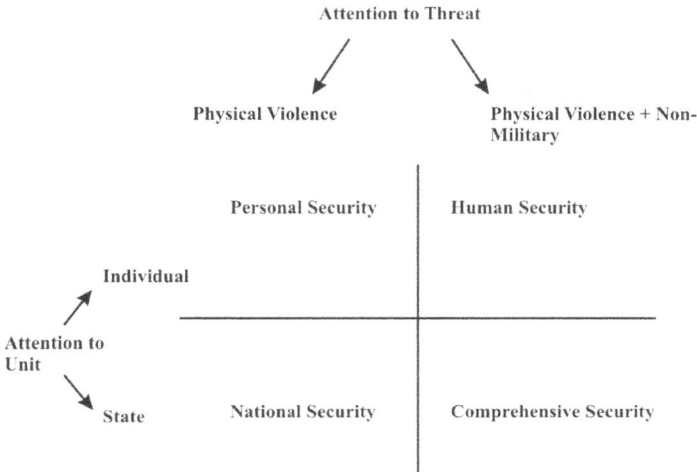

Attention to Threat

Physical Violence

Physical Violence + Non-Military

Personal Security   Human Security

Individual

Attention to Unit

State   National Security   Comprehensive Security

Chart 2: The Evolution of Human Security

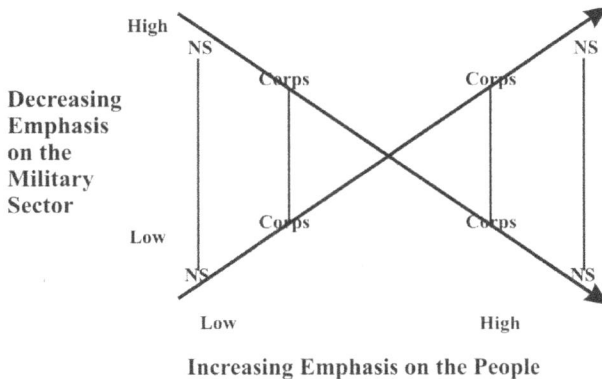

High

NS   NS

Corps   Corps

Decreasing Emphasis on the Military Sector

Corps   Corps

Low

NS   NS

Low   High

Increasing Emphasis on the People

NS: National Security: Corps: Comprehensive Security: CopS: Cooperative Security: HS: Human Security

Illustration Source

Amitav Acharya's article 'Debating Human Security: East versus West', p.8
www.hsph.harvard.edu/hpcr/events/hsworkshop/acharya.pdf

III

Situating Environmental Degradation In The Human Security Matrix

Mathew George

Security has been central to the study of international relations since its inception as a discipline.[1] It has however, not had the same meaning from the beginning. "Security in a general sense is the condition of being protected from or not exposed to danger. It has historically been concerned with safety and certainty from contingency."[2] Traditionally this contingency has meant only the possibilities of external aggression towards the state and hence has limited the role and planning of security apparatus of a state against these. However, the debates on the epistemology of security have lead to the broadening and widening of the concept of security and allowed for newer concepts of security to be established or at least propounded. Human security and comprehensive security have developed from such debates.

Comprehensive security refers to the concept which envisions the prioritising of aspects like economy, politics, humans, environment, energy, food, societal and health. In this way it removes the concept from the normal processes of politics,[3] and starts the process of securitizing them.

---

1   Sheehan, M. (2010). Military Security. In A. Collins, *Contemporary Security Studies* (pp. 169-184). Oxford: Oxford University Press. p.170

2   Barnett, J. (2003). Security and Climate Change. *Global Environmental Change, 13* (pp.7-17). p. 7

3   Šulović, V. (2010, October 5). *Meaning of Security and the Theory of Securitization.* Retrieved January 11, 2011, from Centre for Civil-Military Relations: http://www.ccmr bg.org/Occasional+Papers+and+Analysis/3855/Meaning+of+Security+and+the+Theor y+of+Securitization.shtml

This does not mean that the traditional sphere of security is neglected by comprehensive security; it wouldn't be comprehensive if it did. But rather, there is a focus on all things rather than just one.

The sectors that make up comprehensive security are

- Military

- Economic

- Political

- Human

- Environmental

- Energy

- Food

- Societal

On the other hand, "human security goes beyond the traditional understanding of security as a state-centred concept related to threats and conflict."[4] "The UNDP (1993) Human Development Report indicated for the first time in an official document that the individual must be placed at the centre of international affairs. The Report expressly states that:

...the concept of security must change- from and exclusive emphasis on national security to a much greater stress on people's security, from security through armaments to security from human development, from territorial security to food, employment and environmental security."[5]

In the 1994 UNDP Report, Human Security is referred to as 'first safety from such chronic threats as hunger, disease and repression. And second, it means protection from sudden and hurtful disruptions in the patterns of daily life- whether in homes, in jobs or in communities. Such

---

4 O'Brien, K. (2006). Are we missing the point? Global environmental change as an issue of human security. *Global Environmental Change, 16* (pp.1-3). p. 1

5 Sommaruga, C. (2004). The Global Challenge of Human Security. *Foresight, 6*(4). (pp. 208-211). p. 210

threats can exist at all levels of national income and development.'[6]

The same report also states **seven** components of security. These are,

- Economic security

- Food security

- Health security

- Environmental security

- Personal security

- Community security (societal security)

- Political security.

And in 2005 Annan said that the UN's three key goals were security, development and human rights. He structured this report around three pillars of an emerging human security concept: freedom from want (a shared vision of development), freedom from fear (a vision of collective security) and freedom to live in dignity (under the rule of law, human rights and democracy).[7]

These discussions in to human security saw to it that security now meant that individuals were to be/ should be the primary target of security policies and those decisions should be made to reflect ways of securing the individual. It should be kept in mind that human security and comprehensive security models insist on the development of all the sectors together simultaneously so that the absence of development in one does not hinder the progress in the others.

As the discussion in this chapter proceeds, it will look at the different issues that have influenced research regarding environmental security as well as the need to understand environmental security as an instrumental part of human security and the need for policy makers to think in these terms.

---

6   UNDP. (1994). Retrieved May 07, 2011, from United Nations Development Program: http://hdr.undp.org/en/media/hdr_1994_en_chap2.pdf

7   Brauch, H.G. (2008). Conceptualising the environmental dimension of Human security in the UN. *International Social Science Journal.* 59(s1). (pp. 19-48). p. 19

Talking about environmental security, environmental security means different things to different people. While for some it means to secure precious natural resources that would help the country grow without hindrance from others, to others it means the protection of the environment from human actions. There is also another debate about from who the security should be. If security is about threat, then along with pollution, would a natural disaster come under the purview of environmental security? In which case, we would be protecting against the environment, it being the risk.

In a recent literature review on environment and security, it was suggested that three main approaches can be identified: environmental conflict, environmental security and ecological security.[8] This highlights the different ways to approaches used when trying to understand environmental security. Environmental conflict focuses on the depletion of resources and environmental change and uses the state as the referent object, while environmental security understands this from the individual or sub-state community. Ecological security on the other hand looks at the entire biosphere and understands the environmental insecurity stems from human activity.[9]

However, one should remember that at the end of the day, all these researches focus on bridging the gap between what is understood to be security and the methods adopted to ensure security.

Again, this is also understood in another front as to how to conduct this research with three main approaches.[10] These are (1) The 'military apparatus' approach, (2) The 'redefining' approach, and (3) The 'environmental conflict' approach.

The first approach emphasises the relationship between the military apparatus and the human environment. The second approach can be subordinated under the 'redefining security' tradition, which started long before the current debate on security and the environment. The third

8 Cudworth,E. & Hobden, S. (2011). Beyond Environmental Security: Complex Systems, Multiple Inequalities And Environmental Risks. *Environmental Politics, 20*(1). (pp.42-59). p. 44

9 For further understanding on these, refer Cudworth E. & Hobden S. (2011)

10 Dokken, K. (2001). Environment, security and regionalism in the Asia-Pacific: is environmental security a useful concept?. *The Pacific Review, 14*(4). (pp. 509-530). p.518

approach concentrates on the conflict side of the link between environment and security. [11]

However, climate change, resource scarcity etc are all concerns that countries across the globe are facing. In addition, countries and world bodies are trying to work together to ensure that the environment and its resources are not destroyed.

By and large, it is clearly understood that the environment plays a vital role to the security of the country. However, the increase of the environment's role in the planning of the security apparatus of countries is often lacking. Even though, in the Clinton administration, environmental security or insecurity due to the environment was recognised, steps toward the changing of policies to ensure ecological security was largely overlooked.[12][13]

It is understood now that, no matter what countries do, climate change is inevitable.[14] And that the only two possible concrete actions that states can do are to Adapt and Mitigate. States have no option but to take charge and ensure that their populations are able to adapt to the changing climate and environmental effects in the future, and that whatever these effects may be, that states would be able to mitigate these effects.

Usually, successful mitigation may be understood to be a cost intensive mechanism and that safety mechanisms and institutions, such as the National Disaster Management Authority and the National System for Disaster Management are sufficiently equipped and ready to take care of the citizens of a country should the need arise. However, as was seen in the case of the Hurricane Katrina, not always are rich countries even prepared to deal with the impending climate change scenarios that we may see.

The Mississippi Delta, where Katrina hit, was referred to as the "poster child" for problems threatening the world's deltas, coastal wetlands, and

---

11 *Ibid.* p. 518-519

12 Barnett (2003), *Op. Cit.,* p. 9

13 Brauch (2008), *Op. Cit.,* p. 31

14 Kaechele et al. (2011). Confronting the climate change challenge: discussing the role of rural India under cumulative emission budget approach. *Environmental Science &Policy, 14.* (pp. 1103-1112). p. 1104

cities on the sea.[15] And if steps aren't taken to mitigate the effects of climate change, then we see that more scenarios like Katrina are a possibility. Rising global temperatures (global warming) and the oceans acting as green house gases (GHG) sinks have lead to the increase in the surface temperatures of seas as well. It is also known that warmer sea surface temperatures provide energy that strengthens the intensity of hurricanes.[16] This can only mean that unless we engineer a way to cool the Earth's temperatures and find a reversal to global warming, we find ourselves facing stronger hurricanes and further natural disasters.

"The loss of lives due to cyclones and surge storms impacting large cities on the east coast of India is expected to rise because of increasing rural–urban migration to the coast in recent years."[17] Hurricanes of a category 4 or 5 intensity would devastate the coasts of India, leading to wide spread loss of life and huge economic losses while trying rebuild societies and set economic processes back on track.

The 2011 floods in Thailand also need to be kept in mind while understanding why mitigation or even adaptation are areas where the government needs to invest heavily in the short to medium future. While the floods themselves caused havoc to the tourism industry by cancellation of hotel bookings and so on, long term effects of the floods are still being calculated. Thailand being an exporter of many computer parts, companies and industries are were estimating losses and expecting rises in global prices for parts.[18]

It is now understood that environment plays an important role in the causation of conflict. However, this relation is not a direct one.[19] Environmental resources coupled with other existing factors have been known to trigger conflicts around the world.[20] This research has also been contested by the other side that says that the abundance of environmental

15 O'Brien (2006), *Op. Cit.*, p. 2

16 *Ibid.*, p. 2

17 Adamo, S. (2010). Environmental Migration and Cities in the context of global environmental change. *Current Opinion in Environmental Sustainability, 2.* (pp. 161-165). p. 161

18 'Hard disk and camera makers hit by Thai floods.' BBC World. November 1, 2011. Retrieved December 8, 2011 from http://www.bbc.co.uk/news/technology-15534614

19 Barnett (2003). *Op. Cit.*, p. 10

20 *Ibid.*p.10

resources is the cause of conflicts around the world.[21] However, the in the latter case, this abundance is coupled with regulating or controlling the access to, use of and the distribution of the profits made from these resources.[22]

Knowledge of the role of resources, its scarcity or abundance has influenced discourse in India on the importance of environmental security to ensure national security in terms of securing the sovereignty of the country, arguing that sea level rise could submerge parts of the country and at the same time reduce the area under the country's EEZ and hence its access to precious resources it holds itself entitled to as well as arguing for the security of the economic growth of the country by developing or protecting reserves of energy.

However, "it is perhaps unsurprising that international relations have had a problematic engagement with environmental questions. This is perhaps because a subject that is analytically state centred (albeit with a focus on inter-state relations) has difficulty in dealing with problems that transcend state borders. Despite a broadening of the security agenda, a more traditional approach to thinking about the ways in which environmental issues may impact global relations is apparent: environmental degradation as a cause of conflict. This focus on the environment as a source of conflict has not only been a concern to writers within international relations, but also been an issue discussed by politicians, the popular media and international organizations."[23]

Hence, in the same light, it is not to say that we in India have forgotten or look away from the securitization of the environment. On the contrary, we have argued very much for it. But as Karen O'Brien puts it, "Are we missing the point?"[24] Are we forgetting that India should also try to understand environmental security from the human security perspective?

We may argue for the importance of environmental security, to bolster and safeguard the national security of the country, how climate change could affect the internal peace of the country, or even how this climate

---

21 *Ibid.* p.11

22 *Ibid.* p.11

23 Cudworth, E. & Hobden, S.(2011), *Op. Cit.,* p. 43

24 O'Brien (2006), *Op. Cit.,* p.1

change may affect relations with the neighbours and cause us to focus on strained relations with our neighbours due to climate based migration.[25] But all these still focus on the primary role and importance of securing the state.

The argument here is not discrediting this kind of research. It is of the utmost importance that states need to be made secure. However, we should not forget the importance in securing the human while we secure the state, i.e. the consistent of the state. In this regard, India plays a crucial role in how environmental security may be developed as a model that may be emulated in other parts of the world. The vastness of India presents it with terrains of all kinds and none of them are shielded from the effects of climate change. Successes in the mitigation of possible effects in these diverse regions may allow for steps to be taken in other parts of the world and allows for the growth of a new industry focused on the mitigation of climatic effects, while they also partner with ways for local populations to adapt to the changing climatic situations.

Changes in the climate and environment would require local populations to adapt to new scenarios. Population mobility is a common strategic response for adapting to and coping with environmental risk, stress and hardship.[26] The catastrophic floods in Mumbai, India, in 2005 were caused by an extreme weather event, but the consequences were aggravated by the combination of poor preparedness, vulnerability of poor populations and institutional failure.[27] For India, it is estimated that climate-change induced drought and conflict over scarce resources in the Indian countryside are likely to increase the intensity of rural–urban migration in the near future.[28] It is possible to speculate that should human security be the corner stone for the environmental security policies, robust mechanisms to ensure the security of the individual is designed and implemented. At the same time remembering that environmental security should include the entire biosphere, as, our survival depends on its survival too.

---

25 For more on migration, refer Adamo, S. (2010).

26 Adamo (2010), *Op. Cit.,* p 161

27 *Ibid.* p. 163

28 *Ibid.* p. 163

India argues that it should be allowed to grow, and that on the other hand, there should be reviews and checks in to whether developed nations have adhered to the Kyoto Protocols. However, such arguments have found no favour even with small island nations[29] that stand to lose the most out of climate change and global warming. However, considering that most of these countries would be partially or completely submerged in a few decades time, if the predictions of the IPCC do not speed up, what is the benefit for these countries to back the EU rather than a check on the emissions?

Isn't it possible to think that maybe, these countries have found the only possible answer to their circumstance as migrating? It will be the only solution left to them at some point or another. And where else to migrate to but in places where HDI is higher, and possibly these countries could offer them refuge as their emissions led to their crisis.

Sceptics arguing for the cost intensive, growth impeding factors of such a move need to realise that growth is something that doesn't have an end point. While growth may slow down, there is no point when India or any other country would say, "we've grown enough, let's focus on environmental security now." Else, we would have had active steps taken by the EU, US and other first world countries jumping to ensure the Kyoto Protocols were adhered to.

On the other hand, should India take mitigating steps now, it would be possible for India to continue its growth story even with its own huge internal market with lesser effects from the effects of climate change on markets around the globe. And possibly, to develop technology that would assist in the mitigation of climate change and the adaptation to it.

The example of Thailand should not be forgotten, its growth story has now halted because mitigation measures weren't thought of. How sure can we be that a hurricane will not hit the East coast of India or flash floods stop Mumbai?

The above arguments would summarise that environmental security plays a crucial role on the economic growth story of the country. If that

29 Seth, N. (2011, December 9). Small islands snub India, back EU's vision on climate talks. Times of India. Retrieved from http://timesofindia.indiatimes.com/home/environment/global-warming/Small-islands-snub-India-back-EUs-vision-on-climate-talks/articleshow/11041574.cms

isn't motivation enough, maybe other factors that India is trying to work should be thought of as well.

No one can deny that the food production of the country depends heavily on the environment. What happens to all the steps being thought of to ensure food security for the country when the environment itself isn't under consideration? And what about the people that it is meant to help and the gross loss of lives, solely due to the lack of planning to mitigate climate effects? (http://www.hks.harvard.edu/sustsci/ists/docs/khagram_etal_jhd03.pdf)

It is easily understood now that the environment plays an important part in the security dimension of states. Degradation in the environment directly affects the lives of the citizens, the economic processes the states depend on and the societal norms that states are built on. And it is in the interest of the states to develop means and ways to protect, and improve the environment, both in terms of protecting humans from the effects of the environmental change and the environment from the actions of human beings.

This has been understood to work better if countries were to cooperate with each other in their regions to ensure the protection of the environment. And hence look for regional solutions to problems as well as indigenous localised solutions.

This interdependency can be understood in Buzan's definition, "Environmental security concerns the maintenance of the local and the planetary biosphere as the essential support system on which all other human enterprises depend"[30] Even though his definition seems to concentrate only on the protection of the environment, it could also be read as requiring such sustenance to ensure that the state's resources are protected for its furtherance.

All in all, environment plays an important role in the determining of security for the country. The protection of the environment may be thought of in many ways, but ignorance of the human dimension of environmental security would be a folly in the planning of the security of any state. It is vital for the development of secure societies for the future.

---

30 Sheehan, M. (2006). *International Security-An Analytical Survey.* New Delhi: Viva Books Private Limited., p. 47

IV

An Overview of Environmental Security In South Asia

- S. Utham Kumar Jamadhagni

Environment as a Security Threat

In this new millennium global concerns about sustainable economic development have brought the concept of environmental security into sharp focus. Environmental Security is set to become a leading priority for most countries, especially the developing world, this century. Nations in all regions of the world, if they are to provide for the long-term well-being of their citizens, must find the means to protect the environment in order to ensure continued access to natural resources and the health of their citizenry. But national sovereignty and regulatory policy at the level of individual nations cannot guarantee success in matters related to environmental security. It is now quite apparent that threats to a nation's environmental well-being may not only arise outside its borders, but may prove beyond the reach of corrective measures at the national level. In 1981 the World Watch Institute's Lester Brown first issued a plea to adopt a new and robust concept to national security since threats to security arise more from man's relations with nature-dwindling reserves of critical resources.[1]

Wither security

There are two schools of thought on the debate on the inclusion of environment as part of the security matrix. While one school opines that non-traditional issues like environment are bound to replace military

---

1   Foster, Gregory., Environmental Security: The search for strategic legitimacy. **Armed Forces and Society**, Spring 2001, **27**, 3, 373.

centric view of security (some proponents have called for an enhanced appreciation of the causal relationship between environmental problems and traditional security threats, others have argued for a more basic redefinition of the concept of security in order to embrace and include these environmental threats)[2], there is another body of scholars who cast aspersions on the very meaning of security becoming so ambiguous that it is rendered "meaningless".[3]

For example, rapidly growing demands for a limited supplies of water of internationally shared river systems such as Jordan and Nile rivers, could intensify conflicts among the countries that depend on them, possibly even to the point of war. Large number of refugees fleeing a ravaged environment in their home country also could become a cause of international tension if they severely strained the resources of the country receiving them. More broadly environmental security is any major ecological development that seriously threatens the welfare of human societies, even without increasing the likelihood of war. Thus any issue like depletion of ozone layer, global warming, desertification, deforestation, and the loss of biodiversity – collectively referred to as "global change"[4] – constitute threats to environment.

Environmental security can be understood in two different ways. Resource scarcity and environmental degradation impact upon the quality of life of the citizens, their health, economic productivity and ultimately, security of a nation. These problems can create and intensify international conflicts thereby increasing the likelihood of violence and war. However, it cannot be forgotten that sharing of natural resources like water and other minerals have been the basis of several inter and now even intra-state disputes that have even lead to war. For example one of the main causes for the Iran-Iraq war was the issue of sharing the Shat-al-Arab waterways[5]. Tension abounds in the water sharing of the river Nile in Africa, Jordan in

2 Kenneth T Broda-Brahm, 'Finding protection in definitions: The quest for environmental security', *Argumentation and Advocacy*, Spring 1999, **35**, 4, 159.

3 See Paris, Roland., Human Security: Paradigm Shift or Hot Air? *International Security*, Fall 2001, **26**, 2, for a critique on this.

4 Soroos, Marvin., Environmental Security: Choices for the Twenty-first century. *National Forum*, Winter 1995, 75, 1, 20,

5 The Inventory of Conflict and Environment(ICE) Case Studies Trade and Environment database, Conflict Studies Iran-Iraq War And Waterway Claim http://www.american. edu/projects/mandala/TED/ice/IRANIRAQ.HTM

West Asia and the Ganges and the Brahmaputra in South Asia. The control over mineral rich regions of many countries in Africa have created inter-state civil war-like conditions. Lower riparian states and provinces (often the worst affected) nurse grievances against upstream neighbours over water distribution.[6] A classic example has been the ongoing, yet unresolved Cauvery river water contention between the Indian states of Karnataka and Tamil Nadu.

Environmental refugees are defined as "those people who have been forced to leave their traditional habitat, temporarily or permanently because of a marked environmental disruption that jeopardised their existence and /or severely affected their quality of life"[7] Severe strain on the availability of resources due to over population, scarcity conditions like rainfall failure, drought and even floods and man-made calamities like war could drive people away from their homelands into adjacent regions and at times countries.[8] This gives rise to the problem of refugees and the problems in migrant – local relations. The Chakma refugees from Bangladesh for example posed a serious demographic and resource sharing challenge to eastern Indian states[9]. Non-adoption of eco-friendly practices in agricultural and industrial production has led, especially in developing countries, to trans-boundary ill effects like pollution of water, air and land of contiguous nations. In South Asia, the mining of dolomite in Bhutan has caused severe soil erosion in India and the deforestation in upper Nepal results in siltation problems in Bangladesh.[10] Thus the security of the nation could easily be threatened by environment factors and thus need to be carefully studied. It is thus assumed that environment would continue to play an important role in the political, economic and social fabric of the nation. Though the countries in the South Asian region share many concerns, environmental priorities are not necessarily the same in every case.

---

6   Ashok Swain Water Wars: Fact or Fiction? Futures,2001. 769-81 gives a detailed account of the issue of water scarcity and its impact on national securtity.

7   Arthur Westing, Environmental refugees: A growing category of displaced persons, Envioronmental Conservation, Vol 19, Nr. 3, Autumn 1992, p.203 http://cgt.columbia.edu/files/papers/226_-_Env_refugees.pdf

8   http://www.envirosecurity.org/conference/working/EnvironmentalRefugees.pdf

9   Sanjoy Hazarika Refugees Within, Refugees Without http://www.himalmag.com/96apr/chakma.htm

10 Gurneeta Vasudeva, Environmental Security: A South Asian Perspective, Tata Energy Resources Institute, Arlington, VA, 2000 p.11

Unlike other security threats, which either emanate from within the state or outside it, environmental security is the cumulative effect of actions of many states including one's own, in the areas of population growth, resource extraction and refining, energy production, industry, vehicular traffic and agriculture. As the US State Department position reads: "...Countries, especially in the developing world, face a number of complicated and interrelated trans-boundary environmental challenges. These issues – air quality, water and energy resources, land use, and urban/ industrial growth – either can contribute to political and economic tensions or can be a focus of regional cooperation". [11]

India is located in a region that houses not only some of the world's poorest people, but has a density far above the world average, thus posing severe demographic and resource challenges. Population and poverty combine to deplete precious natural resources and inversely increase their requirement. As a result air pollution; polluted, scarce and low quality of water resources; loss of fertility of land due to degradation; deforestation; harmful effects on special ecosystems like marine ecology etc., and the larger and grave problem of loss of biodiversity that is needed to maintain ecological balance are present and growing concerns.

The inevitable diffusion of technology—from the automobiles, refrigerators, and air conditioners characteristic of rapid basic societal modernization to the cleaner materials, products and the processes characteristic of more mature stages of development – can have both positive and negative impact on the environment. With most of the developed world moving to largely service-based economies, the industrialisation that increasingly will be concentrated in the developing world will also have expectedly pronounced environmental effects. On the one hand, population growth will produce mass markets of poor, uneducated consumers ripe for cheap products produced by outdated, inefficient, polluting manufacturing processes that result in massive waste and environmental damage.

On the other hand, as economic and industrial globalisation advances, as commercial markets become more open to entry and competition, as international environmental standards and compliance mechanisms take hold, and as industry gradually comes to see profitability and competitive

---

11 US Department of State, Environmental Diplomacy. Fact Sheet, Bureau of Oceans and International Environment and Scientific affairs, 20 November 1998.

advantages in cleaner products and manufacturing methods, the result could be a measurable greening of the marketplace. Also the appearance of auto catalytic events like floods, earthquakes, hurricanes, massive oil spills, nuclear or chemical incidents that feed off and accentuate environmental degradation and resource scarcity heighten public awareness and discontent.[12]Developed countries also fear that environmental and resource scarcities in foreign lands especially in poorer developing nations can interact with political, economic, social, and cultural factors and policies to contribute to instability and terrorism.[13]

For example, rapidly growing demands for a limited supplies of water of internationally shared river systems such as Jordan and Nile rivers, could intensify conflicts among the countries that depend on them, possibly even to the point of war. Large number of refugees fleeing a ravaged environment in their home country also could become a cause of international tension if they severely strained the resources of the country receiving them. More broadly environmental security is any major ecological development that seriously threatens the welfare of human societies, even without increasing the likelihood of war. Thus any issue like depletion of ozone layer, global warming, desertification, deforestation, and the loss of biodiversity – collectively referred to as "global change"[14] – constitute threats to environment.

Unlike other security threats, which either emanate from within the state or outside it, environmental security is the cumulative effect of actions of many states including one's own, in the areas of population growth, resource extraction and refining, energy production, industry, vehicular traffic and agriculture. As the US State Department position reads: "…Countries, especially in the developing world, face a number of complicated and interrelated transboundary environmental challenges. These issues – air quality, water and energy resources, land use, and urban/ industrial growth – either can contribute to political and economic tensions

---

12 Foster, 393.

13 Robert Dufant, 'Wither Environmental security in the post-September 11th era? Assessing the legal, organizational and policy challenges for the national security State', **Public Administration Review,** Sep 2002, 62, 115 – 124.

14 Soroos, Marvin., Environmental Security: Choices for the Twenty-first century. **National Forum** , Winter 1995, 75, 1, 20,

or can be a focus of regional cooperation". [15]

Home to about half the world's poorest people[16], at a density far above the world average, South Asia poses severe demographic and resource challenges. Population and poverty combine to deplete precious natural resources and inversely increase their requirement. As a result air pollution; polluted, scarce and low quality of water resources; loss of fertility of land due to degradation; deforestation; harmful effects on special ecosystems like marine ecology etc., and the larger and grave problem of loss of biodiversity that is needed to maintain ecological balance are present and growing concerns of this region.

Topical Significance

The inevitable diffusion of technology – from the automobiles, refrigerators, and air conditioners characteristic of rapid basic societal modernization to the cleaner materials, products and the processes characteristic of more mature stages of development – can have both positive and negative impact on the environment. With most of the developed world moving to largely service-based economies, the industrialisation that increasingly will be concentrated in the developing world will also have expectedly pronounced environmental effects. On the one hand, population growth will produce mass markets of poor, uneducated consumers ripe for cheap products produced by outdated, inefficient, polluting manufacturing processes that result in massive waste and environmental damage.

On the other hand, as economic and industrial globalisation advances, as commercial markets become more open to entry and competition, as international environmental standards and compliance mechanisms take hold, and as industry gradually comes to see profitability and competitive advantages in cleaner products and manufacturing methods, the result could be a measurable greening of the marketplace. Also the appearance of auto catalytic events like floods, earthquakes, hurricanes, massive oil spills, nuclear or chemical incidents that feed off and accentuate environmental degradation and resource scarcity heighten public awareness and

---

15 US Department of State, Environmental Diplomacy. Fact Sheet, Bureau of Oceans and International Environment and Scientific affairs, 20 November 1998.

16 South Asia houses half of world's poor, the Himalayan times, 24 August 2010 http://www.thehimalayantimes.com/fullNews.php?headline= South+Asia+houses+half+of+world's+poor:+Report&NewsID=255081

discontent.[17]Developed countries also fear that environmental and resource scarcities in foreign lands especially in poorer developing nations can interact with political, economic, social, and cultural factors and policies to contribute to instability and terrorism.[18]

Environment – Security linkage

There are two schools of thought on the debate on the inclusion of environment as part of the security matrix. While one school opines that non-traditional issues like environment are bound to replace military centric view of security (some proponents have called for an enhanced appreciation of the causal relationship between environmental problems and traditional security threats, others have argued for a more basic redefinition of the concept of security in order to embrace and include these environmental threats)[19], there is another body of scholars who cast aspersions on the very meaning of security becoming so ambiguous that it is rendered "meaningless".[20]

However, it cannot be forgotten that sharing of natural resources like water and other minerals have been the basis of several inter and now even intra-state disputes that have even lead to war. For example one of the main causes for the Iran-Iraq war was the issue of sharing the Shat-al-Arab waterways[21]. Tension abounds in the water sharing of the river Nile in Africa, Jordan in West Asia and the Ganges and the Brahmaputra in South Asia. The control over mineral rich regions of many countries in Africa have created inter-state civil war-like conditions. Lower riparian states and provinces (often the worst affected) nurse grievances against upstream neighbours over water distribution.[22] A classic example has been

17 Foster, 393.

18 Robert Dufant, 'Wither Environmental security in the post-September 11th era? Assessing the legal, organizational and policy challenges for the national security State', *Public Administration Review,* Sep 2002, 62, 115 – 124.

19 Kenneth T Broda-Brahm, 'Finding protection in definitions : The quest for environmental security', *Argumentation and Advocacy*, Spring 1999, **35**, 4, 159.

20 See Paris, Roland., Human Security: Paradigm Shift or Hot Air? *International Security,* Fall 2001, **26**, 2, for a critique on this.

21 The Inventory of Conflict and Environment(ICE) Case Studies Trade and Environment database, Conflict Studies Iran-Iraq War And Waterway Claim http://www.american. edu/projects/mandala/TED/ice/IRANIRAQ.HTM

22 Ashok Swain Water Wars: Fact or Fiction? Futures,2001. 769-81 gives a detailed account

the ongoing, yet unresolved Cauvery river water contention between the Indian states of Karnataka and Tamilnadu.

Severe strain on the availability of resources due to over population, scarcity conditions like rainfall failure, drought and even floods and man-made calamities like war could drive people away from their homelands into adjacent regions and at times countries. This gives rise to the problem of refugees and the problems in migrant – local relations. The Chakma refugees from Bangladesh for example posed a serious demographic and resource sharing challenge to eastern Indian states[23].

Non-adoption of eco-friendly practices in agricultural and industrial production has led, especially in developing countries, to trans-boundary ill effects like pollution of water, air and land of contiguous nations. In South Asia, the mining of dolomite in Bhutan has caused severe soil erosion in India and the deforestation in upper Nepal results and siltation problems in Bangladesh.[24] Thus the security of the nation could easily be threatened by environment factors and thus need to be carefully studied.

It is thus assumed that environment would continue to play an important role in the political, economic and social fabric of the nation. Though the countries in the South Asian region share many concerns, environmental priorities are not necessarily the same in every case. Table 1 summarises the key environmental concerns of South Asian economies.

Table 1: Environmental priorities for South Asian countries

Country	Land degrada-tion	Water scarcity	Water quality	Air pollution Indoor	Outdoor	Urbani-zation	Marine Environ-ment	Defores-tation
Bangladesh	High	Medium	—	High	Medium	Medium	High	Medium
Bhutan	—	—	Low	High	—	—	—	Medium
India	High	Medium	Medium	High	Medium	Medium	Low	Medium

of the issue of water scarcity and its impact on national security.

23 Sanjoy Hazarika Refugees Within, Refugees Without http://www.himalmag.com/96apr/chakma.htm

24 Gurneeta Vasudeva, Environmental Security: A South Asian Perspective, Tata Energy Resources Institute, Arlington, VA, 2000 p.11

Nepal	Medium	—	—	High	High	—	—	—
Maldives	—	Low	—	—	—	—	High	—
Pakistan	High	Low	Medium	High	—	Medium	Low	Medium
Sri Lanka	—	Medium	—	—	—	—	High	—

Source: CPR Environment Education Centre website www.cpreec.org

Of the many issues the focus here is on the areas of primary concern namely pollution that is affecting air, water and land, Deforestation, damage to the marine environment and overall loss of biodiversity.

Let us see the country-wise status of various environmental parameters, their health and the possible ways that problems are being dealt with.

South Asia occupies 10% of total land area of the world but houses one-fifth of its population, making it the most populous region in the world. Three of the world's top 10 populated countries (India, Bangladesh and Pakistan) are in this region[25].

Bhutan

This landlocked country bordering India and China has a very small population and mountain regions that are uninhabitable. The highlands are highly populated. The fragile ecosystems though well maintained till now face severe strain due to anthropogenic activity. The forests which cover more than half of the country's land area are now being destroyed to make way for agriculture and due to illegal logging of trees[26]. Forest degradation is primarily caused by caused primarily by over harvesting for timber and fuel wood; inappropriate harvesting practices; forest fires; overgrazing; habitat destruction and pollution. The rich biodiversity is also affected by the poaching of animals like tigers, leopards and musk deer hunted for the body parts and other products that allegedly cure diseases. In the wake of these activities, wildlife is forced to survive in increasingly fragmented spaces[27]. This has also endangered mammals like tiger, snow leopard, Asian

25 http://www.internetworldstats.com/stats8.htm

26 http://www.cbd.int/countries/profile.shtml?country=bt#status

27 http://www.globserver.com/en/bhutan/environment

Elephant and wild yak.[28] The mountainous slopes which are naturally eroded during the monsoons face rapid landslides due to deforestation, and development activity like road construction and building of irrigation channels.

With much of the population living in the cities, pollution is another big environmental concern. The primary sources of air pollution emission in Bhutan, according to the Strategy for Air Quality Assessment and Management in Bhutan, are exhaust emissions from diesel and petrol vehicles that are increasing at a rate of 11 to 12% every year, and particulate matter (PM) that is feared to cross the UN limits emitted from brake and tyre wear, resuspended road dust, industrial emissions, smoke from wood stove called bhukaris, wind-blown dust from building construction sites, bare agricultural soil, and road construction areas during the winter dry season, and smoke from forest fires[29]. Waste management is now becoming an environmental issue with increasing urbanisation. A study by the Royal Society of Protection of Nature (RSPN) shows that the capital Thimphu and the second largest town Phuntsholing, together account for 36.70 and 24.76 tonnes of solid waste respectively. The amount of solid waste collected in these two urban centres has more than tripled in the past decade, the study also showed. [30]

Another unique issue is that of Dolomite mining in Bhutan. This is a mineral that is used in steel manufacturing and in horticulture. The mining is not only polluting the rivers but also affecting tea plantations in neighbouring Indian state of West Bengal. The dust that settles on the leaves chokes the tea plants whose production has plummeted over the years. The soil is also turning alkaline unsuitable for the tea plants that grow well in acidic soil. The mining deposits are also polluting nearby rivers killing animals from thirst in the Manas sanctuary. Bhutan is endowed with freshwater from glaciers and glacial lakes. But the glaciers are reported to be receding at an alarming rate of 20-30 metres per year.[31] So the availability of water would soon become an issue. Water quality is

28 http://www.nationsencyclopedia.com/Asia-and-Oceania/Bhutan-ENVIRONMENT.html # ixzz1WcIfmt6b

29 http://www.businessbhutan.bt/?p=3501

30 With urbanisation comes the garbage, Bhutan Times, http://www.bhutantimes.bt/index. php?option=com_content&task=view&id=1413&Itemid=89

31 http://www.bhutanstudies.org.bt/pubFiles/V23-4.pdf

yet another area that needs to be looked at. However Bhutan is the only country that has made a constitutional commitment to maintain 60% forest cover at all times.[32]

Nepal

Nepal is one of the worst pollution affected countries in South Asia. The main problems are air pollution, water contamination, rapid loss of forest cover and waste disposal. The topography of Kathmandu also lends to its pollution level. Located in a bowl shaped valley the city is unable to let out industrial and vehicle fumes. The high level of vehicular emissions is due to the poor maintenance of vehicles, the use of low quality fuel, a weak emission inspection system and poorly managed transportation system. This has had an adverse effect on the health of the common people with COPD on the rise.[33] The alarming rates of pollution much higher than the WHO levels, have increased proportional to the mushrooming number of inferior quality vehicles on the traffic congested roads, together with the unregulated location of industries, particularly brick manufacturing. Brick manufacturing in the winter months is a major source of pollution as the kiln burn coal, a green house gas emitter. [34] Some other polluting industries like tanning, distilling and cement are being relocated from the city. A WHO report earlier deemed Kathmandu to be the most polluted city in Asia. [35]

The Bagmati river which holds deep religious significance for Nepalis runs through Kathmandu. But due to unregulated and untreated discharges it has been polluted. [36] Toxic effluents from industries like tanneries pollute water sources and also affect farming. The high use of banned pesticides like DDT in agriculture contaminates the water endangering animals like

---

32 State of the nation, July 2011 Third annual report of Lyonchhen Jigmi Yoeser Thinley to the seventh session of the first parliament on The State of the nation http://rtm.gnhc.gov.bt/RTMdoc/State_of_nation_2011.pdf

33 S.K.Joshi, Air Pollution in Nepal, Kathmandu University Medical Journal, Vol.1, Issue 4, 2003 p. 231 http://kmc.academia.edu/Sunil/Papers/100253/Air_Pollution_in_Nepal

34 http://www.world-weather-travellers-guide.com/air-pollution-in-kathmandu.html

35 Linda Solomon, Air pollution in Kathmandu off the charts, *The Vancouver Observer*, June 4, 2011 htt p://www.vancouverobserver.com/blogs/publishersplatform/2011/06/04/air-pollution-kathmandu-charts

36 http://www.elaw.org/node/1249

the Gharial crocodile, Gangetic dolphin and blackbuck.[37]

Deforestation and land degradation have not only affected the environment but stifled economic growth and livelihood. Loss of forests has meant increased floods, soil erosion and stagnant agricultural production. Almost half of the forest cover has been lost in the last two decades and the loss is accelerating.

Development has also affected the environment. The setting up of new industrial towns has not only meant population migration from rural areas but more importantly destroyed wetlands that are being filled up to make way for housing[38]. The under-developed infrastructure in these areas gives rise to additional problems like low water quality, waste generation and disposal. The industrial areas lack treatment plants discharging the untreated effluents directly into rivers or streams.[39] This pollutes the groundwater too. The waste generation and disposal is yet another concern. In the capital city of Kathmandu, 150 tonnes of waste is produced every day of which almost half is dumped in rivers.[40] The geomorphology of some regions like Terai region poses a unique challenge. Most communities here rely on tube wells for drinking water access. The region is made of sedimentary layers of sand, gravel deposits interlocked with flood plains carried by rivers making it vulnerable to arsenic contamination.[41]

Bangladesh

Bangladesh is the second most densely populated country in South Asia after Maldives. Bangladesh is now widely recognised to be one of the countries most vulnerable to climate change. Natural hazards that come from increased rainfall, rising sea levels, and tropical cyclones are expected to increase as climate change, each seriously affecting agriculture, water & food security, human health and shelter. Bangladesh now has among

---

37   http://www.wwfnepal.org/our_solutions/conservation_nepal/tal/area/threats/river_pollution/

38   http://www.searo.who.int/LinkFiles/National_Environment_&_Health_Action_Plan_envofhlthissue.pdf

39 Santosh Poudyal, Nepal, p.156 The International Symposium on Management of Industrial EStates through Green Productivity (GP), Penang, 19-21, September 2000 http://www.apo-tokyo.org/gp/e_publi/penang_symp/Penang_Symp_P149-158.pdf

40 http://www.waterhealtheducator.com/Issues--Asia-in-Depth.html

41 ibid

the smallest areas of protected and intact forest in the world, consisting of 1.4% of its landmass.[42] (http://www.adb.org/Documents/CEAs/BAN/BAN-CEA-Jul2004.pdf) The fast dwindling special ecosystem like the mangrove forests called the Sundarbans, threaten the existence of not only keystone species like the Bengal Tiger but have drastically reduced the availability of river fish like the Hilsa directly affecting the livelihood of fishermen and the protein dependence on marine life. Untreated wastes from various industries, garbage from hospitals and disposal of sewage from the city of Khulna into the Bhairab river which flows through the Sundarbans would soon spell doom to the world's largest mangrove forest area[43]. The proposed coal-based power plant at Bagerhat and a shipyard and silo in Chandpai are also feared to add to the woes.

Over population is a unique problem affecting Bangladesh as it is one of the most densely populated areas in South Asia. This has given rise to lack of potable drinking water, insufficient sanitary conditions and a general low standard of living. The crowded cities have meant alarming rates of air pollutants. Dhaka has recorded particulate matter levels at 247 micrograms per cubic metre (mcm) nearly five times higher than that set by the National Ambient Air Quality Standard of Bangladesh.[44]

Water pollution is another serious issue. In Bangladesh, excessive withdrawals of water have led to waterlogging and salinity and to land subsidence in cities such as Dhaka. The untreated waste water from textile and other industries are let into waterways deeply polluting them. The rivers are now being termed 'biologically dead', meaning they are unfit for livestock consumption. Dhaka with four rivers running around it is one of the most polluted cities in the world[45]. Mercury and cadmium, heavy metals have penetrated the ground water creating a health hazard for the millions who depend on it.

---

42 http://www.usaid.gov/bd/programs/environ.html

43 Khalilur Rahman, Pollution threatens the Sundarbans, *The Financial Express*, July 24, 2011 http://www.thefinancialexpress-bd.com/more.php?news_id=143848&date=2011-07-24

44 Shahiduzzaman Khan, Air pollution in city reaches alarming level, Financial express, June 19, 2011 http://www.thefinancialexpress-bd.com/more.php?news_id=139702&date=2011-06-19

45 River pollution in Bangladesh, April 26, 2011 http://www.glocal24.com/river-pollution-in-bangladesh.html

Ship breaking in the port of Chittagong is hazardous and practices fall well short of international standards. Most of the developed world has banned ship breaking in their own countries making economically weak countries like Bangladesh willing victims of the now thriving industry. This dangerous industry of dismantling old unusable ships mostly without the help of technology but bare hands affects the health of workers. The spilling of oil and other chemicals on the beaches has rendered them polluted. The toxic chemicals like asbestos, polychlorinated biphenyls, ozone depleting substances and heavy metals have rendered the soil and water high in concentrations of cadmium, mercury chromium, lead and oil[46]. This is despite a judicial intervention in March 2009 which held that ships must be decontaminated at source before being imported for scrapping, and directed ship breaking companies to set up facilities to separately handle scrap metals, toxic paints, and waste materials, and to manage oil spillage.

Food industry is the worst polluter followed by cement, pulp and paper industry and textile. Among food industry, most of the pollutants come from the sugar mills. In the Sunderbans, an ecosystem common to India and Bangladesh, increasing population pressure together with industrial activity has led to the loss of diversity of both plant and animal species.

Sri Lanka

Sri Lanka is an island nation and is one of the most biodiverse countries in all of Asia. It also has the highest species density. Such a naturally abundant land is now under increased threat of human interventions. From 80% of land being covered with forests in 1800 the present cover is only around 25%.[47] The severe depletion of forests has increased soil erosion, landslides, floods, fauna and flora degradation, and damage to human lives and properties. Wildlife is threatened by poaching. Leopards, monkeys, wild boar, elephants are some of the species that are threatened by this activity. Also, as an island endowed with forests and enchanting coastline, Sri Lanka has its own share of unique problems. The exploitation of the forests and related deforestation, coastal erosion, and the common problems of unsustainable forms of food production have polluted the land, water and

---

46 Bangladeshi ship breakers defy court ruling, June 17, 2011, Al Jazeera website http://english.aljazeera.net/indepth/features/2011/06/201161614573884376.html

47 Ram Alagan, Sri Lankan Environmental Challenges, http://www.gvglobalvision.org/publications/Sri%20Lanka%92s_Environmental_Challenges.pdf

air.[48] The erosion of coasts has not only damaged beaches but also affected costal communities and the conservation of unique eco systems.

While ambient air quality is being monitored and measures like phasing out leaded gasoline, introducing low sulphur diesel, banning the import of two stroke three wheelers and introducing vehicular emission testing,[49] what is of grave concern is the indoor air pollution levels. The use of firewood by more than 70% of Sri Lankan households makes it the principal indoor polluter due to the presence of particulate matter in high levels. This coupled with poor ventilation has led to respiratory diseases in nearly 20% of children in such households.[50]

Urban expansion with inadequate infrastructure has resulted in the proliferation of slums and shanties, and many other urban problems. Moratuwa, Kandy, Colombo, Matale, Gampaha, Negombo are some of the cities that have been battling the problem of waste disposal. Open dumping of waste has polluted ground water sources. Burning of waste pollutes the air. Colombo generates 1500 tonnes of solid waste per day.[51] The lack of waste management procedures has now increased the risk of spread of Dengue fever.

Mangroves are another unique eco system that is found in Sri Lanka. The 6000-7000 hectares of mangroves along Sri Lanka's coastline houses nearly 20 different species. Large mangroves can be found in lagoons such as Kalpitiya, Batticaloa, Madu Ganga, Trincomalee, Jaffna, Potuvil, Panama, and Periyakalappu. The mangroves are home to several flora and fauna varieties that maintain balance in the eco system. Mangroves also help people sustain their livelihoods in fishing, timber, and various other

---

48 http://print.dailymirror.lk/opinion1/45998.html

49 Yatagama Lokuge S Nandasena , Ananda R Wickremasinghe and Nalini Sathiakumar, Air pollution and health in Sri Lanka: a review of epidemiologic studies, *BMC Public Health* 2010, **10**:300 http://www.biomedcentral.com/1471-2458/10/300

50 Sumal Nandasena, Ananda R Wickremasinghe, Nalini Sathiakumar, Fine Particle Air Quality Levels of Sri Lankan Households and Associated Respiratory Conditions: Preliminary Findings of an Ongoing Longitudinal Study,Epidemiology:January 2011 - Volume 22 - Issue 1 - pp S215-S216 doi: 10.1097/01.ede.0000392346.69462.d8 http://journals.lww.com/epidem/Fulltext/2011/01001/Fine_Particle_Air_Quality_Levels_of_Sri_Lankan.654.aspx

51 K.L.S Perera, "An Overview of the Issue of Solid Waste Management In Sri Lanka" in Martin J. Bunch, V. Madha Suresh and T. Vasantha Kumaran, eds., *Proceedings of the Third International Conference on Environment and Health, Chennai, India, 2003*

socio-economic activities.

However, in recent years mangrove forests have been greatly reduced to facilitate commercial activities like tourism, aquaculture and agriculture.[52] The dumping municipal and urban waste, land-filling for housing development, cutting for firewood, and clearing for security reasons in the northern and eastern districts have also caused serious pressure to the mangroves environment. This has intensified flooding and erosion in the lagoon and coastal areas. The 26 December 2004 tsunami was the biggest natural disaster to strike Sri Lanka. It resulted in 38,900 deaths and displaced about 443,000 people on the eastern and southern coasts. Research now shows that the destruction of coral reefs and mangroves actually intensified the destruction illustrating the value of these environmentally significant systems[53].

Pakistan

Pakistan is beset with numerous challenges on the environmental front. Poor natural resource management over many years and continuing high population growth have had a negative impact on Pakistan's environment. Urbanisation, pollution of land, water and air continue to raise concerns. According to Pak-EPA, air pollution levels for the bigger Pakistani cities – Karachi, Lahore and Islamabad – have been recorded seven times higher than those prescribed by the World Health Organization.[54] Most of these cities have huge number of vehicles clogging the roads. Thus vehicular emissions that have become more toxic due to the use of poor quality fuel are the worst air polluters. Due to poor maintenance and usage of outdated models, the vehicular emission accounts for 90% of air pollution[55]. The use of diesel as the main fuel type has further added to the problem. The other polluter is municipal solid waste that is disposed mostly by burning. In Islamabad, the hundreds of tons of solid waste are generated each day is either dumped in low-lying areas or burned. This gives out particulate matter and also produces other carcinogenic pollutants.

---

52 http://cmsdata.iucn.org/downloads/sri_lanka_information_brief_of_mangroves.pdf

53 Water : A shared responsibility, The United Nations World water development report 2, UNESCO, 2006, p. 508 http://www.unesco.org/water/wwap/wwdr/wwdr2/case_studies/pdf/sri_lanka.pdf

54 http://woodsmokeworld1.wordpress.com/2011/04/17/2011-april-17-pakistan-islamabad-air-quality-monitoring-system-resumes-work/

55 kitakyushu.iges.or.jp/docs/mtgs/seminars/theme/uaqm/.../Karachi.doc

Much of the country suffers from a lack of potable water due to industrial waste and agricultural runoff that contaminates drinking water supplies. Poverty and high population growth have aggravated, and to a certain extent, caused, these environmental problems. Industries have polluted streams and rivers and also the Arabian Sea by discharging untreated waste water into them. The river Kabul in North West Frontier Province (NWFP) bears 80,000 m^3 of untreated industrial effluents that cause skin diseases, reduce agricultural produce and decimate fish population[56]. Sugarcane and tanning industries are other major polluters. In Hyderabad in Sindh sugarcane factories dump waste directly into the drains and tanneries near Karachi are yet to completely adopt waste treatment methods. In Pakistan, chemical pollution of the *Ravi* has resulted in the loss of several fish varieties and the loss of livelihoods of tens of thousands of people.[57] The pollution of water bodies has resulted in bacterial contamination making them unsuitable for human consumption.

Pakistan ranks second highest in rate of deforestation. Use of fuel wood and timber are the main causes for this rapid destruction of forests. It is feared that in a decade or so the forest cover would be completely depleted.[58] The devastation caused by the July 2010 floods was aggravated due to the lack of forest cover that would have mitigated the force of the torrent. In the Swat valley for instance, illegal timber logging undertaken by the Taliban helped to fund its activities. While nearly 15% of forest cover was lost during just six years of Taliban control, the clearing of vast forest area along the Indus river in Sindh was for planting cotton, sugarcane and wheat.[59] The *Thar* region of Pakistan and India, and selected watersheds in the Himalayan regions of India and Nepal, are among the worst affected.

Pakistan's 990 km coastline is also being polluted. The transport of oil from the port of Karachi results in an annual rate of 90,000 tons of oily discharge.[60] The dumping of \untreated waste including industrial effluents

---

56 http://www.environment.gov.pk/PRO_PDF/PositionPaper/Water%20Pollution.pdf

57 http://www.defence.pk/forums/strategic-geopolitical-issues/8256-river-ravi.html

58 http://www.illegal-logging.info/item_single.php?it_id=1482&it=news

59 Alex Rodriguez, Pakistan flood crisis blamed partly on deforestation, *Los Angeles Times*, October 13, 2010, http://articles.latimes.com/2010/oct/13/world/la-fg-pakistan-logging-20101013

60 http://saarc-sdmc.nic.in/pdf/workshops/goa/Pakistan/Environmental%20Porblems%20of%20Marine%20&%20Coastal%20Area%20of%20Pakistan.pdf

carrying dangerous chemicals into the sea is another environmental concern. Ship breaking at Gadani and the destruction of the mangroves of the Indus deltaic region are also creating havoc to the coastal environment. In Pakistan, hunting is still pursued as a popular sport. Falcons are smuggled to the Middle East and lizards and snakes are killed for their skins.

Maldives

Maldives a small island nation in South Asia has pollution problems related to the congested city of Male. This is due to the quantum leaps in number of vehicles plying on the streets[61]. Coral mining supplies material to the construction industry. Mining corals reduces coastline protection against normal tide and wave-induced erosion and sand movements and increases coastal susceptibility by effectively increasing water depth making it susceptible to storm induced erosion and flooding. Coral reef depletion also reduces reef fish species [62] Global warming and the associated sea level rise threaten the fragile ecosystems of the

Maldives, where 80% of islands are less than 1 meter above mean sea level. Adapting to the likely consequences of climate change is a key challenge and development imperative for the Maldives.[63] including the depletion and pollution of groundwater resources, environmental decline caused by the inappropriate disposal of sewage and solid waste, and erosion of the coastline from excessive coral reef mining. Areas that continue to need attention include coastal zone management, biological diversity conservation, integrated reef resource management, solid waste and sewage management, pollution control and hazardous wastes management, and sustainable tourism development.

Solid waste management is another environmental problem the island is currently grappling with. The waste and sewage produced in Malé is a major environmental problem as is the accumulation of waste on the other inhabited islands. With no disposal facilities, noncombustible waste, empty

---

61 Asian Development Bank Document, Maldives: Environment Assessment, Sep 2007. http://www.adb.org/Documents/Assessments/Country-Environmental/MLD/ Environment- Assessment.pdf

62 Workshop on Integrated Reef Resources Management in the Maldives - Bay of Bengal Programme, BAY OF BENGAL PROGRAMME, Madras, India,1997 BOBP/REP/76 http://www.fao.org/docrep/X5623E/x5623e0r.htm

63 Maldives 2007–2011, *ADB Country Partnership Strategy*, September 2007 http://www. adb.org/Documents/CPSs/MLD/2007/CPS-MLD-2007.pdf

food bags, water bottles and other plastics are thrown in the ocean.[64] The entire country has only one landfill in Thilafushi island. [65] Development activities like harbour dredging and land reclamation could permanently change the natural environment and substantially damage habitats while activities such as the improper disposal of solid waste and sewage have a slow cumulative impact on the environment. Beach erosion is a serious problem, with 97% of inhabited islands reporting beach erosion and the uncontrolled disposal of solid wastes, including medical waste, is a threat to coastal and marine ecosystems.[66] The loss of habitats of endangered species and the destruction of its coral reefs[67] Marine and coastal environments are also vulnerable to tourism, exemplified by the destruction of coral reefs along the Maldives coast.

India

As the largest country in South Asia, India is beset with a number of environmental challenges. The exploding population, the unquenchable need for resources to house, feed and clothe this population is truly taking a toll on the already exploited and limited natural resources. India is the seventh largest country in the world by area. Along with this large and diverse landmass, are associated problems of over exploitation, resource scarcity, rapid depletion and resultant harmful effects on the environment, the people and finally the well-being of the nation. Pollution due to the rapid urbanisation has irreversibly changed the quality of the air, water and land. In India, stupendous amounts of air pollutants enter the atmosphere per annum. The pollutants comprise of 50 lakh tonnes of particulate matter, 30 lakh tonnes of sulphur dioxide, 10 lakh tonnes of carbon monoxide and 22 lakh tonnes of hydrogen sulphide. Chennai too is one of the four metropolises to suffer the consequences of polluted air, though the greater effect can be felt in north Chennai where the industries are clustered together[68].

---

64 http://www.jica.go.jp/maldives/english/office/about/message.html

65 http://www.env.go.jp/recycle/3r/en/asia/02_03-3/02.pdf

66 http://www.mangrovesforthefuture.org/Countries/Maldives.html

67 http://www.independent.co.uk/news/world/asia/the-march-of-tourism-and-a-threat-to-the-maldives-867629.html

68 Pollution Control Board publishes weekly Pollution Watch Reports of arterial roads and other heavy traffic and industrial areas

Much of India's urban pollution is due to energy generation, other industrial productions and transport systems. In the urban centres, the air pollution level has exceeded the prescribed WHO standards. The air quality standards in small towns are also worsening. It has been estimated that 2.0 million Indians die annually due to air pollution. India is spending nearly Rs. 4,550 crores per year to treat health problems caused by air pollution.[69] Increase in average temperature, acid rain over some cities and indoor air pollution due to wood fires are some of the other problems. Air pollution from vehicles, industries and dust results in respiratory disorders like asthma, bronchitis, bronchial irritation, etc.

India is one of the signatories of the international convention to curb pollution. As a result of this, diesel vehicles and 15-year-old vehicles are to be banned to control vehicular pollution in cities like Delhi, Mumbai, Hyderabad, etc. Vehicular emission checks have been made mandatory for all vehicles. To regulate the pollution levels of industries and their surrounding areas systems like precipitators, scrubbers and filters have to be compulsorily installed. Legal provisions under the Air (Pollution, Prevention & Control) Act have also been made to sue the polluting industries. The whole debate on conversion of diesel-run vehicles to CNG (Compressed natural gas) had to be addressed by the Supreme Court.[70]

To drive a growing economy, India vitally needs energy. However, at present most of her energy needs (nearly 80%) [71]are satisfied by coal-based power generation. Coal when burnt pollutes the air as it emits suspended carbon particles and various gases that lead to global warming. Indian coals, though low in sulpur, contain higher amount of ash (about 35-45%), resulting in the generation of huge quantities of fly ash in India. The annual generation of fly ash has increased from about 1 million tonne in 1947 to about 40 million tonne during 1994 and to about 112 million tonnes at present[72]. Fly ash, combined with emissions from the increased use of coal, is a major environmental concern. It is estimated that about 35-40 million

69 Urban Air Pollution, *Current Science*, Vol. 77, No. 3, 10 August 1999 p.334 http://www.ias.ac.in/currsci/aug10/airpollution.pdf

70 'CNG buses in Delhi', http://www.cleanairnet.org/infopool/1411/propertyvalue-19513.html

71 Industrial pollution in India - A bitter reality, http://www.breakingnewsonline.net/features/8701-industrial-pollution-in-india-a-bitter-reality.html

72 Manifold increase in flyash utilization in India, http://flyashbricksinfo.com/construction/manifold-increase-in-fly-ash-utilisation-in-india.html

tons of fly ash is generated by thermal power plants each year in India, of which a very small percentage i.e., 3.5% is recycled.[73] With a major leap in power generation slated in the coming years, the production of fly-ash is bound to increase. The fly ash is now being utilised as cost-effective construction material in the form of bricks and replacement for cement and other building materials.[74] It is also being used in agriculture, soil treatment etc. This is one instance where a potential pollutant has been turned into a profitable and more importantly environmentally friendly utility.

The pollutants are not only affecting the areas of origin but regions far away too. As early as 1999, a layer of pollutants, now famously called the Asian Brown Cloud, covered parts of northern Indian Ocean, India and Pakistan and parts of South Asia, Southeast Asia and China was observed. The cloud is caused mainly by domestic wood and dung fires plus smoke from the burning of forests and fields for agriculture. In addition vehicle exhausts, power plants and factory chimneys add to the mix. It has led to some erratic weather, sparking floods in Bangladesh, Nepal and northeastern India but drought in Pakistan and northwestern India.[75] The cloud is also said to hasten the melting of the Himalayan glaciers which feed all main rivers in the region, which could lead to large scale droughts in the long run.[76]

Water pollution and scarcity

The availability, exploitation and scarcity of water resources is increasing with growing population and change in consumption patterns are also grave environmental concerns. The effects of land-use, deforestation,

---

73 Romir Chatterjee, Meeta Mehra and Shilpi Banerjee, Environmental Security in South Asia, *TERIGlobe* Vol.2, No.2, February 2000, p.4 http://www.teriin.org/upfiles/pub/papers/ft16.pdf

74 Technology Information, Forecasting & Assessment Council (TIFAC) Techno-Market Survey on Flyash Bricks http://www.tifac.org.in/index.php?option=com_content&view =article&id=434&Itemid=205&limitstart=2 has a comprehensive information on this.

75 Harshal T. Pandve, The Asian Brown Cloud, Letter to the editor, *Indian Journal of Occupational and Environmental Medicine*, Vol. 22(2), August 2008, pp. 93-95. http://www.ncbi.nlm.nih.gov/pmc/articles/PMC2796752/

76 Roger Highfield, Asian Brown Cloud of pollution contributes to global warming, *The Telegraph*, August 2, 2007 http://www.telegraph.co.uk/earth/environment/globalwarming/3302231/Asian-Brown-Cloud-of-pollution-contributes-to-global-warming.html

and discharges of contaminated water into aquifers, rivers, and streams have affected the quality of water. The rapid growth of both agriculture and urbanisation has imposed added pressure on the water resources. This is evident from the trace of the decline in per capita availability of water in our country. In India, the per capita water availability fell from 5177 cubic meters in 1951 to 1820 cubic meters in 2001.[77] In a 2010 report titled 'The Himalayan Challenge: Water Security in Emerging Asia' prepared by the Mumbai based think tank – Strategic Foresight Group it is stated that India's per capita water availability would sharply decline from 1730 to 1240 cubic metres by the year 2030.[78] Estimates for the year 2050 predict acute shortage of water in India.

The exploitation of groundwater for irrigation is yet another area of concern as this has led to extensive depletion of underground aquifers in several parts of the country. In some areas in the Indian states of Rajasthan, Haryana, Punjab, and Gujarat, the over exploitation rate hovers at 100%-260% far above the critical level of 85%[79]. Declining water quality due to contamination from both untreated sewage and industrial effluents affects the health of the people. In India only 10% of wastewater generated is treated. A survey of some of the major Indian rivers showed that while most can support aquatic life, the water they provide is totally unfit for drinking or even for bathing. On an average, less than three-fourths of municipal solid waste is collected and the rest finds its way into sewers or is burnt in the open.

The principal source of water pollution in the less developed areas of the world is sewage. This is a mixture of waste water from households, factories and other establishments. Much of sewage is untreated. An important component is the human excreta which contain 400 different species of bacteria and viruses. The presence of harmful bacteria persists even after treatment. So, reuse of waste water can be done only when the water is chlorinated. Untreated sewage causes water borne diseases and severely affects the health of citizens. It is estimated that almost two thirds of India's fresh water is polluted. Controlling water pollution is a mammoth

---

77 http://www.cseindia.org/dte-supplement/industry20040215/agriculture.htm

78 http://governancenow.com/views/think-tanks/report-warns-huge-capita-water-decline india

79 Gurneeta Vasudeva, Environmental Security - A South Asian perspective, http://unpan1. un.org/intradoc/groups/public/documents/apcity/unpan015801.pdf

task as is evident from the series of Ganga action plans and the repeated failure in dealing with just one river system[80].

Apart from domestic sources the other major concern is the effluents that are dumped from a variety of industries like sugar factories, tanneries, distilleries and paper mills.[81] Waste water from oil refineries contain the chemical phenol which not only has a strong odour but also is poisonous to marine life. The ammonia, urea, phosphate and sulphates discharged by fertiliser industries causes algal bloom which can decimate water based flora and fauna. Other chemical industries dump mercury that is deadly for humans. Another metal that mixes with waste and is extremely harmful is lead that is the principal component of batteries, printing processes, petrol and paste-processing industries, trace and toxic elements such as zinc, copper etc., and effluents from mining industries affect aquatic organisms. Ship breaking industries like the one at Alang also are extremely polluting. The beaches are now black with oil and other sediments[82].

The pattern of water use in India is such that 93% is used by the agricultural sector and 3.73% by the domestic sector. Nearly 80% of the 14 perennial rivers in India are polluted with sewage. Water in which maximum permissible concentration of any single or more constituents is in excess is unfit for drinking and human health. There are definite tolerance levels for water used for different activities such as drinking, bathing, irrigation and industrial purposes. Depending on its use, there are different physio-chemical and bacteriological standards for water.

Water scarcity due to ground water depletion is the major problem in India. The population has tripled since 1950 and the water demand has multiplied to double the sustainable yield of the aquifers. Aquifer depletion could bring down India's potential crop harvest by 25%. More than 230 blocks in our country are facing a severe shortage of water resources. Vanishing wetlands, heavily silted tanks and shrinking reservoirs are the other problems concerned with water resources in India. Water

---

80 For details on action plans refer www.cleanganga.com

81 Read this and related news items on action against effluent treatment plants for not implementing the zero liquid discharge stipulation. Effluent treatment plants in Tirupur ordered closed, the Hindu, January 29, 2011 http://www.hindu.com/2011/01/29/stories/2011012957180100.htm

82 Manish Tiwari, Titanic Junkyard, DOWN TO EARTH, 15 March 1998, New Delhi, India http://www.ban.org/Library/down_to_earth.html

management practices like desilting of tanks, afforestation, creation of percolation ponds, rainwater harvesting systems and irrigation practices like drip irrigation and sprinkler irrigation are the remedies or solutions available to ease the problems of scarcity. To control water pollution, effluent treatment plants must be installed in industries. Water quality monitoring stations must be created in all the major river systems. A legal provision to prevent and control water pollution is also provided in the form of the Water Act.

By 2025, India would be the most populous country in the world with associated risks to health and the environment. About 2.7 billion people, nearly one-third of the expected world's population, will live in regions facing severe water scarcity, says a study by International Water Management Institute (IWMI). Asia and sub-Saharan Africa containing the most heavily populated and poorest regions of the world will be most severely affected.[83] Also, more than half the population of the world will depend on rice as their principal source of food in 2025. However rice requires a lot of water nearly 2000 tons of water are needed to grow one ton of rice. Therefore there is a dire need to adopt new techniques of cultivation like wet seeding, intermittent rice irrigation, land levelling, improved weed management and management of cracked soil. Yields in developing countries are also low at just 2.5 tons per hectare compared to 7 tons by North American and West European countries.[84] Low cost irrigation technology like the treadle pump- a mechanical water pump used to irrigate small tracts of land, need to be used.

Land Degradation

In the continuing struggle to provide food and other basic needs of the nation's burgeoning populace, land degradation has emerged as a vital concern. Soil suffers from varying degrees of degradation on account of rapid deforestation, poor irrigation and drainage practices, and overgrazing. The depletion of land resources through desertification and the loss of nutrient-rich topsoil through water and wind erosion threaten

---

83 Water Scarcity Threatens Food Supply and Environmental Security. *Health & Medicine Week*, Sep 10, 2001. Also see David Seckler, Upali Amarasinghe David Molden,, Radhika de Silva, and Randolph Barker World Water Demand and Supply, 1990 to 2025: Scenarios and Issues *Research Report 19,*1998 http://www.iwmi.cgiar.org/pubs/PUB019/REPORT19.PDF

84 Ibid.

the livelihood of countless millions throughout India. In our country, as much as 27% of soil cover suffers from severe erosion. Another cause of land degradation is mining, which is typically unorganised and unscientific, without any defined environmental management and land reclamation plans. In some cases there are clear trans-boundary impacts. Poor mining practices in the dolomite mining areas of Bhutan, adjoining the state of West Bengal in India, have resulted in increased landslides and soil erosion. The Indian foothills have taken the burden of landslide debris. Little is known about the impacts on groundwater and the pollution of aquifers in the region as a whole, but they are likely to be significant. India has a total land area of about 329 mha, of which only 266 mha is under proper usage. Land degradation and change in land use patterns are the main problems concerning land resources in India. Land is a very valuable but limited resource, as the population increases rapidly. Many highly urbanised cities are faced with acute space problems, as in Calcutta or Bombay. Besides the limited availability of land, 175 million hectares of land are becoming less productive every year. India loses 20 tons of topsoil per hectare in a year due to floods, rainfall and deforestation. 20 % to 50 % of lands under irrigation can go out of cultivation at this rate because of water logging and salinity. In urban areas, land pollution is caused by disposal of solid wastes and discharge of effluents. In rural areas, it is due to intensive agricultural practices and excessive use of chemical fertilisers and insecticides.

Landslides, soil erosion and topsoil loss are common, due to improper land management practices. Pasturelands are overgrazed by an increasing cattle population. Water logging and salinisation of lands are the problems associated with modern agriculture. Due to increase in population density, the per capita land availability has decreased to 0.12 ha. The land area under forests is just 11% as against the required 33%. The Indian government has set up the National Wasteland Development Board to reclaim wastelands. Afforestation programmes like social forestry and joint forest management have been taken up with public participation. More efforts are required.

Agriculture in the Indian context has undergone various phases of transition. With the increasing population pressure, the need for increased food production resulted in the "Green revolution" of the 1960's. At the expense of forestlands, the land under agriculture has almost doubled. The Green Revolution emphasised hybrid varieties, excessive use of fertilisers, insecticides and weedicides, and has now rendered nearly 13 mha irrigated land unfit for agriculture. Groundwater depletion for agriculture is twice the rate of recharge. Agriculture has degraded 125 mha of land with monoculture, salinisation and water logging. Intensive agriculture has converted many fertile lands to waste lands. Presently, the food grain production is 200 million tonnes, which is projected to increase to 240 million tonnes, by the year 2005. The agricultural sector contributes to almost 30% of the GDP and employs 64% of the total workforce in the country.

Urbanisation

The population of India has tripled since independence. It has crossed the one billion mark leading to a population density of 290 persons/km². Urban areas of some densely populated areas have a population of even 700 - 6500 persons/km². The major effect of this population explosion is "resource crisis". Roughly 20% of the absolutely poor people live in 3 Asian countries of which India is one. Almost half of the population in our country lives below the poverty line. Every year, the population grows at the rate of 2.2%. One fifth of the Indian population lives in rural areas. The migration into cities and towns is at the rate of 2% every year. This migration has led to urbanisation and 40% of the migrant population lives in slums. Dharavi, the largest slum settlement in Asia, is in our country.

Nearly 40% of India's urban population lives in one-room houses, which contain an average of 4-6 persons. The food production is just enough to feed this population. Poor management and storage practices have resulted in wastage of bumper crop yields to pests or simply let to rot. Much of the finite, non-renewable resources (land, water and fuels) are disappearing at an alarming rate due to over-exploitation and unplanned development. If our population does not stabilise at this stage, even a second Green Revolution would not be able to satisfy the hunger of our people. In India, 80% of the migrant population in urban centres does not have access to safe drinking water. Urban slums, garbage and sanitation are the problems associated with urbanisation. The "quality of life" becomes a critical question. This problem can be combated if proper urban planning is adopted in all cities and towns. Developments should lead towards sustainable eco houses and eco towns.

Waste Management

Waste is generally defined as "something, which is not put into proper usage at a given time". As the population increases, the amount of waste generated also increases. The accumulation and improper disposal of waste leads to environmental pollution and accelerates the spread of communicable diseases. Of the 52,000 tonnes of solid waste generated per day, only 2,832 tonnes of waste gets to Waste can generally be categorised according to its origin as domestic waste, industrial waste and hospital waste.

Domestic waste production is the main problem pertaining to India. All the cities and towns produce large amounts of solid waste whose disposal is the main problem. Every Indian on an average generates about 250 - 300 gm. of waste per day. Mumbai, the largest garbage generator in India, produces about 5000 metric tonnes of waste per day. [85] Improper disposal of this waste results in diseases like diarrhoea, malaria and even epidemics like plague. It provides a good breeding ground for vectors, which carry fatal diseases. Waste management aims at curtailing the waste from the initial stage of production. Wastes could be managed by making the manufacturing process efficient, reusing the waste generated and by recycling the waste products.

Sufficient research findings are available for adequate design of sanitary landfills, which are effective in keeping the surface and ground water free from toxic leaching. Waste management will relieve the stress on the natural resources and provide a clean and sustainable environment.

Deforestation

On account of industrial and agricultural expansion as well as trade in forestry products, deforestation remains a major concern in India. India has already lost more than 75% of its forest cover. Conversion to forest land to agricultural use is the principal reason. Building of new dams across rivers and projects like inundations for irrigation and hydroelectric power projects, and construction of new urban areas, industrial plants, roads, power lines, and paper and pulp industries has also resulted in loss of forests. Mining of products like coal and other minerals has also led to cutting down of forests. The illegal logging for timber in protected forest areas has

---

85 Data Sabale, 'Clean Mumbai Campaign', http://www.bombayfirst.org/citymag/vol1no3/article-18.htm

also added to the woes. The problem of deforestation in India is aggravated by the method of exploitation namely sequential exploitation meaning the cutting of trees that are most accessible or near urban areas and then when all of these have been cut seeking remote patches of forests to denude. In this manner much of some states have been completely rendered bereft of forest cover. Not only is deforestation reducing the available forest produce drastically it is severely affecting the wildlife population too. As the forests shrink the wild animals are increasingly coming into contact with humans in their search for food destroying plantations, crops, and even harming people. Water resources in forests are getting polluted rendering rivers and streams dry. Lack of trees, that help the top soil to remain in place, especially in mountainsides, causes landslides and avalanches. These create environmental havoc completely upsetting normal life and imposing huge economic costs for restoration and repair of roads and other damaged infrastructure. For example, the frequent and massive landslides in the Nilgiris area of Tamilnadu are due to the drastic reduction in forest cover caused by the mushrooming of unplanned tea estates[86]. The reason is the same all over India whether it be Karwar in Karnataka or Uttarkasi in Uttarakhand. Unsustainable means of development and destruction of forests is affecting the overall well being of the population in general.

Marine Ecology

The seas and oceans surrounding India have also been subject to exploitation of resources, pollution, through dumping of untreated effluents from industries and cities in India's coastal regions. In particular, the chemical, paper, and sugar industries are major polluters of the marine environment. Agricultural run-off has also contributed to ocean pollution. An estimated 1800 tons of pesticides enter the Bay of Bengal annually[87] and increased use of pesticides in some areas has resulted in contamination of mollusks and fish species. The depletion of mangroves due to shrimp farming in coastal swamps increases the risk of destruction due to tsunamis or others tidal waves. Over fishing and unregulated fishing using huge trawlers has rendered many areas with no fish. Despite a ban on fishing during the

---

86 S. Vasantha Kumar and D. V. S. Bhagavanulu, Effect of deforestation on Landslides in Nilgiris District - A case study, *Journal of Indian Association of Remote sensing*, Vol.36 No.1, March 2008, pp.105-108

87 Environmental Guidebook on the Enclosed Coastal Seas of the world, Centre for Environmental Management of Enclosed Coastal Seas, Japan 2003 p.109 http://www.emecs.or.jp/guidebook/eng/pdf/17bengal.pdf

spawning season the situation is far from satisfactory. Frequent crossing of the international boundary in search of more fertile fishing grounds has often brought conflict with Sri Lankan naval personnel and even fishermen. The depletion of coral reefs has upset the delicate ecological balances of the seas. Coral reefs are unique systems that help to nurture a myriad variety of fish. They also guard the islands and mainland from destructive waves and other marine disturbances. Mining of rare elements like Thorium etc from the sands of beaches across India are making them unusable.

Oil spills are yet another major threat to ocean resources. Approximately 5 million tons of oil is deposited in the Arabian Sea every year; another 400 000 tons is added to the Bay of Bengal.[88] With the growth of tanker traffic in the Indian Ocean and increased offshore exploration and development, the threat of oil spills will undoubtedly increase. There have been a spate of collisions or groundings of ships near Mumbai's shores leading to oil spills. The cargo ships MSC Chitra and MV Khalijia-III collided in August 2010 spilling oil spanning 2 miles.[89] A ruptured pipeline of an oil company caused another oil spill early this year.[90]

Ship breaking is yet another industry that has directly affected the health of our seas. The dismantling of old, unseaworthy ships is now a third world occupation. The dangerous and harmful chemicals and other substances that are released during the process of ship breaking are detrimental to the health of the workers as well as the marine habitat. Vast stretches of beaches in Alang, Gujarat are black with oil and other liquid that have spilled. The unscientific methods adopted in removal of materials like PCBs and such others impact upon the health of the fish and other marine animals. Ingesting these harmful chemicals make the fish unfit for consumption and could also spread diseases to humans who intake contaminated sea food.

---

88 Assessment of biological characteristics of coastal environment of Murud (Maharashtra) during the oil spill 17 May 1993, *Indian Journal of Marine Sciences*, Vol 24, December 1995, p.196 http://drs.nio.org/drs/bitstream/2264/2287/2/Indian_J_Mar_Sci_24_196.pdf

89 Efforts on to check worst oil spill in Arabian Sea, *The Navhind Times*, August 9, 2010 http://www.navhindtimes.in/india-news/efforts-check-worst-oil-spill-arabian-sea

90 ONGC pipeline leak causes oil spill off Mumbai coast, Business Today, January 21, 2011 http://businesstoday.intoday.in/story/ongc-oilfield-spills-oil-off-mumbai-coast/1/12627.html

Loss of Biodiversity

Within the Asia-Pacific region, overall habitat losses have been the most acute in the Indian subcontinent. The underlying causes are international trade in timber, introduction of non-native species, improper use of agro-chemicals, excessive hunting and poaching, etc. India houses not only the second highest number of people on earth but also India's biological diversity is one of the most significant in the world, since India has only 2% of the total landmass of the world containing 6% of the world's wildlife. India has a great diversity of natural ecosystems from the cold and high Himalayan ranges to the seacoasts, from the wet north-eastern green forests to the dry north-western arid deserts, different types of forests, wetlands, islands and the oceans. India consists of fertile river plains and high plateaus and several major rivers, including the Ganges, Brahmaputra and Indus. India is home to 33% of the life forms found in the world and is one among the 12 mega diverse countries of the world. The rich diversity can be attributed to the different geographical zones, tropical climate and its position. The biological wealth of India is estimated to include 45,000 plants and 65,000 animal species. 60% of this wealth can be found in the Western Ghats, which is one of the hotspots of diversity in India, and in the marine habitats. Logging, poaching and over exploitation are completely threatening to destroy rare and endemic species. The tiger, elephant and many other animals are now in the brink of extinction.

Precious biodiversity is also being lost due to habitat alteration, construction of dams, converting forestlands to agricultural lands and natural calamities. The common problems are habitat disturbance and destruction, introduction of exotics, exploitation, marine pollution, and natural disasters like floods, earthquakes and forest fires. Each ecosystem stands to suffer from different sets of problems. For instance, destruction of wetlands is due to siltation, eutrophication, encroachment and tourism.

Conclusion

While this chapter has attempted to highlight the most pressing environmental problems that individual countries face, it is neither comprehensive nor exhaustive. The objective here is to bring to notice the enormous strain and stress our common environment has come to bear due to the unscrupulous acts of humans in the name of development and existence. While non-renewable resources like water and fossil fuel deposits are fast vanishing, the region has to bear the developmental costs too. In the name of development, large tracts of the already greatly reduced forests are being destroyed and villages and tribal areas that mostly depend on forests or forest based resources are being rendered uninhabitable. This results in migration towards urban areas, which in turn places insurmountable pressure on the meagre land and water available there. On the agricultural front poor crop management, repeated and indiscriminate use of pesticides and fertilisers, water scarcity and low soil fertility are reducing farm yields affecting the livelihood of farmers, even costing their very lives.

Urban environments with dense population, lack of adequate space, infrastructure and disproportionate resource distribution contribute to tense social and dismal economic conditions that might lead to unrest and violence. Vehicular pollution due to the burgeoning numbers and lack of stringent environmental safety measures in the past has raised air pollution levels to an all time high. Lack of water management has led to abhorrent civic conditions and non-availability of potable water in some parts of South Asia. Ground water levels have reduced drastically and only ad hoc measures are being adopted. Waste management is becoming another mammoth problem in urban agglomerates. Due to deforestation, silting of water bodies and over exploitation of land and even the sea, fragile eco-systems are vanishing and many rare birds and animal species have become or are nearing extinction.

Recent years have witnessed the emergence of a number of national and local responses to environmental problems in countries of the Indian subcontinent. These initiatives have taken the form of development of national environmental action plans, environmental regulation, and some effort to seek market-based remedies. In some countries, intervention has taken the form of decentralisation and devolution of power to local/ provincial governments for environment planning and management, as well as increased support for grass-roots organisations such as associations of water-users in the design and implementation of solutions.

Given the gravity of common concerns in the region, there is an urgent need for an agenda to implement remedial action among countries of the region. Not only should the South Asian countries act nationally they should also utilise significant opportunities for cooperation in the search for remedial and regulatory responses within the region. Some mechanisms like the SACEP are in place. However, more robust exchanges over an entire range of fields like surveys, research, problem solving, pilot testing and evolution of practicable, effective, regional plans, modules and systems including physical and ideational levels is the need of the hour. Success stories in specific issues like watershed management, rainwater harvesting, sustainable development could be replicated across national territories. Networking of professionals, academics, researchers, scientists, policy makers and concerned citizens throughout the region using the electronic media could pave way for joint development of solutions, sharing of research outputs, experimental data. This could strengthen our response to some of the most debilitating environmental challenges the region of South Asia faces to make environmental security a reality.

V

Endangered Indian National Security By Consequences of Environmental Degradation

Prof Y. Yagama Reddy

Approaches to Issues Concerning Security and Environment

The history of 20th century has amply dealt with security-related issues on the lines of military alliances and strategic arms and armaments, balance of power and geopolitical equations— all have portrayed military threat to the security of a territory or nation-state. Cooperative security has been evolved as a complementary mechanism to comprehensive security in dealing with a post-Cold War environment increasingly challenged by non-military threats to the security at all levels[1]. But, for a long period, the non-conventional/non-military threats like socio-economic problems including poverty and social vulnerability and ecological crisis had hardly been perceived as tangible threats to national security. In fact, many scholars look at environmental security as a component of sustainable development than as a dimension of "traditional" national security[2] . There has been of late a shift in the focus from traditional security conflicts to the implicit concerns emanated from the environmental management. Homer-Dixon and Blitt (1998), for instance, highlighted the imminent links between the

---

1   Dewitt, David B., "Common, Comprehensive, and Cooperative Security in Asia-Pacific," *The Pacific Review*, 7(1), 1994.

2   Najam, Adil, "The Environmental Challenge to Human Security in South Asia," (pp. 225-247), in Thakur, Ramesh and Wiggen, Oddny (ed.), South Asia in the World: Problem Solving Perspectives on Security, Sustainable Development, and Good Governance, United Nations University Press: Tokyo: 2004., p.239

environment and security in their **Ecoviolence,** brought out by the Peace and Conflict Studies Programme at the University of Toronto. Listed in it are the circumstances of environmental scarcity capable of:

1. Producing civil violence and instability as a result of scarcity of renewable resources,

2. Creating demand and unequal distribution as a consequence of degradation and depletion of renewable resources,

3. Prompting the capture of valuable resources by the powerful groups leaving the marginal groups in the lurch,

4. Impinging on economic development and contributing to migrations,

5. Weakening governmental institutions and states,

6. Widening the existing socio-economic distinctions,

7. Generating reaction in the form of ethnic conflicts, insurgencies and coups d`etat, and

8. Causing significant indirect effects on international community.[3]

Although environmental security is treated throughout the literature as being distinct from national security, theoretically it does fall mostly within the sphere of national security and therefore "...national security is no longer about fighting forces and weaponry alone. It relates increasingly to watersheds, croplands, forests, genetic resources, climate, and other factors rarely considered by military experts and political leaders. This methodology and conceptual framework, what is termed as 'methodological pluralism,' was defended against challenges from the traditional and unilateral approaches advocated in some quarters[4].

Deterioration of environmental quality — manifesting in the form of water contamination, soil degradation, deforestation and urban pollution

---

3   Homer-Dixon, T. F. and Blitt, J. (eds.), Ecoviolence: Links among Environment, Population, and Security, Rowman & Littlefield: Lanham, Md., 1998.

4   Schwartz, D.M., Deligiannis, T. and Homer-Dixon, T.F., "The Environment and Violent Conflict", in Diehl and Gleditsch, V.P. (eds.), Environmental Conflicts, Westview Press, Boulder, Colorado: 2001., p.291

— is initially a threat to human well-being, and eventually to human security[5]. Despite perceptible differences over positioning the environment concerns at the centre stage of security agenda, the arguments of Soroos (1994) deserve mention. At the conceptual level, security implies freedom/ protection for human well-being from serious threats, may it be, military, economic, resource, food or environmental realms. Theoretically, the argument is basically on empirical cause-and-effect relationship focusing on the potential of major environmental changes to generate and intensify conflict between and within states. From the point of political premise, the nexus between environment and security seeks to advance the environmental cause for the potential security problems. The threat being posed by the modern civilisation to the primacy of environmental values is an exemplary normative agreement. In the context of debates and discourses on the environment and security, Ullman (1983) offered a vivid definition:

> *A threat to national security is an action or sequence of events that (1) threatens drastically over a relatively brief period of time to degrade the quality of life for the inhabitants of the state, or (2) threatens significantly to narrow the range of policy choices available to the government of a state or to private, non governmental entities (persons, groups, corporations) within the state.* [6]

Political Ecology

Industrialisation of previously agricultural economies, urbanisation of rural societies, economic liberalisation, development goals to catch up with globalisation are the global trends leading to a host of environmental consequences manifesting in pollution of water bodies, degradation and conversion of agricultural land, poor urban air quality, declining of aquatic resources and alike. The concerns over environment have long been debated at various levels over space and time. The holistic understanding of the environmental issues needs a multi-disciplinary approach. The classical concept environmental determinism becomes untenable inasmuch as environmentalism at present cultivates a sphere of overlapping interests and discourses capable of sensitizing a broad spectrum of the population to common cause[7]. It logically assumes the form of environmental governance

---

5   Najam, 2004, p.226

6   Ullman, R.H., "Redefining Security," *International Security*, 81 (3), pp.129-153, 1983.

7 , Hirsch, Philip and Warren, Carol, The Politics of Environment in Southeast Asia:

at regional, national and global levels. This simply means application of ecology to the art of governing. Political ecology, as is broadly known, attempts to study the interdependence among political units and the interrelationships between political units and their environment. Explicitly, this study takes into account the political consequences of environmental change as well as environmental consequences of political decision-making[8]. This is vindicated by the UN Conference on Environment and Development held in Rio de Janeiro in 1992 which recognised environment as an issue that could not be constrained by borders of nation-state.

The concepts of both development and security have been transformed to meet strategic realities. Development, viewed as a process often accompanied by unintended consequences, is not necessarily a public good. Similarly, security is no longer presumed as defence of a nation's territory by armed forces against military threat, inasmuch as threat to the state or its people is possibly expected from many other factors. Thus, as Dewitt and Hernandez (2003) advocate, development and security are the policies dependent on a mix of factors.[9] In the context of broadening of the concept of security beyond military threats as to encompass, among various sources, environmental degradation, there have been policy recommendations adopted by the nation-states to ensure protection of the environment. The international community has got itself sensitised to environmental issues since 1960s and begun to interpret environmental degradation and its impact on the security of nations as non-military threat.

The link between environment and security has of late begun to garner the support. This proposition envisages the process of environmental degradation leading to the deterioration in security position rather a threat to the national security. It bespeaks of the link between the national values and environmental values; explicitly, environmental degradation endangers important national values. Although varied in intensity, no part of the globe has ever remained free from environmental degradation in one or other form of the four Ds-- *d*eforestation, *d*esertification, *d*estruction of

---

Resources and Resistance, Routledge, London: 1998, p.21

8   Tiwari, 2007, p.176

9   Dewitt, David B. and Hernandez, Carolina G., "Defining the Problem and Managing the Uncertainty," (pp. 2-14), in Dewitt, David B. and Hernandez, Carolina G., Development and Security in Southeast Asia, Vol. I: The Environment, Ashgate Publishing Co., Hants, England: 2003, p.4

habitat and species, and decline of air and water quality, as evident from multitude of sources cited by Dewitt and Hernandez (2003). Environment, the earliest and most pervasive source of human conflict, is a source of security concern as well[10]. Levy (1995) focused on the link between environmental degradation and security threat to nation on the existential, physical and political lines. Though Levy was skeptical of the argument that the environmental degradation would threaten national values and thereby the security (*existential* view), he concurred with the proposition of *physical* link between environment and the security; of course through a prescription of a policy combining "containment" and "coexistence". Similarly, Levy termed the *political* threat from environmental degradation (in the form of environmental refugees, resource wars and alike) as weakest; but considered environmental degradation as an important casual factor in sparking regional conflicts.

Environmental Stress and Food Security

Environmental degradation was perceived as a national security issue in Robert Kaplan's analysis, entitled "*The Corning Anarchy*"[11]. The argument of Kaplan has begun to capture popular attention and create unison of interest between the two schools of thought — conventional security threat vis-à-vis environmental security concerns (Mathew, 2000 and Levy, 1995). While elaborating environmental security as the minimisation of environmental damage, Pachauri, Vice Chairman, Inter-governmental Panel on Climate Change (IPCC), looks at national security "as not simply a measure of military power or geopolitical strength, rather it encompasses major social, cultural and human dimensions." Pachauri further elaborated that economic-vulnerability and resource-dependency are at the base of the nexus between the environmental change and the potential for violence and insecurity in the developing world (*Environmental Security...*, 2000). The connection between environmental degradation and human security often portrays poverty as the casual motivator of environmental stress as well as the important manifestation of human insecurity, eventually leading environmental degradation to violent conflict[12]. The resultant 'environmental stress,' which Pachauri viewed as a reflex of exacerbated poverty, is well identified in five areas -- increased land degradation

10 Najam, 2004, p.226

11 Kaplan, Robert, "The Corning Anarchy," *Atlantic Monthly* (February), 1994, pp.45-76

12 Najam, 2004, p.237

owing to struggle for food and basic needs, worsened pollution impacts, global climate change consequences, risk-prone water and air quality, and deforestation. Air pollution, deforestation, agricultural mismanagement, wanton use of water, over-harvested fisheries, oil spills and callousness in waste disposal are a host of factors contributing to the environmental degradation with various magnitudes of consequences on ecosystems and human environment at local, regional, national and global levels.

The growth of global population— from about 1.0 billion in 1825 to about 1.65 billion in 1900, and then to 6.0 billion at the turn of 20th century— and an increased consumption of resources have made the globe vulnerable to environmental changes. Cleo Paskal of Energy, Environment and Development Programme, Chatham House, linked the large scale population growth to complex and far-reaching environmental changes, such as groundwater depletion, deforestation, exhausted farmland, stress on urban infrastructure, over-fishing[13]. The increasing demand for agricultural products of the burgeoning population is quite alarming in that an annual population growth of 80 million requires an annual increase of 26 million tonnes of food grains. In other words, the demand for food grains in 2020 is estimated at about 2500 million tonnes. The increase in agricultural production from 740 million tonnes in 1950 to about 1900 million tonnes in 1995 was accomplished by both extensive and intensive agricultural practices. Despite the claims of progress in tackling the grave issues of hunger and malnutrition, "India is home to the world's largest food insecure population" occupying 66th rank among the 88 countries surveyed by Washington based international Food Policy Research Institute (*Wikipedia: the free encyclopedia*). Endemic mass hunger, often resulting in starvation deaths, has coexisted with food grain stocks. As further extensification of agriculture is likely to contribute about 7 per cent (50 million tonnes) on global scale, intensification seems to be the option for increasing production, projected at about 4.0 tonnes / hectare (2020) as against 2.8 tons / hectare (1995) or 1.15 tons / hectare in 1951[14]. Conversion of productive cropland to non-farm uses is likely affect the food production. Less affluent countries import food grains; desperate people denied of access to food would move as economic migrants to food-

---

13 Paskal, Cleo, UK National Security and Environmental Change: A Policy Brief for the IPPR Commission on National Security for the 21st Century, Institute of Public Policy Research, April 2009, p.3

14 Tiwari, 2007, pp.230-01

secure countries

Economic liberalisation, unleashed in 1991, has brought in a paradigm shift from subsistence grain production (staple food crops) to commercial farming (cash crops). This policy – a form of neocolonialism biased to agribusiness multinational corporations – has led to the mass displacement of mainly small and marginal farmers who are being deprived of livelihood opportunities and employment generation in the traditional farming sector. The fact that India has 14.2% of landless people and poverty ratio of 39.2% (Planning Commission) subscribes to the prevalence of starvation-epidemic in India. The resultant 'agrarian crisis', was manifested in farmers' suicides to the tune of 150,000 during 1997-2005 (Afsar, 2008), including 5,000 in Andhra Pradesh alone during 1998-2004. The widespread farmers' suicides bear testimony to desperation and frustration as well as to precarious food security; and stands as rhetoric of lofty claims like "shining India" and "booming Indian economy." The National policy for Farmers (2006) therefore underscores "the need to focus on the economic well-being of the farmers, rather than just on production" (Swaminathan, 2008). Food security in India rests in 'million person jobs and livelihoods, rather than in million tonnes of food grains. This is a fact based on the workforce of about 60 per cent of the total being engaged in agriculture-related activities that constitute the largest private sector-enterprise (Swaminathan, 2001), contributing 18 per cent to GDP.

Agriculture and Forest Lands

In view of spatial distinctions in physiography of India, diversity in bioclimatic phenomena is rather incidental to India, so much as in the land use pattern, deforestation and water resources. India's land area accounts for 2.5 per cent of the earth's land surface. Over half-a-century, agricultural land registered substantial increase from 118 million hectares (mha) (1951) to 142 mha (2000), keeping pace with the increasing population[15]. India has a forest cover of 63.7 mha or 19.39 per cent of the total geographical area of 329 mha. But, this represents a phenomenal decrease of forest cover form 65 per cent of the total land area (214 mha) in the first quarter of 20th century[16] (). India had since independence lost three fourths of its forest cover of about 164 mha. Even the claim of forest area in 72.5 mha (22 per

---

15 Dash, Sushil Kumar, Climate Change: An Indian Perspective, Centre for Environment Education, Ahmedabad: 2007, pp.135-36

16 Dash, 2007, pp.135-36

cent of the total land area) in mid-1980s was later revised as to put the forest cover at 19.52 per cent of the total land area (Yagama Reddy, et. al., 1990). Forest degradation still continues so much so that the loss of best (closed) forest cover during 1990-2000 was estimated at 38,089 hectares (ha) (FAO, 2000), or even in its extreme end the loss was put at 188,900 ha during the same period of time (MOEF, 1999). About 11 million hectares of tropical forests are destroyed annually and another 6 mha got desertified in the developing countries. This is amply evident from the increase in the extent of agriculture land from 118 mha (1951) to 142 mha (2000), as opposed to the decrease in the forest land from 132 mha (1950) to 64 mha (2000) (Yagama Reddy et. al., 1990; Dash, 2007). The more the population-pressure on land (1.42 ha/person in 1800 through 1.37 ha in 1901 to 0.20 ha in 1981), the more the encroachment into forest lands[17].

The ubiquitous phenomenon of forest decline owed much to fodder famines, over-grazing of forest lands and illicit extraction of forest wood for fuel and industrial purposes; and it set in motion a chain of reactions— soil erosion, flooding and siltation, recurrence of droughts and threat to bioclimatic life— eventually leading to the formation of waste lands which is a manifestation of environmental degradation. The population pressure-on-agricultural land encroaching-into-forest land, undisputedly a negative nexus, portends the eventual rather inevitable environmental degradation. The combination of factors leading to phenomenal decline in forest cover simply testifies to the perception of forests as timber mines rather than ecological resources that need to be protected. Of some solace is the modest increase of 389,600 ha under the afforestation programme during the two decades between 1980 and1999[18].

Forest degradation together with such other factors as drought, inappropriate agricultural practices, over-exploitation of land, accelerated soil erosion, salinisation of soils, increase in surface runoff leading to reduction in soil moisture and decline in the plant species-diversity would result in land degradation, a precursor to desertification. About 18.74 per cent of area in India is found vulnerable to desertification affecting the livelihood of 250 million people and rendering about 100 million people

---

17 *The Hindu*, 5 May 1987, p.17; Sharma, R.C., Population Trends, Resources and Environment: Handbook on Population Education, Dhanapat Rai & Sons, Delhi: 1975.

18 Dash, 2007, 137

vulnerable to displacement from the peripheral region of dry lands[19], besides threatening food security. About 1/3 of land area (about 107.30 mha) in India is affected by various forms of land degradation, predominantly by water erosion, forest degradation and wind erosion[20].

Pressure on available Water Resources

India has 4 per cent of fresh water resources of the world's total. Out of the India's annual precipitation of 4,000 billion cubic meters (bcm), about 1,869 bcm takes the form of surface run off into rivers. Together with 690 bcm of surface water, about 1,122 bcm of water is available for 1.166 billion population. India's projected population of 1.6 billion in 2050 will make demand for 14,476 bcm of water and 450 million tonnes of food grains[21]. According to United Nations Environment Programme (2002), the per capita water availability in India (1,249 m^3 / year / person) falls far short of the global average and is far less than other South Asian countries, save Bangladesh. Water situation in India is worse, with eight of the 20 river basins facing water deficit threatening the lives and livelihoods of over 200 million people, whose number is expected to reach the mark of 900 million by 2025[22]. Spatio-temporal variations in the range of 100 mm to 1,170 mm of annual rainfall are well pronounced, given the fact that 80 per cent of rainfall occurs during the summer monsoon spreading over 100 days. Yet, 91 districts would face drought, even as 83 districts experience flooding. Climate change-induced erratic weather, which parched the heart of India, is destroying agriculture and plunging the poorest farming families into crippling debt.

Pollution Hazards

Through the medium of capricious winds, atmospheric pollution transcends geographical and political boundaries. The ever increasing air pollutants, essentially a man-made legacy, were attributed to the emissions

---

19 Dash, 2007, pp.122-123

20 Adeel, Zafar and Piracha, Awais, "Critical Links between Environment and Development in South Asia," (pp.205-224), in Thakur, Ramesh and Wiggen, Oddny (ed.), South Asia in the World: Problem Solving Perspectives on Security, Sustainable Development, and Good Governance, United Nations University Press, Tokyo: 2004, p.212

21 Dash, 2007, pp.117-18

22 Dash, 2007, p.118

in alarming proportions by both stationary and mobile sources[23]. Automobiles and industries depending on fossil fuels pump several billions of carbon monoxide, sulphur dioxide and oxides of nitrogen into the air, besides other pollutants like lead, suspended particulate matter (SPM) and polycyclic aromatic hydrocarbons (PAHCs). The levels of sulphur and carbon in fuels are more in India than the international standards. Apart from poor fuel quality, fuel adulteration is quite alarming in India. Stratospheric ozone depletion is essentially a man-made crisis erupted by the release of chlorofluorocarbons (CFCs) that inhibit the atmospheric ability to shield the earth surface from ultra-violet radiation responsible for increased risks of cancer, cataracts and respiratory ailments as well as lower crop yields. Water pollution is yet another concern in India. The highly polluted 13 major river basins have their perceptible impact on 85 per cent of population in their respective river-catchment areas covering 80 per cent of land area[24]. Besides rising incidence of water-borne diseases and skin diseases, the polluted river water has affected the fishing resources, crop yields and ground water aquifers. Indiscriminate application of pesticides with organochlorines (such as dichloro-diphenyl trichloro-ethane and benzene hexachloride) and organophosphates (like monocrotophos and melathion) has resulted in excessive accumulation of pesticide residues in food items such as milk, rice, maize, wheat, cauliflower, bananas, apples and grapes. Pollutants discharged by the coastal cities have caused destruction to the coastal wetlands supporting the life system. Chemical wastes, in the from of sewage and mining waste, are responsible for the falling fish catches, besides causing damage to the mangroves which are known for their proven efficacy in containing soil erosion and acting as barriers against cyclones.

Industrial solid and hazardous waste materials, filling to the extent of 1.0 meter deep across 96 sq. km every year, have increased the levels of toxins (like cyanide and chromium), capable of causing respiratory ailments and contaminating the groundwater[25]. To make the polluted environment further worse, the urban garbage largely composed of hazardous plastics and metals, to a tune of 80,000 tonnes every day, is indiscriminately dumped on the river banks with total disregard to the imminent consequences of

---

23 Prasad, K.S.S. and Yagama Reddy, Y., "Levels of Air Pollution in the Indian Cities," Environment & Ecology, 6 (4), pp. 933-37, 1988, pp.933-37

24 India Today, 1999

25 Dash, 2007, p.127

environmental degradation (*India Today*, 1999). As per the survey of the United Nations (2000), open-dumping accounts for 60 per cent of the urban waste disposal practices in India.

Some of the notable changes of global warming in the recent years are equally important for discussion on environmental degradation. Yes, there are studies indicating the warming of surface mean annual air temperatures, with apparently well pronounced variations in meteorological parameters like fog days, snow ablation and snow fall, rainfall amount and rainy days, monsoon depressions and cyclonic storms. Agriculture and related activities-- which constitute the single largest component of India's economy - contribute 1/3 to GDP, provide employment to 2/3 of the total workforce and make up 1/5 of the total exports. Agricultural productivity is vulnerable to climate changes either directly or indirectly. It is estimated that the costs of climate change in India "could amount to as much as 9-13% of GDP compared with a world without climate change" [26]. The catastrophic consequences of food crisis would threaten national sovereignty, not necessarily on account of external threats, but due to internal strife. It would be then a geopolitical contest among the nations neither for gaining control over a parcel of land, nor even for a market; but invariably for gaining access to the food-source country.

The increased emission of CO_2 and the anticipated rise in temperature and rainfall would result in decreased crop yields in central and southern parts of India. CO_2 is the main greenhouse gas and about 290 billion tonnes of carbon have been released into the atmosphere since mid-1970s. The wealthiest 10 per cent of people in developed countries emit 7.5 times more CO_2 than the 10 per cent of poor people in developed countries, and 155 times CO_2 than the poorest 10per cent of people in developing countries. With 5 per cent of CO_2 emissions in 2003, India ranks fourth among the largest polluters, viz., the United States (22%), China (16%), Russia (6%) and Japan (5%). Climate change would tend to dislocate the summer monsoon rhythm which has direct influence on the rain-fed crops and direct pressure on irrigation and soil water levels, and thereby on the crop growth. Dislocation rather failure of monsoon rhythm and increased evapo-transpiration in India have resulted in depletion of groundwater

---

26 Stern Review Report 2007, as quoted in Halden, Peter, Geopolitics of Climate Change: Challenges to the International System, FOI Swedish Defence Research Agency, Stockholm, Sweden: 2007., p.92

levels, as evident from the fact that half of the 21 million irrigation wells got dried up. If temperature increase leads to upward soil water movement giving rise to salts-accumulation in the upper soil layers, sea level rise leads to salt-water ingression in the coastal lands, rendering them degraded soils.

Global Warming—Sea Level Rise—Consequences

Climate change is projected to increase global mean surface temperature in the range of 1.1 to 6.4°C by 2100 and the sea level by 18-59 cm that pose myriad risks. A mean annual increase in temperature just by few degrees would set in motion a chain of reactions. Of much significance is the mean sea level rise, due to global warming, in the range of 10-25 cm over the last 100 years[27]. One meter rise in sea level on the Indian coastline of about 6,500 km would inundate 170,000 mha of potentially productive agricultural land (IPCC, 1922); at the extreme end, the inundated area is projected at about 570,000 mha covering 7.1 million people as victims (JNU, 1993). Halden (2007, p.49) looks at the geopolitics of climate change from the view point of degradation of ecosystems and human habitats as a consequence of warmer climate and changed precipitation patterns.

It is of much relevance to make a mention of the possible intra-regional migration flows in the event of coastal lands becoming liable for inundation by the sea level rise. The much expected global warming would have its adverse impact on South Asia. If the rise in temperature induces melting of Himalayan glaciers, the source of Asia's biggest rivers, there would be enormous drainage through the Himalayan-origin Rivers including Brahmaputra, the Indus and the Ganges flowing into the Indian sub-continent. Concurrent melting of the polar ice-caps and glaciers around the world would lead to the rise in global sea level resulting in submergence of low-lying areas including river deltas, coastal plains and small and low-lying islands. Consequently, the densely populated coastal based cities would face the risk of getting inundated, besides losing the agriculturally productive lands in the coastal fringes. If it were the case, parts of Bangladesh, Sri Lanka, Pakistan, Maldives and several parts of India would be the worst victims of rising sea level that would ignore the political frontiers. In that event, unclear rather disappeared borders would become contested boundaries becoming highly susceptible to proxy war, centering on water and land resources (Pai, 2008).

---

27 Dash, 2007, p.115

Climate Refugees

This trans-border population displacement creates intra-state violence arising out of diversified population groups differentiated by religion, sectarian faiths, language and ethnicity. There shall also be inter-state conflicts on account of disputed claims for resources— river waters and exclusive economic zones (Subramanyam, 1989). The effects of climate change on migration may increase the risk of civil conflicts between groups (Barnett, 2003). The geopolitical ramifications of climate change include large scale movement of 'climate refugees' leading to skirmishes, battles and even wars due to resource constraints[28]. An authority on the linkages between environmental degradation and violent conflict, Homer-Dixon, is reported[29] to have pointed out that 'the disputes concerning environmental degradation would lead to the ethnic clashes' on the lines of migration and social cleavages and the 'civil strife, caused by environmental scarcity, affecting economic activity, livelihood, elite behaviour and state responses. Halden (2007, 149) further outlined the 'paths to violent conflict under conditions of climate change': firstly, the political actors could exploit climate change-induced strains, for example migrants, to gain or retain power in internal power struggle; and the other one on the lines of 'subsistence conflicts' over scarce resources, for instance land and water between the 'haves' and 'have-nots.'

Capricious Citizenship- Vote Bank Politics

The climate-change makes India to become a centripetal stage for intra-regional migration from all other SAARC countries. The illegal immigrants, constituting 30 percent of Assam's population of about 26 million, are at the centre stage of Assam politics, especially in 40 out of 126 Assembly constituencies (Upadhyay, 2005; Kumar, 2005). Yet, the expediency of the vote bank politics has made political parties turn blind eye towards illegal migrants in Assam even as they have become a formidable a national threat. In a similar fashion, thanks to the captive vote bank politics in West Bengal, Bangladeshi infiltrators constituted 17% of the electorate in as many as 56 Assembly constituencies[30]. This 'capricious

28 Barnett, Jon, "The Geopolitics of Climate Change," Geography Compass, 1(6), pp.1361-75, 2007, pp.1362-64

29 Halden, Peter, Geopolitics of Climate Change: Challenges to the International System, FOI Swedish Defence Research Agency, Stockholm, Sweden: 2007, p.50

30 *Pioneer* 6 October 1992

citizenship' of transnational migrants has churned chauvinism. All along with the xenophobic reactions against these transnational migrants, they are blamed for many problems faced by Indians, like unemployment, environmental degradation, domestic and international terrorist activities, escalated crime and lawlessness. No doubt, India's large population, poverty and limited resources could hardly afford to take on Bangladeshis burden; and India would become an arena of geopolitical game often provoking the interference of other external powers. In the context of the South Asian regional security complex, dominated by history of the India-Pakistan border skirmishes, climate change will have a major security policy implication. Bangladesh will occupy the centre stage of the debates on climate change and exploit the crisis to its advantage. Climate change will become an excuse for Bangladesh to continue its policy of *lebensraum*.

Nexus between Environmental and Security Crises

Climate factors played a forgotten role in geopolitical theories of early 20th century. Though Spykman (1944) made a case for climatic primacy in his geopolitics, he treated geographical location of a state as of utmost importance in defining its problems of security. For him, climate factors set the limits to agricultural production which, in turn, conditions the economic structure of the state and thereby the basis for the power of the state. In his address to 12th Conference of Parties to the United Nations Framework Convention on Climate Change at Nairobi on 15 November 2006, the UN Secretary General, Kofi Annan, cautioned:

> *Climate change is not just an environmental issue…. It is an all-encompassing threat. It is a threat to health. It could imperil the world's food supply. It could endanger the very ground on which nearly half of the world's population live. Climate change is also a threat to peace and security.* (Barnett, 2007).

Environmental degradation, as is to be logically viewed, presages a threat to national security. No longer should security threats be perceived strictly in military terms, but in a more holistic fashion. ….national security and environmental security are related — though not identical — concepts on the theoretical level. Environmental change and degradation are thus fundamental to national security concerns because many environmental problems pose direct threats not only to individuals but to nations as well. Environmental degradation, constituting a security risk, implies environmental resource-scarcity and environmental resource-degradation.

VI

Security Implications of Climate Change – An Indian Perspective

- Lalitha Ramadorai

"Few threats to peace and survival of the human community are greater than those posed by the prospects of cumulative and irreversible degradation of the biosphere on which human life depends. True security cannot be achieved by mounting buildup of weapons (defence in a narrow sense), but only by providing basic condition for solving non-military problems which threaten their survival." [1]

- Brandt Report, 1980.

Changing Paradigm of National Security in India

India's peninsular shape provides her a land frontier that exceeds 15,000 kms and a coastline of 7,600 kms. Our country shares land borders with seven countries and maritime boundary with five countries. She has an Exclusive Economic Zone of over 2 million square kms.[2] Her island territories are thousands of kilometers away from the mainland and are closer to her South East Asian neighbours. Being the world's largest democracy in one of the most unstable regions of the world, security has always been top most priority for India.

National Security in India has traditionally focused on external challenges; most notably threats posed by our hostile neighbours and has mainly involved the military-centric protection of our territories

---

1 Brandt, W., *North-South – A Programme for Survival*, Report of the Independent Commission on International Development Issues, Pan Books, London, p.115, 1980.

2 http://mod.nic.in/samachar/july15-01/html/ch1.htm

and population. Though the external military aggressions from Pakistan and China forms the core of India's security concerns even today, newer challenges have emerged. These so called 'non-military threats' include religious fundamentalism, financial turmoil, deadly pandemics, mass migration, drug and human trafficking and natural disasters. Unlike the external challenges that threaten the sovereignty of a nation, the non-traditional threats affect life, health, prosperity and freedom of individuals (collectively referred to as 'human security'), society and states, and in extreme cases can create the condition for conflicts and armed violence.

Environmental degradation is also being perceived as one of the non-military threats faced by humanity in recent times. Environmental problems such as dwindling water and energy supplies, land degradation and desertification, disappearing biodiversity and climate change threaten human survival more than military action ever could. This is attributed to the fact that these resources are the cornerstone of human survival and form the support system on which all other human activities depend – whether political, social, cultural or economics.

Environmental stresses also poses threat to national security by increasing the prospects of conflicts. This is particularly true for poor and marginalised communities, where degradation can limit economic options and force the already impoverished to seek for their livelihood in newer lands. The multiple effects of environmental problems, including economic decline, large population movements can weaken the state's capacity to address the people's demands and in turn to maintain their confidence on the system. This can result in weakened states; support for extremism and in extreme cases armed conflicts. As emphasised by the United Nations Commission on Environment and Development – *"The immediate cause of any mass movement may appear to be political upheaval and military violence. But the underlying causes often include the deterioration of the natural base and its capacity to support the population"*.[3]

In India, environmental degradation is arguably one of the prominent and immediate threats to national and human security at present times, which is unlikely to be matched by any foreseeable type of military engagement. India's spectacular economic growth averaging 6-8 %

---

3 World Commission on Environment and Development, *Our Common Future (The Brundtland Report)*, Chapter 11,Oxford University Press, New York, USA, 1987, http://www.un-documents.net/ocf-11.htm

annually over the past decade or so has produced an impressive increase in the standard of living for hundreds of millions of Indian citizens. At the same time, this development has had severe ramifications for the natural world. The country has only 21.05% of total area under forest cover[4]; 246 species of plants and 413 species of native animals are presumed extinct or threatened with extinction[5]; almost 70% of India's surface water resources and a large proportion of her ground water reserves are contaminated[6]; in urban areas water and air pollution levels have skyrocketed and undermine human health. In terms of loss of territory, of the total land expanse of 329 million hectares, nearly 141 million hectares (43%) are subject to soil and wind erosion, while another 34 million hectares are affected due to water logging, salinity, ravines, alkaline and arid soil, etc.[7] Thus, it can be reasonably concluded that the security of India and Indians is at great risk from various environmental stresses.

This chapter examines the environmental dimension of security in India with a special focus on the impacts of climate change. The chapter argues as to why climate change should be treated as a serious issue that threatens human and ultimately national security.

Climate Change – The Background

Climate change is defined as a long-term (typically decades or longer), significant variation the average weather a region experiences. It is not a new phenomenon to planet earth. The earth's climate has changed before, many times throughout its history. There have been ice ages interspersed with warmer interglacial periods. The last ice age ended about 7000 years ago, marking the beginning of the modern climatic era and more importantly, the human civilisation.

Most of the climatic variations in the past have been attributed to natural causes such as variation in solar output, meteorite impact, tectonic processes, volcanic eruptions and changes in the earth's orbit. Ecosystems

---

4 India's forest cover declines, *Down to Earth*, February 8, 2012, http://www.downtoearth. org.in/content/india-s-forest-cover-declines MacKinnon, J., and MacKinnon, K., *Review of Protected Areas Systems in the Indo-Malayan Realm*, IUCN, Gland, Switzerland, 1986.

5 http://data.iucn.org/dbtw-wpd/edocs/RL-2009-001.pdf

6 Jain, S.K., Agarwal, P.K., Singh, V.P., *Hydrology and Water Resources of India*, p. 997, 2007.

7 Vyas, V.S., *Changing Contours of Indian Agriculture*, NCAER, New Delhi, p.18, 1999.

have adapted continuously to these natural changes in the climate and flora and fauna have evolved in response to the gradual change in their physical conditions, or have become extinct. The current climate change, however is different and significant because most of it is very likely human-induced and is occurring at a rate that is unprecedented.

Since the beginning of the industrial age, an increasing world population has made more widespread use of fossil fuels to aid economic development as well as to augment human comfort and convenience. We have assembled an array of machinery, all of which produce carbon dioxide and other gases that have altered the composition of the atmosphere in a way that the atmosphere is retaining an increasing amount of heat.

Under normal conditions, when the sun's rays warm the earth's surface after having first passed through the earth's atmosphere, about a third of it is radiated back into space (infrared radiations). Some is then trapped or absorbed by the greenhouse gases like carbon dioxide, methane, nitrous oxides, etc. and about half is absorbed by the land, sea, trees, etc. But the recent buildup of carbon dioxide in the atmosphere traps in heat that otherwise would be reflected back into space, driving the warming of the atmosphere as well as the earth's surfaces (both land and sea). This in turn has many other effects such as changes in the rates of evapo-transpiration and in the amounts and distribution of precipitation.

The best evidence of climate change over the past century or more has come from surface temperature recorded around the world. Although the trend has not been regionally uniform, there is consensus that the average global surface temperature has risen 0.74 °C between 1906 and 2005, with "most of the warming observed over the last fifty years".[8] The decade 2001-2010 was the warmest decade ever recorded in all continents of the globe, with the warmest year being 2011.[9]

---

8 Trenberth, K.E., Jones, P.D., Ambenje, P., Bojariu, R., Easterling, D., Klein Tank, A., Parker, D., Rahimzadeh, F., Renwick, J.A., Rusticucci, M., Soden B., and Zhai, P., Observations: Surface and Atmospheric Climate Change, in *Climate Change 2007: The Physical Science Basis*, Contribution of Working Group I to the Fourth Assessment Report of the Intergovernmental Panel on Climate Change, Solomon, S., Qin, D., Manning, M., Chen, Z., Marquis, M., Averyt, K.B., Tignor, M., Miller, H.L., (eds.), Cambridge University Press, Cambridge, United Kingdom and New York, NY, USA, p. 237, 2007.

9 WMO annual Statement confirms 2011 as the 11th warmest on record, , 23 March 2012, http://www.wmo.int/pages/mediacentre/news/

Consistent with the warming, global sea levels also increased at an average rate of 1.8 mm/year between 1961-2003, with contributions from thermal expansion, melting glaciers and ice caps, and the polar ice sheets. The rate of sea level rise was faster over the period 1993-2003, when sea level rose by as much as 3.1 ± 0.7 mm / year.[10] The world's mountain glaciers and snow cover have receded in both hemispheres, and the Arctic sea ice extent has been continuously shrinking by 2.7 percent per decade, since 1978.[11] The continent of Antartica has been losing 100 cubic kilometers of ice every year since 2002.[12] Extreme hydrological events, such as droughts, hurricanes and floods also appear to be becoming common.

By using best estimates from various modelled scenarios, Inter-Governmental Panel on Climate Change (IPCC) projects that these changes are likely to intensify in the near future. The global mean surface temperature is to increase between 1.1 and 6.4°C by the end of the 21st century. The global mean sea level is projected to rise between 0.18 and 0.59 centimetres.[13]

Although these predicted temperature increase may not seem very large, but as Sir John Houghton (Former Chairman of the Scientific Assessment for IPCC) observes, *"Between the middle of an ice age and the warm periods in between the ice ages, the global average temperature changes by only 5 or 6°C. If a 2.5 °C rise is experienced, this 'represents about half an*

---

10 Bindoff, N.L., Willebrand, J., Artale, V., Cazenave, A., Gregory, J., Gulev, S., Hanawa, K., Le Quéré, C., Levitus, S., Nojiri, Y., Shum, C.K., Talley, L.D., and Unnikrishnan, A., Observations: Oceanic Climate Change and Sea Level, in: *Climate Change 2007: The Physical Science Basis*, Contribution of Working Group I to the Fourth Assessment Report of the Intergovernmental Panel on Climate Change, Solomon, S., Qin, D., Manning, M., Chen, Z., Marquis, M., Averyt, K.B., Tignor, M., Miller, H.L., (eds.), Cambridge University Press, Cambridge, United Kingdom and New York, NY, USA, 2007. p.411.

11 Lemke, P., Ren, J., Alley, R.B., Allison, I., Carrasco, J., Flato, G., Fujii, Y., Kaser, G., Mote, P., Thomas, R.H., and Zhang, T., Observations: Changes in Snow, Ice and Frozen Ground. In: *Climate Change 2007: The Physical Science Basis*. Contribution of Working Group I to the Fourth Assessment Report of the Intergovernmental Panel on Climate Change, Solomon, S., Qin, D., Manning, M., Chen, Z., Marquis, M., Averyt, K.B., Tignor, M., Miller, H.L., (eds.), Cambridge University Press, Cambridge, United Kingdom and New York, NY, USA, p.339, 2007.

12 http://climate.nasa.gov/keyIndicators/index.cfm#seaLevel

13 Summary for Policymakers, In: *Climate Change 2007: The Physical Science Basis*, Contribution of Working Group I to the Fourth Assessment Report of the Intergovernmental Panel on Climate Change, Solomon, S., Qin, D., Manning, M., Chen, Z., Marquis, M., Averyt, K.B., Tignor, M., Miller, H.L., (eds.), Cambridge University Press, Cambridge, United Kingdom and New York, NY, USA, p.13, 2007.

*ice age' in terms of climate change. For this to occur in less than 100 years.....
is very rapid change. Adapting to this will be difficult for both humans and
many ecosystems".*[14]

India's Vulnerability to Climate Change

As increasing scientific evidences reveal the rate and the extent of climate
change, we have began to realise that it holds potentially serious implications
for international security. The unusually ferocious floods, droughts and
storms we have seen across the world in recent years show all too clearly
how vulnerable we are to climatic extremes and how devastating they can
be. Hurricane Katrina clearly demonstrated as to how even the world's
most powerful country can be torn apart by natural disasters.

India, though not a major contributor of greenhouse emissions, is seen
as one of countries most at risk due to climate induced changes – a function
of the country's reliance on climate dependent sectors (such as rain-fed
agriculture). With an economy closely tied with its natural resource base
and a majority of its population - 700 million - being involved in climate-
sensitive sectors, including agriculture, forestry and fishery[15], there are few
greater threats to India's security than climate change. Climate change by
affecting water availability, food security, diseases prevalence and coastal
sea level – could increase forced migration, raise tensions and trigger
conflicts. The country is in fact being seen as one of global 'hot-spot' for
climate change[16], given its location and its limited capacities to respond to
adversities of climate change.

Climate Change Predictions for India: Hotter, Wetter and Unpredictable Weather

Observations over India show that the mean annual surface air temperature
has increased by about 0.57°C in the period 1901-2003. [17] While this is only

---

14 Sir John Houghton, *Global Pollution and Climate Change,* briefing prepared for The
John Ray Initiative, http://www.jri.org.uk/brief/climatechange.htm.

15 Sathaye, J., Shukla, P.R., and Ravindranath, N.H., "Climate Change, Sustainable
Development and India : Global and National Concerns", *Current Science,* Vol. 90, No.3,
p.318, February 2006.

16 Ehrhart, C., and Thow, A., *Humanitarian Implications of Climate Change – Mapping
Emerging Ttrends and Risk Hotspots,* UN Office for the Coordination of Humanitarian
Affairs and CARE International, August 2008.

17 Kothawale, D.R., and Rupa Kumar, K., "On the recent changes in the surface temperature

a marginal increase, the advanced models now predict an increase 2-5°C by the end of this century.[18] The Indian report to the UNFCCC says that at the end of the century the "annual mean temperature rise ranges from 3.5-4.3°C. [19]The warming is predicted to be more pronounced in winters than during the monsoon season.[20] Also, the northern parts of India will be warmer compared to the south.

In India, the south-west monsoon (between June and September) and the northeast monsoon (between October and November) are the primary sources of rainfall. Climate change is likely to bring significant changes in the monsoon patterns and thus, the precipitation levels. Most studies using Global Climate Models and Regional Climate Models suggest an increase in the rainfall during the summer monsoon, with heavy rains occurring over fewer days. The weather is also likely to become more unpredictable.

Table 1: Studies about the projected Precipitation levels over India during the 21st Century

Rainfall Projections	References
Precipitation increase of approximately 20%. Increase in heavy rainfall days during the summer monsoon period and an increased inter-annual variability.	1
Increase in frequency of heavy rainfall events.	2

trends over India", *Geophysical Research Letter*, Vol. 32, L18714, 2005.

18 Sumana Bhattacharya, Lessons Learnt for Vulnerability and Adaptation Assessment from India's First National Communication, BASIC Project September 2007, p.2 http://www.basic-project.net/data/final/Paper07India%20Lessons%20for%20VA%20from%20First%20National%20Communicat%85.pdf

19 http://envfor.nic.in/downloads/public-information/2ndNational_Communication_2_UNFCCC.pdf

20 Lal, M., Nozawa, T., Emori, S., "Future Climate Change Implications for Indian Summer Monsoon and its variability", *Current Science*, Vol. 81, No. 9, p.1204, 2001.

Rainfall Projections	References
Increase of about 7 to 10% in annual mean precipitation. Decline of 5–25% in winter precipitation. Increase in monsoon precipitation is 10–15%. Monsoon season over northwest India – increase of 30% or more in rainfall by 2050. The western semi-arid regions of India could receive higher than normal rainfall in a warmer atmosphere. Decrease in winter precipitation between 10 and 20% over central India by 2050.	3
Decrease in number of rainy days over a major part of the country. This decrease is more in the western and central parts (by more than 15 days), while near the foothills of the Himalayas (Uttaranchal) and in northeast India, the number of rainy days may increase by 5–10 days. Increase in rainy days intensity by 1–4 mm/day, except for small areas in northwest India, where rainfall intensities may decrease by 1 mm/day.	4

These climatic changes will have a series of consequences in India, the prominent ones being discussed in this section.

Threatened Water Supplies

The increase in temperature is likely to make surface water evaporate more quickly, thus affecting surface water flow. Though an increase in precipitation in Mahanadi, Brahmani, Ganga, Godavari and Cauvery basins is projected under the climate change scenario, total run off for all these basins is not likely to increase. This may be due to the increase in evapo-transpiration on account of increased temperatures and other factors such as the distribution of rainfall. A decline in total run off for all river basins is predicted, except Narmada and Tapi. A decline in the runoff by more than two-thirds is projected for the Sabarmati and Luni basins, which may lead to severe drought conditions in the region under future climate change scenario.[21] The evapo-transpiration shows an increase of nearly 10% for Brahmaputra, Indus and Luni river basins. Only Cauvery and Krishna show decline in evapo-transpiration rates.[22]

Climate change is also likely to impact the Himalayan region, popularly referred to as the 'Water Tower of Asia'. The region has the largest concentration of glaciers outside the polar caps. It provides around 8.6 X 10[6] cubic meters of water annually[23] and is the source of innumerable rivers including Ganga, Brahmaputra and Indus, which form the lifeline of millions of people in the Indian sub-continent. Today, the glacial abode is shrinking at a much faster rate of 48.2m a year[24] compared to an earlier estimated rate of 10-15 meters a year.[25] The fear that the glaciers in the Himalayas are actually receding faster than in any other part of the world and are likely to disappear by the year 2035,[26] has been disproved by latest studies that put them "changing at the same rate as the global average".[27]

---

21 Ministry of Environment and Forests, Government of India, *India Initial National Communication to the United Nations Framework Convention on Climate Change,* Chapter 3, 2004, http://www.natcomindia.org/pdfs/chapter3.pdf

22 See Note 216

23 Dyurgerov, M.B., and Meier, M., "Mass balance of mountain and sub-polar glaciers: A new global assessment for 1961-1990", Arctic and *Alpine Research,* Vol.29, No.4, pp.379-391,1997; & Rai, S.C., and Thomas, J.K., *An Overview of* **Glaciers, Glacier** *Retreat, and Subsequent Impacts in. Nepal, India and China,* **WWF** Nepal Program March, **2005,** http://assets.panda.org/downloads/himalayaglaciersreport2005.pdf

24 Glaciers in the Himalayas are shrinking rapidly says study, The Hindu, July 18, 2012 http://www.thehindu.com/sci-tech/article3654044.ece?homepage=true

25 Watkin, K., *Human Development Report 2007/2008 - Fighting Climate Change: Human Solidarity in a Divided World,* UNDP, Palgrave Macmillan, New York, p.96, 2007.

26 Rai, S.C., and Thomas, J.K., *An Overview of* Glaciers, Glacier *Retreat, and Subsequent Impacts in. Nepal, India and China,* WWF Nepal Program. March, **2005,** http://assets.panda.org/downloads/himalayaglaciersreport2005.pdf

27 The melting of Himalayan glaciers: fact or fiction?, The Why files, 23 August 2012 http://whyfiles.org/2012/himalayan-glaciers/

Table 2: *Retreat of Important Glaciers in the Himalayas

Glaciers	Location	Period	Average retreat of the Glaciers (meters /year)
Bada Shigri	Himachal Pradesh	1977-1995	36.1
Bada Shigri	Himachal Pradesh	1890- 1906	20.0
Chota Shigri	Himachal Pradesh	1970-1989	7.5
Triloknath	Himachal Pradesh	1969-1995	15.4
Kolhani	J&K	1857-1909	15.0
Kolhani	J&K	1912-1961	16.0
Machoi	J&K	1906-1957	8.1
Zemu	Sikkim	1977-1984	27.7
Gangotri	Uttaranchal	1935-1976	15.0
Gangotri	Uttaranchal	1985-2001	23.0
Gangotri	Uttaranchal	1977-1990	28.0
Milam	Uttaranchal	1909-1984	13.2
Pindari	Uttaranchal	1845-1966	135.2

*(**Source:** Rai, S.C., and Thomas, J.K., *An Overview of* **Glaciers**, **Glacier** *Retreat, and Subsequent Impacts in. Nepal, India and China*, **WWF** Nepal Program. March, **2005;** *and* Climate Change 2007 – Impacts, Adaptations & Vulnerability, Fourth Assessment Report of the Intergovernmental Panel on Climate Change, Working Group II, 2007)

It is likely that the accelerated melting of glaciers will cause an increase in river levels over the next few decades, initially leading to higher incidence of flooding and land-slides. But, in the longer term, as the volume of ice available for melting diminishes, a reduction in glacial runoff and river flows is to be expected. The Ganga, Indus and Brahmaputra could even become seasonal rivers. In case of the Ganga, the loss of glacier melt water would reduce July-September flows by two-thirds, causing water shortages for 500 million people and 37 per cent of India's irrigated land.[28] The flow of the Indus, which receives nearly 90% of its water from the Himalayas, could decline by as much as 70% by 2080.[29] Assessments for the only 'He-river' of the country also draw such grim pictures. The average run-off in the Brahmaputra basin is likely to decline by 14-20% once the snow melt

28 See Note 25

29 See Note 24

effect has passed.[30] Also, as a result of the rainfall being distributed over few days, there would be floods during the monsoon season will also mean that much of the monsoon rain would be lost as direct run-off resulting in reduced groundwater recharging potential.

Decline in Agricultural Productivity

Climate is an important determinant of agricultural productivity in India. Changes in the key climatic variables - maximum and minimum temperature, rainfall, relative humidity and sunshine hours, which govern crop growth, will have a direct impact on the quantity of food produced.

The wheat crop has already been a victim of temperature rise in recent years. The country's wheat production has stagnated in the last 10-15 years and this is being attributed to climate change. Wheat crops give maximum yield with a day temperature 26 degrees centigrade and night temperature 12 degrees C, relative humidity 68% and sunshine of 8 hours. The yield (grain number and weight) is seen to reduce drastically due to prolonged high temperatures.[31] For example, a 2012 study in Rajasthan shows that at least 2.49 quintals of wheat per hectare is lost for every degree of temperature increase.[32]

In India, wheat is already being grown at the limit of heat tolerance and further rise in average temperature during the growing season (December – March) can affect yields. Studies conducted by the Indian Agricultural Research Institute have pointed to a possible loss of 4-5 million tonnes in overall wheat production with every a degree centigrade increase in temperature throughout the growing period, estimated for 2010-2030 period.[33] Simulation studies of impact of climate change on rice yield in Punjab (the state contributes 60% of rice towards the grain pool) also show a drop with the rice in temperature. It could decrease by as much as 6% for

---

30 See Note 24

31 Nicolas, M.F., Gleadow, R.M., and Dalling, M.J., "Effects of drought and high temperature on grain growth in Wheat", *Australian Journal of Plant Physiology*, Vol.11, 1984,pp.533-66.

32 http://articles.timesofindia.indiatimes.com/2012-06-18/jaipur/32297886_1_climate-change-milk-production-heat-stress

33 Parsai, G., "Rise in temperature will impact crops: Study", *The Hindu*, July 25, 2007, http://www.hindu.com/2007/07/25/stories/2007072561421600.htm

every degree rise in the case of rice yield.[34]

Table 3: *Rice Crop response to variation in Temperatures in Punjab

Climate Scenario	Tem-perature Change (degrees C)	Crop Dura-tion (Days)	Grain Yeild (kg/ha)	Grains (m⁻²)	Grains (Ear⁻¹)	Max (Leaf Area index)	Biomass (kg /ha)	Straw (kg/ha)
		(% deviation over normal scenario)						
Extreme	+ 2.0	-3.3	-8.4	-8.4	-12.4	-3.9	-7.4	-6.4
Greater Warm	+ 1.5	-2.6	-8.2	-8.2	-8.3	-3.9	-6.5	-4.7
Mod-erate Warm	+ 1.0	-2.0	-4.9	-4.9	-6.1	-2.4	-3.6	-2.2
Slight warm	+ 0.5	-1.3	-3.2	-3.2	-2.4	-1.1	-1.3	-0.7
Normal	Normal	153	6136	18846	494	6.2	10220	4943

*(**Source:** Mathauda, S.S., Mavi, H.S., Bhangoo, B.S., Dhaliwal, B.K., "Impact of projected Climate Change on rice production in Punjab", *Tropical Ecology,* Vol. 41, No.1, pp.95-98, International Society for Tropical Ecology, 2000)

The impact does not end with the food crops. Climate change is warming oceans, rivers and lakes and this is likely to threaten fish stock, already under pressure from over fishing, pollution and habitat loss. On the basis predicted sea surface temperature model for the years 2000-2100, a decrease of fish catch in the Indian Ocean has been predicted.[35]

Indirect effects of climate change on food productivity pertain to catastrophic events such as floods, droughts and sea water inundation,

---

34 Changing Asian monsoon would adversely impact kharif yield: Study, The Times of India, March 5, 2012 http://articles.timesofindia.indiatimes.com/2012-03-05/developmental-issues/31123921_1_kharif-crops-monsoon-rainfall-climate

35 Biswas, B.K., Svirezhev, Y.M. and Bala, B.K., "A model to predict climate change impact on fish catch in the world oceans", *Systems, Man and Cybernetics,* Part A, IEEE Transactions, Vol.35, Issue 6, pp. 773-783, November 2005.

which are projected to increase in frequency as a consequence of climate change leading to huge crop losses and also making large patches of arable land unfit for cultivation. The value of production loss from drought is especially very large. In three states of eastern India - Jharkhand, Orissa and Chattisgarh – where rain-fed rice is grown widely, the average production loss of rice during drought years is estimated to be 5.4 million tonnes – over 30% of the annual production in non-drought years. In severe drought years, the loss can rise as high as 40-50%.[36]

Other indirect impacts of climate change on agricultural productions may include changes in the pest scenario, soil moisture storage, irrigation water availability, mineralisation of nutrients.

Rising Sea Levels – Coastal Areas at Risk

The impact of global warming-induced sea level rise has great significance for India due to its extensive low-lying coastline, inhabited by more than 10 million people.[37] India been identified as one of the 27 countries most vulnerable to rising sea levels.[38]

Projection studies indicate that the oceanic region adjoining the Indian sub-continent may warm up at its surface by about 1.5 - 2.0 degrees centigrade by the middle of this century and by about 2.5 - 3.5 degrees centigrade by the end of the century, when sea levels may rise by about 15 - 38cms and 46-59 cms respectively.[39] The rising sea is likely to inundate low-lying lands, erodes shorelines, exacerbate flooding and increase the salinity of estuaries and aquifers. It is also expected to make the coastal regions more vulnerable to extreme weather (such as tropical storms and cyclones) as well to destroy important ecosystems such the mangroves. Many places on the western shores like Khambat and Kutch in Gujarat, Mumbai and

---

36 Pandey, S. and Bhandari, H., "Drought perpetuates Poverty", *Rice Today*, p.37, April – June 2006, http://beta.irri.org/news/images/stories/ricetoday/5-2/RF_Drought%20 perpetuates.pdf

37 Patwardhan, A., Narayanan, K., Parthasarathy, D., and Sharma, U., "Impact of Climate Change on Coastal Zones", In : Shukla, P.R., Sharma, S.K., Ravindranath, N.H., Garg, A. and Bhattacharya, S., (eds.) *Climate Change and India : Vulnerability Adaptation and Assessment*, Universities Press, p.329, 2003.

38 UNEP, "Criteria for Assessing Vulnerability to Sea Level Rise: A Global inventory to High Risk Area", Report H838, p.51, 1989.

39 Lal, M., and Aggarwal, D., "Climate change and its impacts in India", *Asia-Pacific Journal of Environment & Development*, Vol. 7, No.1, pp.1-41, 2000.

parts of the Konkan coast and south Kerala could be inundated. A one or two metre rise in sea level could inundate areas ranging from 169 to 599 sq.km in the coastal regions surrounding Kochi.[40]

Studies on the potential impact of a 1-meter rise in sea level along the Indian coasts provide an idea about the land which could be inundated, and the population which could be affected. It has been suggested that a total area of 5763 sq.km. along the coastal states of India i.e. 0.41% of India's total land area could be inundated and almost 7.1 million, i.e. 4.6% of the coastal population could be directly affected.

Table 4: *Potential effects of a one meter sea level rise on India's Coastal area and population

State / UT	Coastal Area (Million hectares			Population (Millions)		
	Likely to be			Likely to be		
	Total	Inundated	Per-centage	Total	Affected	Percent-age
A.P	27.504	0.055	0.19	66.36	0.617	0.93
Goa	0.370	0.016	4.34	1.17	0.085	7.25
Gujarat	19.602	0.181	0.92	41.17	0.441	1.07
Karnataka	19.179	0.029	0.15	44.81	0.25	0.56
Kerala	3.886	0.012	0.30	29.08	0.454	1.56
Maharash-tra	30.771	0.041	0.13	78.75	1.376	1.75
Orissa	15.571	0.048	0.31	31.51	0.555	1.76
Tamil Nadu	13.006	0.067	0.52	55.64	1.621	2.91
W. Bengal	8.875	0.122	1.38	67.98	1.6	2.35
Andaman & Nicobar	0.025	0.006	0.72	0	0	0
India	139.594	0.571	0.41	416.74	7.1	1.68

*(**Source:** Department of Environment and Forests, Jawaharlal Nehru University, *Impact of Greenhouse Induced Sea level rise on islands and Coasts of India*, New Delhi, 1993)

---

40 Rising sea levels threatens India's coastal areas, *The Indian Express*, June 3, 2012 http://www.indianexpress.com/news/rising-sea-level-threatens-indias-coastal-areas/957360/

Sea level rise may have other significant impacts on the coastal areas and in turn the coastal communities, in almost every aspect of their lives. The rise will affect agricultural productivity and food by increasing the intensity of salinity intrusion (due to soil degradation and reducing availability of fresh water) in the dry season and the depth of the flooding in the wet season from tidal fluctuations. Sea level rise may also increase the risk of health hazards by spreading communicable diseases such as diarrhea. It may also adversely affect coastal ecosystems and structures, leading to loss of recreational beaches and other tourism infrastructure. Coastal infrastructure, tourist activities and onshore oil explorations are also at risk.

Table 5: *Fraction of land likely to be affected in case of a 1 meter rise along the coasts of various Indian states

State	Cultivated Land	Cultivable Land	Forest Land	Land not available for agriculture (human settlements, trade, etc.)
Gujarat	0.03	0.08	0.00	0.89
Maharashtra	0.39	0.21	0.09	0.31
Goa	0.65	0.03	0.00	0.31
Karnataka	0.51	0.13	0.13	0.23
Tamil Nadu	0.39	0.39	0.00	0.21
Orissa	0.68	0.15	0.05	0.12
West Bengal	0.74	0.04	0.00	0.22

*(**Source:** Karthikeyan, C., Gupta, K.R., and Jaganathan, D., *A Textbook of Agricultural Extension Management,* Atlantic Publishers and Distributors, p.30, 2008)

The states of West Bengal and Orissa are already bearing the wrath of sea level change, the effects being most visible in the river deltas. The rising sea levels have already caused two islands from the Indian stretch of the Sundarbans – Suparibhanga and Lohachara - to vanish from the maps. The loss of the two islands rendered over 10,000 people homeless. Other islands have also lost considerable lands to the rising sea. The Sagar islands lost around 4 sq.km, Dalhousie (3.2 sq.km.), Bulcheri (2.7 sq.km.), Jambudweep (1.1 sq.km), Ghoramara (0.6) and Bhangaduani (3.7 sq.km.). It is predicted that the sea levels could go up by 3.5mm a year over the next few decades. This could wash out 15 percent of the islands, displacing around 70,000 people by 2020.[41]

Orissa too has been an early victim of sea-level rise and coastal erosion. The villages most affected by climate change are the coastal ones in Kendrapara district. The worst victim among these is the Satabhaya and Kanhupur villages that are on the verge of being wiped out completely. Satabhaya village (cluster of seven villages) occupied an area of 320 sq.km. as per 1930 land records. The 2000 records indicate that this area has now been reduced to 155 sq. kms with five of the seven villages being eaten up the sea.[42] About "187 kilometres of the 480 kilometre coastline has been exposed to erosion"[43].

Vulnerability to Extreme Events

Extreme climate events are a source of mounting concern across the world and in India too. In recent years, the number of people affected by climate disasters such as droughts, floods and storms has been rising. Though direct attribution of extreme climatic events to climate change is impossible, almost every disaster is accompanied by speculations about possible link with climate change. As climate science develops it will provide clearer insights into the relationship between climate change and weather system outcomes. However, current evidences point very clearly in one direction – that climate change will increase the risk of exposure to climate disasters.

41 Karthikeyan, C., Gupta, K.R., and Jaganathan, D., *A Textbook of Agricultural Extension Management,* Atlantic Publishers and Distributors, 2008, pp.144-45.

42 Kar, M., "Life turns vulnerable in Odisha Coast", *Kalinga Times*, July 25, 2008, http://www.kalingatimes.com/orissa_news/news3/20080725-Life-turns-vulnerable-on-Odisha-coast.htm; and http://orissanewsfeatures.sulekha.com/blog/post/2007/11/orissa-the-worst-victim-of-global-warming-and-climate.htm.

43 Waves east into coastal villages, The Telegraph, July 26, 2012 http://www.telegraphindia.com/1120726/jsp/odisha/story_15771318.jsp#.UEcNM7JlSdw

Table 6: Events of Extreme Weather in India in the recent past

Year	Event
2001	Severe drought in Orissa. 11 million people affected in more than two-thirds of the state's districts. Traditionally drought free districts like Sundergarh and Kendrapara also affected.[5]
2004	Floods in north eastern states including Bihar, Tripura, Assam and Arunachal Pradesh. Over 30 million people affected.[6]
2005	Mumbai recorded an unprecedented 944 mm rainfall in a 24 hour period (July 26 & 27) leading to the loss of about 736 lives.[7]
2006	Severe Floods in Surat (Gujarat)[8], Barmer (Rajasthan)[9] and Srinagar (Jammu & Kashmir).[10] Drought in Assam. Nearly 8.17 lakh farmers in 19 districts were affected. Over 5 lakh hectare of crop damaged.[11]
2007	Heat wave across the country during the months April – June, resulting in 72 fatalities.[12] During the south-west monsoon 2007, 24 states / UT reported damage in varying degree were affected by heavy rains, floods, cyclonic storms, etc. 61.2951 million population, 7.255 million hectare cropped area and about 2.660 million houses were affected besides loss of 3,494 lives of people and 1,04,423 cattle heads.[13]
2008	The 2008 monsoon season caused a series of flood in various states of India. Countrywide the death toll was about 2,400.[14] The Kosi flood of Bihar was declared a national calamity.
2009	Heaviest ever floods inundate Southern states of Karnataka, Andhra Pradesh and Kerala killing 270 people and rendering millions homeless[15]
2010	Cloudburst in Leh on August 6 followed by flashfloods and mudslides leaving 1000 dead and more than 400 injured[16]
2011	Cyclone Thane devastates Tamilnadu and Puducherry with 140 km speed winds uprooting trees and leaving 46 dead and damaging crops.[17]

Threats to Health

Overwhelming evidence shows that climate change presents a grave threat to human health - from extreme weather-related disasters to wider spread of such vector-borne diseases as malaria and dengue. In India, global warming is expected to expose people to various health risks including temperature related illnesses, vector borne diseases, water borne diseases and malnourishment due to food shortages. This may have a serious impact on the already inadequate public health infrastructure of the country. The most vulnerable to all these will be those living in poverty with high incidences of under nutrition and also higher exposure to infectious diseases.

Table 7: *Known effects of weather / climate and potential health vulnerabilities due to climate change

Health Concerns	Vulnerabilities due to Climate Change
Temperature related morbidity	Heat and cold related illnesses Cardiovascular illnesses
Vector-borne diseases	Malaria, Filaria, Kala-azar, Japanese encephalitis and dengue
Effects of Extreme weather	Diarrhea, cholera and poisoning caused by biological and chemical contaminants in the water (even today about 70% of the epidemic emergencies in India are water-borne). Damaged public health infrastructure due to cyclones/floods. Social and mental health stress due to disasters and displacement.
Health effects due to, insecurity in food production.	Malnutrition and hunger, especially in children

*(**Source:** Ministry of Environment and Forests, Government of India, *India's Initial National Communication to the United Nations Framework Convention on Climate Change*, p.116, 2004)

Changes in the climate may alter the distribution of important vector species (for example mosquitoes) and increase the spread of such diseases to newer areas that lack a strong public health infrastructure. Among the vector-borne diseases malaria is of considerable concern for India. The National Vector borne disease control programme of India in early 2012, reported that 9.75 million cases and 40,297 deaths annually were attributable to malaria[44]. This is a phenomenal rise form the two million cases and a 1000 deaths per year reported till recently. [45] Temperature increase projections are going to worsen the malaria situation in the country in various ways like faster rate of development of mosquitoes, faster rate of digestion of blood meal and an increased frequency of feeding. As a result malaria will be seen in newer areas such as Himachal Pradesh, Uttarakhand, J&K & Sikkim, which are relatively malaria free now.[46] Since the people living in these states are not as immune to malaria as inhabitants of traditionally endemic states. Therefore, the fatality rate in newer areas is likely to be much higher. In fact climate change is being seen as one of the factors responsible for the re-emergence of chikungunya in India in 2006 and the widespread occurrence of dengue in the recent years.[47]

Climate Changes as a Security Threat

It is quite apparent from the above section that climate change will limit the availability of key resources such as water and arable land and these will become even scarcer as the population increases. Translated into a simple fact, this would mean that the carrying capacity of many areas could be reduced over a period of time, leading to extreme competition for resources. Climatic events such as sea level rise, flooding and storms could also lead to the displacement of millions. Under certain conditions, such as poor governance, high poverty levels and existing ethnic and religious divisions, these stresses may turn violent.

44 India to raise Malaria toll figure 40-fold, *The Times of India*, February 4, 2012 http:// articles.timesofindia.indiatimes.com/2012-02-04/india/31024354_1_malaria-deaths-malaria-like-high-fever-malaria-infection

45 Dash, A.P., Valecha, N., Anvikar, A.R. and Kumar, K., "Malaria in India: Challenges and Opportunities", *Journal of Biosciences*, Vol. 33, No.4, pp. 583-92, November 2008.

46 Bhattacharya, S., Sharma, C., Dhiman, R.C., and Mitra, A.P., "Climate change and Malaria in India", *Current Science*, Vol. 90, No.3, February 2006.

47http://news.indiainfo.com/2008/04/07/0804071817_chikungunya_kerala_due_climate_change_who.html,;http://www.asiaone.com/Health/News/Story/A1Story20090313-128275.html and http://timesofindia.indiatimes.com/India/Dengue_cases_doubled_last_year/articleshow/3953262.cms

This section argues that climate change presents a security threat to India in the following ways:

THREAT 1 – Conflicts over Diminishing Water Resources

With population more or less trebling over the last four decades, average annual per capita water availability has reduced from 5177 cubic meters in 1951 to about 1820 cubic meters in 2001.[48] The availability has further reduced with the Ministry of Water resources citing 2011 census data at 1545 cubic meters[49]. Thus, India is now falling below the 'water stress' line of 1700 cubic meters. (See figure)

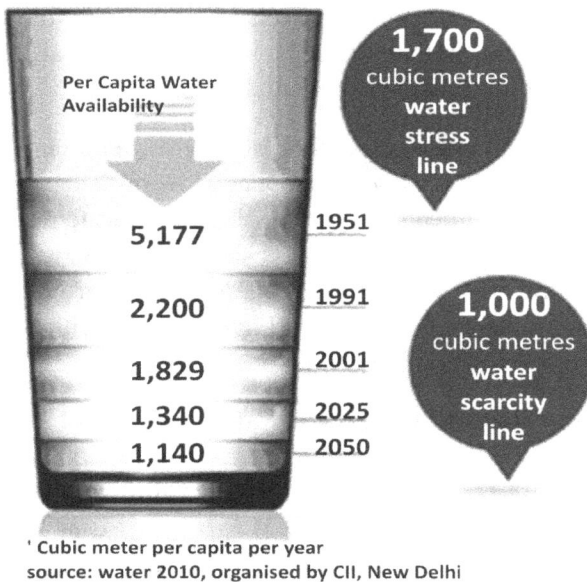

Per Capita Water Availability

1,700 cubic metres water stress line

5,177	1951
2,200	1991
1,829	2001
1,340	2025
1,140	2050

1,000 cubic metres water scarcity line

' Cubic meter per capita per year
source: water 2010, organised by CII, New Delhi

Source:http://articles.economictimes.indiatimes.com/2011-12-20/news/30537977_1_water-conservation-ground-water-water-shortage

However water problems are ever increasing. Climatic change projections show that India's water problems are only likely to worsen as more rain is expected to fall in fewer days and also due to the rapid melting of the Himalayan glaciers. It is in fact predicted that the per capita

---

48 Ministry of Water Resources, Government of India, "Water Resources of India and World", *Newsletter on Fresh Water Year 2003*, 2003.

49 Per capita water availability, Ministry of water Resources, April 26, 2012 http://pib.nic.in/newsite/erelease.aspx?relid=82676

availability will come down further to 1341 cubic meters in 2025 and 1140 cubic meters in the year 2050, leading to water stress of an unprecedented scale.[50]

The impact of increased water scarcity as a result of climate change will have two facets. Firstly, intra-state conflicts will increase. India is already facing a number of conflicts over water access and distribution between various states and also communities. Of India's 28 states, as many as 15 have had water disputes or are fighting over various river water projects.[51] The row over river Cauvery between Karnataka and Tamilnadu, river Godavari between Maharashtra and Karnataka, rivers Ravi-Beas between Punjab and Haryana, river Narmada between Madhya Pradesh and Gujarat are famous ones. These conflicts are being bitterly fought at all levels, imposing very high economic and environmental costs.

Also, with climate change, population growth and increased demand progressively reducing the water supplies, Governments will have to make increasingly difficult decisions on how best to allocate resources between various sectors of the economy (agriculture, industries, etc.), between urban and rural areas and between different ethnic groups. Just as in case of the states, the sharing of water within each community can become the focus of protests and conflicts.

Table 8: Some Recent Examples of Water-related Violence in India

Region	Conflicts
Dispute between Tamilnadu and Karnataka on sharing of the waters of River Cauvery	**1991:** Violence broke out in Karnataka after the centre notified the interim award of the Tribunal, 23 people killed in Bangalore. Thousands of Tamils flee the state.[18] **2002:** Continuing violence over the allocation of the river water. Riots, property destruction and several injured.[19] **2007:** After the final verdict was delivered, a state-wide bandh in Karnataka. A wave of protests in the state.[20]

---

50 http://pib.nic.in/release/release.asp?relid=23826

51 http://www.forumfed.org/en/products/magazine/vol8_num1/india_special.php

Region	Conflicts
Gujarat	**2000**: Water riots were reported in some areas of Gujarat to protest authorities failure to arrange adequate supply of tanker water. Police are reported to have shot into the crowd at Falla village near Jamnagar, resulting in the death of 3 and injuries to about 20, following protests against the diversion of water from the Kanakavati dam to Jamnagar Town.[21]
Chennai	**2001**: Triggered by acute water shortage, an armed group including women damaged vehicles and looted shops on Angappa Naickken Street, Mannady, Chennai.[22]
Kashmir	**2002**: Two people were killed and 25 others injured in Kashmir when police fired at a group of villagers clashing over water sharing. The incident took place in Garend village in a dispute over sharing water from an irrigation stream.[23]
Sriganganagar, Rajasthan	**2004**: Two-months long farmer agitation over reduction in the supply of irrigation water in the Phase I area of the Indira Gandhi Canal in North-west Rajasthan, Six farmers killed. [24] **2006**: Revival of the agitation by farmers. Hundreds, including women were injured and 1 farmer killed when the police resorted to lathi charge and fired teargas and rubber bullets to disperse the crowd. Curfew imposed in many villages in the district and army called in.[25]
Tonk, Rajasthan	**2005**: Five persons were killed and several injured when police opened fire on farmers agitating for release of water from Bisalpur Dam.[26]
Bhopal, Madhya Pradesh	**2009**: Three members of a family killed over a water dispute on May 13.[27]

Region	Conflicts
Tamilnadu and Kerala row over Mullaiperiyar Dam	**2011 :** Amid concerns over a breach in the 116 year old dam, pilgrims from Tamilnadu visiting Sabarimala were stopped or sent back. Kerala businesses were attacked in some parts of Tamilnadu.[28]

Secondly, bilateral conflicts dealing with rights and the sharing of transnational river water will also occur. Already some of India's troubles with her neighbours are about water: with Bangladesh over the Ganga-Brahmaputra-Meghna river system, with Nepal over Kosi and other rivers, with China over the mighty Brahmaputra and with Pakistan over the Chenab River and Baglihar dam. A shrinking quantity of water (whether as a result of reduced water supply or increased demand) will almost inevitably complicate India's relations with its neighbours, making it hard to negotiate new or adhere to peace agreements. For example, water disputes have in fact worsened relations between India and Pakistan. Recently Pakistan blamed India for withholding millions of cubic feet of water upstream in Indian administered Kashmir in the Baghliar dam in order to produce hydro electricity. Pakistani President Asif Ali Zardari had in fact commented - "The water crisis in Pakistan is directly linked to relations with India. Resolution could prevent an environmental catastrophe in South Asia, but failure to do so could fuel the fires of discontent that lead to extremism and terrorism."[52] Pakistan in fact took the issue to the International Court of Arbitration and got a stay on all further work on the Kishenganga hydelpower project in 2011.[53] Many in fact believe that a war over water rights between nuclear-armed rivals India and Pakistan is a real possibility in the near future.

THREAT 2 – Food Insecurity

The Food and Agriculture Organization (FAO) defines food security as: 'when all people, at all times have physical, social and economic access to

---

52 Buncombe, A., and Waraich, O., "India is stealing water of life, says Pakistan", *The Independent*, UK, March 26, 2009, http://www.independent.co.uk/news/world/asia/india-is-stealing-water-of-life-says-pakistan-1654291.html

53 Brahma Chellaney, Water treaties and diplomacy: India faces difficult choices on water, The Economic Times, May 10, 2012 http://articles.economictimes.indiatimes.com/2012-05-10/news/31655856_1_indus-waters-treaty-indus-system-teesta-water-sharing-treaty

sufficient, safe and nutritious food to meet their dietary needs and food preferences for an active and healthy life".[54] In includes the availability of food and the ability to access food. While the availability depends on local agricultural productivity (and to some extent imports), the ability to access depends on people ability to grow or buy food. Climate change is likely to impact both these dimensions of food security. Agricultural productivity will be affected by rise in temperature, change in the carbon dioxide levels, pest intensity and shifting rainfall patterns. Sea level rise and extreme weather events, such as floods and droughts are also likely to have negative consequences for crop cultivation. This in turn could lead to a drastic increase in the food prices.

The negative impact of climate change on production will also cause negative shocks in household incomes, thus affecting people's ability to buy food. This can be significant considering the fact that agriculture is the principal source of income for about 52% of India's population.[55] Food security is already a core electoral issue in India and a highly emotive one too. The sharp surge in food prices during 2007-08 led to a wave of protests in various parts of India.[56] Even in the recent General Elections, the issue of skyrocketing food prices occupied great prominence. There were several populists move by various political parties to make food accessible to the poor.

A wide-scale drop in agricultural production and loss of livelihood due to climate change is likely to leave many individuals and communities financially overstretched and hard pressed to feed themselves adequately. There are already about 230 million people suffering from hunger or under nourishment in India.[57] This number is likely to increase manifolds due to climate change in the near future. The IPCC projects that about 50 million people are at the risk of hunger by 2020 in Asia alone[58], with the Indian

---

54 Food and Agriculture Organization of the United Nations, *Rome Declaration on World Food Security and World Food Summit Plan of Action*, World Food Summit, Rome, 13-17 November, 1996.

55 http://indiabudget.nic.in/es2008-09/chapt2009/chap71.pdf

56 http://www.thehindu.com/2007/08/31/stories/2007083160640300.htm ; and http://www.reuters.com/article/newsOne/idUSDEL27488220080415

57 Food and Agriculture Organization of the United Nations , *The State of Food Insecurity in the World 2008 – High Food Prices and Food Security – Threats and Opportunities*, p. 48, 2008. ftp://ftp.fao.org/docrep/fao/011/i0291e/i0291e05.pdf

58 http://www.cbsnews.com/stories/2007/04/10/tech/main2666760.shtml

continent being one of the worst affected.

Also, as people suffer from starvation and hunger, they are likely to erupt into violent protests and would also assault others they deem responsible for their plight. For example, large-scale riots broke out in West Bengal during October 2007 over shortage of food and widespread corruption in the public distribution system. The protesters burned hundreds of ration shops, accusing the owners of selling government-subsidised food on the lucrative black market. 3 ration distributors committed suicide and hundreds went into hiding fearing their lives[59]. In August 2008, food riots erupted in the state of Bihar in August 2008 when flood affected villagers fought among themselves over limited supplies of food at the Flood Relief Centres.[60] Bihar witnessed riots over soaring food prices again in 2010 with crowds attacking trains and protesting on the streets that shops remain closed.[61] Food riots were witnessed in the Sunderbans among the victims of Cycloe Aila in 2009.[62]

Over a period of time such incidences could cause wider social unrest and undermine political stability of states, depending on a range of other social, economic and demographic factors. For example, the acute famine in Mizoram in 1958-59 during *mautam* (a cyclic phenomenon that occurs every 48 years during which bamboo plants flower causing a considerable increase in the rodent population, which devastate the crops) redefined politics in the state, which of then a part of the state of Assam. The administration in Shillong (then capital of Assam) was indifferent to the threat posed by the rats. It failed to grasp the severity of the food shortages in the Mizo Hills and the gravity of the crisis it had triggered. Activists of the Mizo National Famine Front (MNFF), which was working to provide relief to the famine-stricken people, were enraged by the government's apathy. They turned to armed struggle against the Indian state to express their rage. The MNFF became the Mizo National Front (MNF) and spearheaded a secessionist movement. The insurgency raged for over two decades and ended in 1986 with the signing of a peace accord. The Central Government

59 http://in.reuters.com/article/topNews/idINIndia-29970920071012

60 http://www.financialexpress.com/news/Food-riots-erupt-in-floodhit-Bihar/354041/

61 Food riots as India prices soar, *Gulf Daily News*, January 29, 2010 http://www.gulf-daily-news.com/NewsDetails.aspx?storyid=269501

62 Ray, A., and Chakraborti, S., "Rush for relief sparks food riots in Sunderbans", *The Times of India*, June 10, 2009.

granted full statehood to Mizoram in 1987. Food shortages could also lead to increased tensions among neighbours. For example, in 2008 relations between India and Bangladesh soured when Indian authorities banned the export of rice to Bangladesh in order to contain the rise in domestic prices.

THREAT 3 – Destabilizing Population Movements and Conflicts

Climate change is likely to cause population movements (temporary displacements as well as long-term migration) by making some places less viable to live; by causing food and water supplies to become more unreliable, undermining livelihoods; through sea level rise and flooding that reduces available land; and by increasing the frequency and destructive power of storms and floods. Estimates for the number of 'climate migrants' vary, but perhaps the best estimate given by Norman Myers and Jennifer Kent in 1995 suggests as many as 150-200 million people by the middle of the century would be displaced by disruptions in monsoon and other rainfall regimes, by drought of unprecedented severity and duration and by rise in sea level and coastal flooding.[63]

In India, one-fourth of India's population lives within 50 km of the coastline. The average coastal population density is 432 persons per sq.km. as against 256 persons per sq.km. for the rest of India.[64] Virtually all mega cities located by the sea, including Mumbai, Chennai and Kolkata. Many of these cities are at an average elevation of 2 -10 meters. A 3-5 meters rise in the average sea level in the future, could inundate large chunks of these urban centers leading to major migration waves. It is likely that population movements will occur towards the interior of the country, especially to other large urban settlements. Under these circumstances, it is cities like Delhi, Bangalore. Hyderabad, Pune and Ahmedabad, which already have serious resource constraints, will have to accommodate a large number of migrants. This could lead to increased competition for resources and employment in such areas between the migrants and the receiving population. Besides this the migrants or refugees are perceived to alter the local culture and customs and this may even lead to the eruption of ethnic

---

63 Stern, N. H., *The Economics of Climate Change – The Stern Review*, Cambridge University Press, p. 77, 2007, http://www.hmtreasury.gov.uk/d/Chapter_3_How_climate_change_will_affect_people_around_the_world_.pdf

64 Ministry of Environment and Forests, Government of India, *Report of the Expert Committee on Coastal Regulation Zone Notification, 1991*, February 2005, http://mssrf.org/rm/reports/crz_report_prof/crz_report.pdf

tensions. For example, in 2008 migrant workers from North Indian states of U.P. and Bihar were repeatedly attacked and assaulted in Maharashtra for taking up jobs from the locals. Hindi-speaking migrant workers have also been regular targets in the north eastern states, especially in Assam. The workers from the north east went back to their homes in thousands after fears of reprisals for the clashes between Bodo tribals and Muslim migrants occurred in Kokhrajar district in July 2012.[65]

Besides sea level rise, extreme climatic events will also prompt people to flee their homes. A large proportion of the population lives in disaster prone areas, with few resources in reserve. About 16% of India's total area is prone to drought of varying degree and approximately 50 million people annually are affected by droughts. About 68% of sown land is susceptible to drought.[66] Drought and water scarcity are especially going to produce a sizeable population of climate migrants, who would be forced to move to newer areas in search of livelihood and employment. The recent cyclonic storm Aila saw nearly 50,000 people move out of the Sunderbans into the interiors, mainly Sonarpur near Calcutta.[67]

Many of such displaced people (especially the poor and the marginal such as landless agriculture worker) could finally end up in the refugee camps and urban slums, characterised by high population densities, closed quarters, poor sanitation and insufficient food supply. Such difficult living conditions, discrimination and of livelihood may prompt many of these people to take up unlawful means of survival. Thus, the slums and refugee camps are likely to become easy breeding ground for organised crime, terrorism, fanaticism, drug dealing, sex trade and diseases (such as AIDS).

Climate change could also escalate tensions between India and her neighbours over the issue of migration. Mass migration into India is indicated from Sri Lanka, Maldives, Nepal, Pakistan and particularly Bangladesh. Climate change and associated coastal flooding could force millions of people from low lying Bangladesh to flee their homes in

65   Nandita Haksar, Dissecting the Bodo-Muslim Clashes and Attacks on North-East People, *Mainstream*, Vol l, no 37, September 1, 2012 http://www.mainstreamweekly.net/article3665.html

66 National Academy of Agricultural Sciences, *Disaster Management in Agriculture*, Policy Paper 27, July 2004

67 http://www.telegraphindia.com/1090621/jsp/calcutta/story_11137129.jsp;   and

   http://www.telegraphindia.com/1090614/jsp/calcutta/story_11105736.jsp

search of safer lands. Bangladesh is in fact being seen as 'ground zero' for the impacts of climate change. It is projected that a 45 cm sea level rise by 2050 may inundate about 10-15% of Bangladesh, displacing about 35 million people from the coastal districts.[68] This might trigger widespread migration into India.

India already has about 5 million Bangladeshis living illegally and this is a constant source of tension between the two countries. In north-east India especially in Assam, the demographic invasion by the Bangladeshis (dominated by Muslims) is so much prevalent that the local people fear they would be completely wiped out by the Bangladeshi migrants. Even the Guwahati High Court in a statement noted that "*that illegal Bangladeshis have intruded every nook and corner of Assam, including forest land..........* *they have even intruded upon the most sacred Xattra land......the day is not far off, when the indigenous people of Assam, both Hindus and Muslims and. other religious groups will be reduced to minorities in their own land*".[69] This has resulted in several clashes between the local communities and the migrant population during the past few decades affecting the stability and economic development of the region. Also, there are reports that many of migrants are being recruited by Islamic extremists groups to organise terrorist activities in India and are believed by many to be behind the recent bombings in the state.[70]

THREAT 4 – Climate Change as an obstacle in India's Economic Growth, thereby worsening Poverty and Social stability

India seems to be well on path to becoming one of the leading players in global economy with a remarkable growth rate. If this trend were to be sustained, economic projections indicate that by 2050, India would become the world's second largest economy after China and surpassing the United States.[71] However, climate change could drastically undermine India's

---

68 http://www.adb.org/Documents/Economic_Updates/BAN/2008/QEU-Sep-2008.pdf

69 Talukdar, S., "Bangladeshis in Assam have become kingmakers: Court", *The Hindu*, July 29, 2008.

70 http://www.hindu.com/2008/04/21/stories/2008042160291300.htm; http://ibnlive.in.com/ news/ advani-links-blasts-to-illegal-bangladeshi-immigrants/77068-3.html; and   http:// timesofindia.indiatimes.com/Terror_on_Day_One_5_killed_67_injured_in_Guwahati/ articleshow/3922558.cms

71 Murali, D., "Overtaking US on the growth expressway?", *The Hindu Business Line*, January 25, 2007.

economic growth, thus having negative consequences for the country's development and poverty alleviation plans. According to the Stern Review, the cost of climate change in India could be as high as a 9-13% loss in GDP by 2100 compared to a no climate change scenario.[72]

Rising temperatures, wetter climate, rising sea levels and extreme environmental patters will affect all sector of the economy, with the worst hit being the climate-dependent ones such as agriculture and forestry. The productivity and profitability of the India's agriculture sector, which constitutes about 18% of our GDP (2007-08), will be reduced. India is in fact projected to lose between 7-17% of its income from agriculture because of climate change.[73] This could prove significant as these sectors play a vital role in maintaining India's economic growth and also to provide jobs for our ever expanding population.

Table 9: *Estimated Economic Impacts of Climate Change on India in 2100 with a 2.5 degrees warming

Sector	Damages (Billion USD)
Agriculture	53.2
Energy	21.9
Water Resources	1.2
Coastal Resources	0.1

*(Source: Solanki, B., *Carbon Disclosure Project 2007 - India*, WWF India, p.12, 2007, http://assets.wwfindia.org/downloads/cdp_report_india_2007_2.pdf)

The last few years actually revealed as to how weather can play havoc with Indian agriculture sector. In many parts of India, erratic rainfall made life hell for farmers, pushing hundreds of them to end their lives. In Maharashtra alone, 4453 farmers committed suicide in 2006.[74] Almost all the farmers who committed suicide had huge debts, which they were

---

72 Stern, N.H., *The Economics of Climate Change – The Stern Review*, Cambridge University Press, p. 92, 2007 (http://www.hm-treasury.gov.uk/d/Part_II_Introduction_group.pdf)

73 http://economictimes.indiatimes.com/News/Economy/Agriculture/India_may_lose_up_to_17_of_its_farming_income_due_to_climate_change/rssarticleshow/ 3371195. cms

74 Katakam, A., "Vidarbha waits", *Frontline*, Vol.26, Issue 08, April 11-24, 2009.

unable to repay due to crop failures resulting from lack of rainfall. In the years to come with climate change drastically affecting agricultural yields, the pressure on people to take such extreme step may increase.

Another shock to India's economy will be in the form of climate related disasters The World Bank estimates that natural disaster losses during 1996-2001 amounted to 13.8 USD or 2% of India's GDP and consumed 12% of the Government Revenue during the same period.[75] Given their increasing frequencies, such losses could play a key factor in preventing economic growth in the country. A single disaster can completely negate the economic growth of several years. This was well brought out during the July 2005 floods in Mumbai, India's commercial capital, caused by a record level precipitation within 24 hours. The floods resulted in estimated losses of over 450 crores of rupees.[76] Disasters could also disrupt the livelihood of people overnight, affecting their financial stability

Besides this, episodes of heat cramps, exhaustion and heat stroke would affect the population, especially the poor section of the society involved in physical labour. The frequent outbreak of diseases such as malaria would also affect the workforce, resulting in loss of man days and wages. The occurrence of diseases would result in an increase in expenses on health care by individuals, further deteriorating their financial position. A correlation between a country's level of economic development and its vulnerability for civil wars/conflicts is widely recognised.[77] If climate change results in increased poverty and widespread loss of livelihood, the risk of violent conflicts will also increase.

THREAT 5 – Political Instability in South Asia & Impacts on India's National Security

Climate change could intensify ethnic and regional conflicts in South Asia which could also pose severe national security threats to India. Climate change induced challenges could break down political stability in already vulnerable states including Pakistan, Nepal and Sri Lanka. This

---

75http://www.ndmindia.nic.in/WCDRDOCS/DRM%20&%20The%20role%20of%20 Corporate%20Sector.pdf and http://www.tribuneindia.com/2003/20030626/biz.htm#2

76 "Rain havoc causes Rs.1,000 crores loss", *The Hindu*, July 28, 2005, http://www.hindu. com/2005/07/28/stories/2005072809291800.htm

77 Collier, P., and Hoeffler, A., "Greed and grievance in Civil War", Oxford Economic Papers, Vol. 56, No.4, pp.563-95, 2004.

could prompt insurgency in the region. For example, water shortages and rising levels could sharpen Pakistan's inter-provincial conflicts. Sindh is vulnerable because of its large coastal population susceptible to sea rise and its agricultural lands, which depend on Indus River for irrigation. A perception that it is being exploited by insensitive Punjab could trigger off violent separatism. Baloch separatists could take advantage of the situation in Sindh to escalate their own insurgency. In the worst case scenario, such conflicts could stretch and cause the collapse of Pakistan, therefore having serious implications for India.[78]

Table 10: *Impact of Climate Change on ongoing conflicts in South Asia

Conflict System /Impact Mechanism	Glacial Recession	Rising Sea Level	Extreme Weather	Net Assessment
Jammu & Kashmir	High	-	Medium	Risk of war, motivated in part by the quest for water resources
India- China border	High	-	Medium	Risk of natural disasters in India, worsening Indo-China relations
Bangladesh ethnic invasion	High	High	High	Risk of mass migration into India
Sri Lankan Civil War	-	High	Medium	Risk of mass migration and of ethnic conflict
Nepal Civil War	High	-	High	Risk of natural disaster and mass migration into India

*(Source: Pai, N., 'Climate Change and National Security: Preparing India for New Conflict Scenario', *The Indian National Interest Policy Brief*, No.1, April 2008)

---

78 CENTRA Technology Inc. and Scitor Coorporation, *India: The Impact of Climate Change 2030 – Geopolitical Implications*, 2009

Climate change could pose some direct threats to India's national territory. As pointed out by Dr. R.K. Pachauri recently, the melting snow in the northern Himalayas could open up passages through which terrorists could infiltrate into India.[79]

THREAT 6 - Direct Impact on India's Defence Infrastructure

Climate change also has the potential to impact military operations & their infrastructure. Throughout history the weather has played an important part in planning and fighting wars. It is crucial to the success of troop deployment, attack or defence. Nearly 2,500 years ago the Chinese general Sun Tzu proclaimed: *'Know yourself, know your enemy, your victory will never be endangered. Know the ground, know the weather; your victory will then be total'.*[80] Extreme temperature and rainfall may affect military readiness and their ability to co-ordinate operations.

The use of military forces in handling extreme environmental events, whose frequencies are predicted to rise, will deprive them of time to train for their war-fighting mission. This is also likely to cause greater wear and tear of military equipment and diversion of various resources. During the Kosi floods in Bihar, around 30 columns of the defense forces including the Indian army and navy personnel were involved in evacuation. 10 Indian Air Force helicopters were engaged in air-dropping food packets.[81] The army and paramilitary forces again played a vital role in rescue and relief operations during the recent Cyclone Aila that devastated the Sunderbans.[82] Defense bases along the coasts affected by rising sea level and other extreme climatic event in a similar manner as the Indian Air Force base in Car Nicobar was completely wiped out during the 2004 tsunami.

Conclusion

National Security has been traditionally defined in terms of threats to a country's territory and to the population from a clearly defined enemy.

---

79 "Climate Change could help terrorists against India", *The Times of India*, June 27, 2009. http://timesofindia.indiatimes.com/India/Climate-change-could-help-terrorists-against-India/articleshow/4710313.cms

80 Sun Tzu, *The Art of War*, 500 B.C., Chapter 1, Laying Plans, X. Terrain, No.31, 1910.

81 "Flood situation eases a little in Bihar", *The Hindu*, September 03, 2008, http://www.expressindia.com/latest-news/Flood-situation-eases-a-little-in-Bihar/356932/

82 http://www.hindu.com/2009/06/13/stories/2009061356371400.htm

Such threats could be tackled by strong military capabilities and diplomatic skills. The concept of national security has however expanded in recent times with a growing recognition that threats to India's security extend beyond military threats to include issues that potentially threat human survival and well-being.

One such threat that is redefining the traditionally understood definition of security in the 21st century is Climate Change. It presents India with a range of daunting challenges - how to meet the water and food demands of its 1 billion plus population, how to increase adaptability of communities to droughts and floods, how to distribute increasingly scarce resources among different sections of the society and how to expand its economy in spite of potentially adverse and unpredictable weather. As outlined in this chapter, if left unchecked, these challenges could interact with a host of other factors – poverty, marginalisation, population growth, health pandemics (like HIV / AIDS) and poor governance – leading to political instability, failed states and armed conflicts. Thus, there is an urgent need to revisit and reinforce India's national security strategies and defence policies, giving greater priority to climate change. This could also lead to greater prioritisation and enhanced support for climate change mitigation and adaptation in the country.

'I think the environment should be put in the category of our national security. Defence of our resources should be put in the category of our national security. Defence of our resources is just as important as defence abroad. Otherwise what is there to defend?'[83]

– Robert Redford, 1985

References (used in Tables)

1   Bhaskaran, B., Mitchell, J.F.B., Lavery, J. R., and Lal, M., "Climatic Response of Indian subcontinent to doubled CO_2 Concentration", *International Journal of Climatology*, Vol. 15, No.8, pp. 873–892, 1995.

2   Lonergan, S., "Climate Warming and Indi"', In: Dinar, A., et al (eds.), *Measuring the Impact of Climate Change on Indian Agriculture*, World Bank Technical Paper No. 402, Washington DC, 1998. pp33-67

83 Garcia, G.D., "People", Time, September 90, 1985, http://www.time.com/time/magazine/article/0,9171,959782,00.html

3   Lal, M., Nozawa, T., Emori, S., "Future Climate Change Implications for Indian Summer Monsoon and its variability", *Current Science*, Vol. 81, No. 9, p.1205, 2001.

4   Rupakumar, K., Krishna Kumar, K., Prasanna, V., Kamala, K., Deshpande, N.R., Patwardhan, S.K. and Pant, G.B., "Future Climate Scenarios", In : Shukla, P.R., Sharma, S.K., Ravindranath, N.H., Garg, A., and Bhattacharya, S. (Eds.), *Climate Change and India: Vulnerability Assessment and Adaptation*, Universities Press (India) Pvt Ltd, Hyderabad, p. 462, 2003.

5   http://www.greenpeace.org/india/campaigns/choose-positive-energy/what-is-climate-change/climate-change-a-case-study-o

6   http://news.bbc.co.uk/2/hi/south_asia/3888953.stm

7   Katakam, A., Bavadam, L., and Bunsha, D., "High Water and Hell", *Frontline*, Vol. 22, Issue 17, August 2006, http://www.hindu.com/fline/fl2217/stories/20050826006000400.htm

8   David, R., and Rupera, P., 'Surat's flood toll could cross 200', *The Times of India*, August 12, 2006.

9   Bhagat, H., "Doomsday? Not Yet, say experts", *Tehelka*, Sep 16, 2006, http://www.tehelka.com/story_main19.asp?filename=Ne091606Doomsday.asp

10   Bukhari, S., "Flood situation eases in Jammu & Kashmir" *The Hindu*, September 07, 2006, http://www.hindu.com/2006/09/07/stories/2006090714140300.htm

11   Talukdar, S., "Assam seeks Central team to assess Crop Damage", *The Hindu*, August 18, 2006 http://www.hinduonnet.com/2006/08/18/stories/2006081802191400.htm

12   Srivastava, S., Champati Ray, P.K., Shakya, B., Joshi, D.D., and Kumar, R., *South Asian Disaster Report 2007*, SAARC Disaster Management Centre, New Delhi, p.74, 2008, http://saarc-sdmc.nic.in/pdf/publications/sdr/chapter-7.pdf.

13   Srivastava, S., Champati Ray, P.K., Shakya, B., Joshi, D.D., amd Kumar, R., South Asian Disaster Report 2007, SAARC Disaster Management Centre, New Delhi, p.32, 2008., http://saarc-sdmc.nic.in/pdf/publications/sdr/chapter-7.pdf

14 http://www.cnn.com/2008/WORLD/asiapcf/09/23/india.floods/index.html

15 http://articles.cnn.com/2009-10-05/world/india.flooding_1_flood-waters-flood-hit-andhra-pradesh?_s=PM:WORLD

16 http://www.imd.gov.in/doc/cloud-burst-over-leh.pdf

17 India repairs damage after Cyclone Thane kills 42, The Economic Times, January 1, 2012 http://economictimes.indiatimes.com/news/news-by-industry/et-cetera/india-repairs-damage-after-cyclone-thane-kills-42/articleshow/11327209.cms

18 Satish Kumar, B.S., "Paeceful Protests", *Frontline*, February 10-23, 2007, http://www.hinduonnet.com/fline/fl2403/stories/20070223002901700. htm

19 http://www.hinduonnet.com/2002/09/09/stories/2002090904431100.htm; and http://www.hinduonnet.com/2002/09/08/stories/2002090804090600.htm

20 http://www.hinduonnet.com/2007/02/13/stories/2007021314490100.htm; and http://www.hinduonnet.com/2007/02/06/stories/2007020613750300.htm

21 Gleick, P., "Water, Globalisation and Global Security", *GCSP Policy Brief No. 16*, p.12, Dec 2006 and Dasgupta, M., "Water Riots a new worry in Gujarat", *The Hindu*, December 25, 1999.

22 Shivakumar, S., "Water Crisis triggers Violence", *The Hindu*, August 27, 2001 http://www.hinduonnet.com/2001/08/28/stories/0428401w.htm

23 Gleick, P., "Water, Globalisation and Global Security", *GCSP Policy Brief No. 16*, p.13, Dec 2006.

24 http://www.hinduonnet.com/thehindu/2004/10/28/stories/200410281482 1100.htm;   http://www.hindu.com/2004/12/13/stories/2004121310930500. htm;   and http://www.hindu.com/2004/12/07/stories/2004120710440500. htm

25 http://www.hinduonnet.com/fline/fl2322/stories/20061117001904700. htm;http://www.hinduonnet.com/thehindu/thscrip/print.pl?file=2006 110111560500.htm&date=2006/11/01/&prd=th&;   and   http://www. hinduonnet.com/thehindu/thscrip/print.pl?file=2006102902200500. htm&date=2006/10/29/&prd=th&

26 http://www.hinduonnet.com/fline/fl2214/stories/20050715002204600.htm

27   Chibber, N., "Fight for water ends in murder", *Down to Earth,* June 30, 2009. http://www.downtoearth.org.in/full6.asp?foldername=20090630&filename= news&sec_id=4&sid=4

28   Violence in Tamilnadu and Kerala over Mullaiperiyar Dam row, *The Economic Times*, December 8, 2011 http://articles.economictimes.indiatimes. com/2011-12-08/news/30490516_1_mullaperiyar-dam-new-dam-dam-issue

VII

War, Peace, And Climate Change

– P.K.Gautam

Introduction

Since the days of Thucydides, the causes of war and conditions for peace have been an ongoing and a never ending academic and policy inquiry. Thucydides discusses geography's effect on state's propensity for war, and concludes that sea-based states (e.g. Athens) are more war prone than land-based states (e.g., Sparta).[1] What is also generally known is that people from arid and difficult regions where resources are not plentiful take recourse to war for resources. Contemporary research and accumulated body of knowledge on why wars take place list out a number of causes. Though no one single cause can be attributed to wars, two inter-related variables providing anecdotal and empirical evidence are now very much in the public imagination as the likely drivers of violent conflicts now and in the future. The first is natural and renewable resource scarcities brought about by imbalance in the supply /demand and environmental degradation due to population growth fuelling greater consumption. The second is the looming threat of an abrupt or adverse climate change in the very near future.

What is unique and in a way different from other investigations is that the science of climate change is already given and accepted as evidence that there will be adverse changes and impacts due to climate

---

1   Richard A. Matthews, Michael Brklacich, and Bryan McDonald, " Analyzing Environmental, Conflict, and Cooperation", in *Understanding Environment , Conflict, and Cooperation* , Division of Early Warning and Assessment, United Nations Environmental Programme, Nairobi, 2004, pp.5-15.

change.[2] Nevertheless, one new feature in the international system that we now also have is a number of workable international institutions, norms and procedures that permit and facilitate peaceful resolution of conflicts between nations. Combined with this is the realisation that peace is essential for economic growth. Thus there are two set of forces at work. One is the looming crisis due to climate change brought about by humans which is impacting on resources, livelihood and the very carrying capacity of the planet. This can trigger violent conflict(s) such as war. The second is the realisation of peace, cooperation and integration between nations. This chapter will provide insights from some current historic research on climate change /resource scarcities and war. It will conclude with policies for peaceful resolution of future conflict situations.

Some Current Historic Research Inference

It needs to be noted that that not all civilisations ended due to wars brought about by environmental degradation, resource scarcities and climate change. Severe tectonic disturbances by earthquake in 2000 BC affected the course of the Indus, which helped dry the Ghaggar-Hakra rivers. Modern remote sensing confirms the theory that dramatic shifts in river courses might have created floods that could have cut off food production areas from cities of the Harappan Civilisation. [3] During the Mature Harappan period, about 2500 BC, there was a great rise in the amount of rainfall, but by the beginning of the second millennium BC, it had dropped markedly with damaging effect on food production, further resulting in de-population of cities. One of the reasons for the unpredictability of the rainfall was the extreme deforestation and loss of tree cover caused by burning charcoal in brick- baking kilns. In sum, shifting rivers, rainfall decline, and insufficient food led to a slow but inevitable collapse of the Indus system. It was a combination of civil unrest, weak central authority, resultant outmigration, and by about 1700 BC Mohenjodaro became a ghost town. [4]

Why Mongols expanded their empire between 1190 and 1258 AD? One possible reason could be climatic. Yale historian Valerie Hansen

2   UN Framework Convention on Climate Change, Fourth *Assessment Report: Summary for Policymakers of three working groups and synthesis report*, 2007 has provided updated scientific evidence.

3   Burjor Avari, *India: The Ancient Past, A History of the Indian sub- continent from c. 7000 BC to AD 1200*, London/ New York, Routledge, 2007, pp.53-54.

4   Ibid.

avers that a steep and regular decline in the mean annual temperature in Mongolia between 1175 and 1260 resulted in less grass for Mongol herds, prompting the Mongol to conquer new territories. [5] David Zhang, geography professor at the University of Hong Kong links the 13th century drought as a reason for the Mongols to invade China.[6] So does Andrew R.Wilson writing in *Orbis* when declining temperatures and rainfall in the late 11th century (after several centuries of warmer and wetter medieval warm period) propelled the Mongols outwards for wars of conquest . [7]

Using insights from anthropologists, palaeontologists and palynologists, Jared Diamond similarly documents the demise of the Polynesians from Easter Island due to deforestation and other ecological problems and warfare as a result. He calls it ecocide: people inadvertently destroying the environmental resources on which their societies depend and narrates the story of the demise of the ancient Maya, the Greenland Vikings and present day problems in Rwanda, Haiti and the Dominic Republic. Climate change is a new complication.[8]

These examples could possibly be termed as anecdotal by some critics. Hard scientific data is required to reconstruct and interpret the past. Recent work on China led by David D. Zhang has attempted to explore relationship between climatic change and war by comparing high-resolution paleo-climatic reconstruction with known war incidences in the last millennium. 1672 wars from 1000 to 1911 AD were used as data base (See Dynastic Chronology in China at Table 1).

*Table 1: Dynastic chronology in China

Legendary Sage Emperors	2852 – 2255 BCE
Hsia(Xia)	2205- 1766
Shang	1766 – 1045

5   As quoted in Nayan Chanda, *Bound Together: How Traders, Preachers, Adventures and Warriors Shaped Globalization*, New Delhi, Penguin/Vikings, 2007, p.184

6   See Reuters, *The Hindustan Times*(New Delhi), November 23, 2007.

7   Andrew R . Wilson, " War and the East", *ORBIS, A Journal of World Affairs*, Vol.52., No.2, Spring 2008, pp.358-371.

8   Jared Diamond, *Collapse : How Societies Choose to Fail and Succeed*, London, Penguin Books, 2005.

Chou(Zhou)	
Western Chou(Zhou)	1045 – 770
Eastern Chou(Zhou)	770 – 256
Spring and Autumn	722 – 481
Warring States	403 – 221
Ch'in (Qin)	221 – 207
Former Han (Western Han)	206 BCE – 8 CE
Later Han (Eastern Han)	23 – 220
Three Kingdoms	168- 280
Six Dynasties	222- 589
Sui	589- 618
T'ang (Tang)	618- 907
Five Dynasties	907 – 959
Sung	960 – 1126
Southern Sung	1127- 1279
Yuan (Mongol)	1279- 1368
Ming	1368- 1644
Ch'ing(Manchu) (Qing)	1644 – 1911

* **Source:** Ralph D. Sawyer, *The Tao of Deception*: Unorthodox Warfare in Historic and Modern China, New York, Basic Books, 2007, p.xv.

A strong correlation was established between climatic change, war occurrences, harvest level, population size and dynastic transition. During the cold phase, China suffered more often from frequent wars, population decline and dynastic change.[9] The journal *Science* also has a similar research which shows the waning of the Asian monsoon rains that helped bring down the Tang dynasty in 907 C.E.[10]

9   David D. Zhang, C.Y. Jim. George C-S Lin, Yuan – Qing He, James J. Wang and Harry F. Lee, "Climatic Change, Wars and Dynastic Cycles in China Over the Last Millennium", *Climatic Change*, Vol. 76, Nos 304, June 2006, pp.459- 477.

10 Richard A. Kerr, "Chinese Cave Speaks of a Fickle Sun Bringing Down Ancient Dynasties: *Science,* 7 November 2008, Vol322, Issue 5903, pp.837-838.

As result of recent scientific breakthroughs in establishing precise paleo-climatic records, this experiment was extended to study global and continental levels between AD 1400 and AD 1900, during the Little Ice Age. The proposed hypothesis of the study posits that long-term climate change has significant direct effect on land – carrying capacity (as measured in agricultural production). Fluctuation of the carrying capacity in turn affects the food supply per capita. A shortage of food resources in populated areas increases the likelihood of armed conflicts, famines, epidemics and reduction in population size. In the same manner as Northern Hemisphere (NH) temperature variations, the incidence of warfare in the NH, Europe, Asia, and the arid areas of the NH (i.e., the arid zone from Eurasia to North Africa) in A.D. 1400 – 1900 tends to follow a cyclic pattern with a turbulent period followed by relatively tranquil one. [11]

Case of India

In India not much of historic data in terms of climate history based on paleo-climatic records, detailed documentation of wars, record of agricultural production and population data have been complied for analysis and interpretation. [12] One study on northwest India due to changes in the Indian summer monsoon concludes that: 'The Indian summer monsoon reached the peak of its intensification in the early Holocene 10,000- 7000 cal years before BP and thereafter weakened gradually. Several major rivers, including the Indus were flowing with full vigour during this time. The abundant summer rain in the early Holocene helped early people to augment their agricultural practices and grow a variety of cereals, lentils and grains. This brought about a change in the living style of the people from hunting, gathering and pastoralist to subsistence economy, one centred around settled agriculture and domestication of wild animals. Weakening of the summer monsoon led to the beginning of arid phase in South Asia ~ 5000 – 4000 cal yrs BP. This triggered a chain of change in agricultural

---

11 David D. Zhang, Peter Brecke, Harry F. Lee, Yuan- Qing He, and Jane Zhang, " Global climate change, war, and population decline in human history", *Proceedings of the National Academy of Sciences* , vol. 104,No. 49, December 4, 2007, pp.19214-19219.

12 Prof David Zhang when queried about India responded by e mail on 06 March 2008. In his study wars in India during the last millennium were included. According to Prof Zhang, the wars in India do not reflect temperature cooling because the country is sub- tropical and tropical where the cooling did not lead to environmental crisis. The situation was the same as in Southern China. Dr Zhang is now preparing an article about comparison between India and China under temperature change

practice and food habits in South Asian population. In some cases, societies adapted to monsoon failure by constructing ponds, dams, and other rain harvesting structures. In other situation people migrated eastward towards Ganga plain, where rainfall was sufficient to sustain burden of new influx of human population."[13] The chronology of the change as given in table in the study (Table 2) does give an indication of climate change with response like adaptation, mitigation and migration.

*Table 2: Chronology of events in the Indian subcontinent during the Holocene

Cal yr BP	Climate in the Indian Subcontinent	Agriculture	Population response
AD 1800 onwards	Increased global warming causing high variability in the southwest monsoon	General increase in agricultural production	Widespread floods in the north and northeast drought in the west and northwest
AD 1400-1800	Little Ice Age, weak southwest monsoon, widespread droughts	Decreased agricultural production	Great famines in India, widespread population migrations
AD 700 – 1200	Medieval Warm Period, wet phase in India	Increase in agricultural production	Height of prosperity, increasing trade with Europe and Middle East, beginning of invasion by Islamic invaders

---

13 Anil K. Gupta, David M. Anderson, Deep N. Pandey and Ashok K. Singhvi, " Adaptation and human migration, and evidence of agricultural coincident with changes in the Indian summer monsoon during the Holocene", *Current Science*, Vol. 90, No.8, 25 April 2006, pp.1082-1090. The Indo- US joint project was based on proxy records of monsoon winds from marine sediments from Arabian sea, land records from southern Oman and Tibetan plateau. Previous palynological and archaelogical evidence was used. Another study in *Current Science* though strictly speaking is not on climate change but has studied the rise and fall of Vijayanagar Empire in 13th – 16th century AD based on trade in natural resource. See K.N. Ganeshaiah, R. Uma Shaanker and R. Vasudeva, " Bio- resource and empire building : What favoured the growth of Vijayanagra Empire?', *Current Science*, Vol. 93, No. 2, 25 July 2007, pp. 140 – 146.

1700 onwards	Increasing strength of summer monsoon	General increase in agricultural production	Strengthening of economy, increased trade with Europe and the middle East
4000 – 3500	Intensification of dry phase, weakening of southwest monsoon, widespread droughts	Mixed agriculture, both *rabi* (winter) as well as *kharif* (rainy) season crops were grown; *kharif* crops included maize, millet, rice and a variety of lentils.	Indus people migrated to the east towards Ganga(Ganges) plain, fall of Indus civilisation
7000- 4000	Transitional phase with moderate rainfall, southwest monsoon shows step- wise weakening	Wheat and barley were main crops with a shift towards *kharif* crops	Rise of Indus civilisation; people start migrating to newer areas; traces of human settlement in Thar deserts as early as ca 4800 cal yrs BP
10,000 – 7000	Humid phase, strong southwest monsoon, major rivers like Indus in their full splendour	Winter crops like wheat and barley were main crops grown in Indus region	Traces of first human settlement ca 9000 cal yrs BP in the Indus region near Mehrgarh(now in Pakistan)

*Source: Anil K. Gupta, David M. Anderson, Deep N. Pandey and Ashk K. Singhvi, " Adaptation and human migration, and evidence of agricultural coincident with changes in the Indian summer monsoon during the Holocene", *Current Science*, Vol. 90, No.8, 25 April 2006, p.1083.

Strangely enough, though scholars may thirst for historic data: one event that is still fresh in our memory is the famous Bengal famine in 1943 which killed between two and three million people. The drought was attributed to Monsoon failure. Amartya Sen's insight that famines have as much or more to do with authoritarian politics as they do with climate fluctuation and crop yield,[14] famously explains this food security episode. But as Jeffrey Sachs has cautioned, we need to treat the idea that democracies never have famines now with caution as evidence in rain-fed Africa shows that drought can cause famine in democracies. [15] The Director General of the Food and Agricultural Organization assessed that climate change can cause India a loss of 125 million tonnes or equivalent or 18 % of the country's rain fed production.[16]

Should absence of historic data on correlation with climate change and war on India compel us to ignore the issue? Absence of long-term historic evidence due to non availability of data should not deter us. We should rather use our imagination and see the future with modern tools of scientific data. Using the scientific evidence as given by the Intergovernmental Panel on Climate Change (IPCC) on the forthcoming adverse impacts of climate change over the next few decades we can visualise projections, scenarios and contingencies. Appropriate policies for cooperation and peace can be implemented in the region.

Policies

How can we overcome the risks in order to avoid the achieve conditions of peace? A beginning at the regional level would be a practical way of addressing the issue. A country is unlikely to declare war on the USA, the leader of the global axis of pollution, for having caused drought or floods, abrupt climate change and water scarcities. Rather even though the floods in shared international river system may not be just due to climate change, but other reasons, as current history suggests, countries may have a good reason to accuse their neighbours and ratchet up the issue as one more reason for warlike stance. With climate change now juxtaposed, floods and droughts are going to increase in frequencies and intensities.

The risks of water, food, disasters and migration need to be seen in a holistic manner. While by 2000, 130 multilateral environmental agreements

---

14 Jeffrey Sachs, *The End of Poverty: How We Can Make It Happen in Our Lifetime*, New Delhi, 2005, Penguin Books, p.175.

15 Ibid.

16 *The Hindu* (New Delhi), August 8, 2007.

had been agreed upon by the countries,[17] the number of these has climbed to over 250 in the past decade.[18] It is the ripe time that regional countries now attempt to develop a security regime on climate change .This exercise is bound to be tough as even before conflicts occur we attempt to address them. Some areas where countries in the region would need to share in knowledge creation and then incorporate in national policies are suggested.

Himalayan Eco-System

China, Pakistan, Nepal, Bhutan and Bangladesh need to take initiatives to have a comprehensive dialogue on the state of degradation of Himalayan ecosystem and the likely outcomes. How will the water budget get impacted and what needs to be done jointly may be a good preamble. A regional data, information and early warning ecological intelligence system may be the first step incorporating existing data. Gaps in knowledge and the related field stations for measurement need to identify. Geo-scientific inputs also need to be shared when we talk of borders.[19] The second step is countries need to spell out adaptation action plans so that common features can be compared. Scientific studies need to simulate disaster events that may have cross border implications. Common understanding of floods and why it takes place will be a good first step. Myths and unscientific arguments should no more inform deliberations.

International Rivers and Treaties

There is a need to begin scientific work in a non incremental manner. Complete study of Himalayan glaciers is a gigantic task. China for instance discovered 42 shrinking glaciers in Tibet in 2007 in the Qinghai- Tibet plateau.[20] In 2011,[21] it was found that they were shrinking faster than ever affecting three major river systems namely Yangtze, Lancang and Yellow river. Besides remote sensing it needs sustained field work and "ground

---

17 John Baylis and Steve Smith, *The Globalzation of World Politics : An introduction to international relations*, New Delhi, Oxford University Press, Second Impression, 2006, pp. 451-478.

18 WTO, 2012 http://www.wto.org/english/tratop_e/envir_e/envir_neg_mea_e.htm

19 U. Raval, *Current Science*, Vol. 93, no. 8, 25 October 2007, p. 1047.

20 *Hindustan Times*(New Delhi), September 26, 2007.

21 Glaciers on China's Qinghai-Tibet Plateau melting fast due to global warming, English. xinhuanet.com, October 21, 2011 http://news.xinhuanet.com/english2010/china/2011-10/21/c_131205294.htm

truthing".[22] Recent studies indicate that glacial lake outburst flood (GLOF) will increase. Besides there is fragmentation of glaciers leading to its disintegration. Even radioactive fallout residue in now not found as there is no accumulation of snow. In one study, no radioactive fallout (from 520 atmospheric tests in 1950s and 1960s) was found implying Tibetan ice field has been shrinking over the last 50 years. Loss of ice field is a disaster waiting to happen.[23] A two track approach is suggested. The first, to study the impact of climate change on river flow on treaties such as Indus Water Treaty (between India and Pakistan over the Indus basin), Ganga Water Treaty (between India and Bangladesh on the Ganges at Farakka barrage) and the Mahakali Treaty (on Mahakali/Sarda river between India and Nepal) . In the second track common understanding must be reached on rivers on which there is no treaty like the Brahmaputra (China, India and Bangladesh). The clichéd water war hypotheses can be falsified if a new approach is taken for agriculture, irrigation and water use intensities.

Food Security

Historic evidence abounds in food shortages and war. In the case of India, Pakistan, Nepal and Bangladesh, by 2015 the population is expected to reach figures of 1302.5, 190.7, 32.8 and 180.1 million. One popular book of Lester Brown is "Who will Feed China?" Chinese authorities and academics dismiss this alarm by mentioning that as along as markets exists food can be bought. It is pointed out that there is ample supply of food in world market, and the future of food security will be taken care of by genetically engineered crops. [24] While this may hold for China, food deficit countries are insecure. In 2007 unprecedented drought in Australia and unfavourable weather conditions in Argentina, Ukraine and southern Russia had sharply reduced wheat output. The year 2008 more

22 I am thankful to Dr Prateek Sharma of The Energy Research Institute (TERI), New Delhi for explaining the term "ground truthing" which means   for example that just remote sensing is not sufficient and   that physical measurement and confirmation is needed. Translated into practical terms it means that the remote and rugged border regions need to have humans trained and deployed to undertake this new ecological task.

23 KS Parthasarathy, " Missing footprint of A – bomb fallout in Himalayan ice fields", *The Hindu* (New Delhi), January 31, 2008. The author quotes research of Prof Lonnie Thomson of Ohio State University. According to the study, 12,000 cubic metres of fresh water is stored in glaciers throughout the Himalayas.

24 Yushi Mao, " There is No Food Crisis in China", *China & World Economy* , Vol. 13, No. 1, January – February 2005. The author mentions that even Japan imports 25 million tonnes(MT) per year which is more than 20 MT per year import by China.

people joined the world's hungry as food prices soared and stocks became low. In India, an estimated quarter of the entire world's hungry or nearly 213 million go hungry everyday.[25] Genetically modified technology may provide solution, provided there is no negative ecological impact of its use as an unintended consequence. The most practical methods is to focus on water use intensities in agriculture and attempt to change the crops according to the best ecological needs. This may also bring down demand for water for agricultural use which is over 80 %. Combined is the need for planting bio fuels as opposed to food crops, feed or agro- forestry. This requirement competes with arable land. Loss of biodiversity also has made us lose the diversity in plant and animal breeds. Monoculture has made us vulnerable as we now lack resilience such as having water tolerant crops or crops suitable for arid conditions. This revival of traditional knowledge could also be an area of cooperative framework.

Migration

Though migration is a historic process, it has lead to social tensions and insurgencies in the case of India's north east as result of migrants from erstwhile East Bengal, East Pakistan and contemporary Bangladesh. One way is to look at it from the perspective of international political economy. Cheap labour has been an important factor in movement of people. But if identity gets overwhelmed then violence is bound to take place in receiving country. Combined is the spread and export of terrorism with smuggling. Though a fence is in the process of being erected along the Indo- Bangla border, it is unlikely that it will form a wall which can not be infiltrated. With sea level rise, more and more of coastal areas would be inundated forcing further inland migration. Both India and Bangladesh have to now face this reality. A dialogue is long overdue.

Climate Related Disasters

Frequencies and intensities of natural disasters will increase. Floods and drought will be more common. Greater cooperative disaster preparation between countries will benefit all countries. Best way to overcome disasters made worst by human interference is to study drainage congestion and the neglect of flood plains and take remedial action. Urbanisation, roads,

---

25 Superpower? 230 million go hungry daily, *The Times of India*, January 15, 2012 http://articles.timesofindia.indiatimes.com/2012-01-15/india/30629637_1_anganwadi-workers-ghi-number-of-hungry-people

communication networks and infrastructure have changed the nature of terrain. Cushions such as wet lands or seasonal rivers have been encroached. Thus natural events have been changed into nature's devastating fury. The Kosi floods in Bihar in August 2008 will remain as trigger events to take stock of the increasing disasters. However it cannot be attributed to climate change. Rather it is a man made disaster due to embankments and drainage congestion and poor workmanship and operation and maintenance of structures. But such disasters will increase in future due to climate change related impacts.   An integrated dialogue between neighbouring countries in managing and reducing disasters needs to be carried out. Watershed restoration by planting suitable ecologically friendly trees in any case need not wait and must be done in an emergency mode.   What needs to be done is to see what would have happened had there been no anthropogenic climate change and then superimpose it on climate change models.   For example, a report in *Scientific American* showed that about eight per cent of the rain that hurricane Katrina dumped onto New Orleans in 2005, can be attributed to global warming. [26]

Abrupt Climate Change

The possibilities of sudden ecosystem breakdown such as monsoon failure or release of vast quantities of methane from permafrost in Tibet (a "giant burp") due to warming also must be considered. The impact of such extreme events or ecosystem tipping points also known as abrupt climate change events would be devastating, though the probability of their occurrence is (hopefully) low and uncertain with our current knowledge.   In what time frame and how long will the effects impact is one area which needs joint research.

Historic Research

There is a need to initiate joint historic projects to understand causes of war and conditions for peace in the region. Climate, population and food related studies may generate new insights, more so on how problem was overcome or not overcome and how we now need to react to the future projections. Barring the colonial period under the British, comprehensive records do not exist of wars, and battles. Projects to record our military history must be initiated by organisations such as the Centre for Armed

26 Kevin E. Trenberth, " Warming Oceans, Stronger Hurricanes, *Scientific American* India, July 2007, pp. 26-33.

Forces Historic Research of the United Service Institute of India or the Historical Section of the Ministry of Defence as a first step. This then should be extended to include other records such as economy, population, food production, and climate.

In the final analysis as has been eloquently pointed out by historian Arnold Toynbee, one needs to get rid of the *karma* that the institutions of war have cumulated by effects of past acts.[27] Our knowledge and wisdom of understanding of causes of war should not allow the self fulfilling prophesy that next war will be over water or land or climate change. We need to deconstruct the militarisation of environmental security.

---

27 Arnold Toynbee, *Surviving the Future*, New York/London, Oxford University Press, 1971, pp. 109-110.

VIII

Impact of War on Environment

– Ajey Lele

"Only the dead have seen the end of war".

- Plato

Doings of the war and help the suffering population to cope up. But, the damage these campaigns cause to the environment are difficult to restore.

'Some scientific studies have succeeded in quantifying the greenhouse gas emissions of the wars and the climate change. Such emissions associated with the wars normally go unreported. There is a need for states to understand that their every action on the battlefield or the preparation for waging a war adversely impacts environment. It is a known fact that warfare negatively impacts specific ecosystems. Hence, it is essential to incorporate ecological science into military planning and improved rehabilitation of post war ecosystem services[1].

Issues related to human rights have been at the centre stage of various debates related to modern day war fighting. It has become a global norm that the civilians should *not* be military targets. In the 21st century the states involved in war fighting fully understand their responsibility towards avoiding *collateral damage. Now, there is a need for global community to factor in the issues related to environmental degradation due to war fighting in their pre and post war planning.* Mankind is tampering with the environment knowingly or unknowingly for last many centuries. Man's

---

1   Gary E. Machlis and Thor Hanson, "Warfare Ecology" *BioScience* September 2008, Vol. 58 No. 8, p.729. http://www.eurekalert.org/images/release_graphics/pdf/Machlis%2009-08.pdf

approach towards life could be said to be the biggest causative factor for the degradation of the environment. This approach mainly involves casual approach towards environmental issues, commercial interests, and rampant and unethical usage of natural resources. One human activity which has adversely impacted environment for many years but unfortunately has gone unnoticed is the role played by various military campaigns since time immemorial.

We have witnessed wars of various types and durations. Few wars have been small wars lasting few days involving two countries and fought over a limited geographical area. However, in some cases wars have been fought in different continents involving many countries and lasting for many months/years. All such military offensives over the years have disturbed the balance of environment in some form or other. Various war waging tactics like mountain warfare, jungle warfare, desert warfare etc have degraded environment. The shear movement of troops, movement of military hardware like armoured vehicles, artillery guns, and big ships polluting coastal region or aircrafts flying in air has made their own contributions towards damaging the environment. The weapons fired during military campaigns constitute of many poisonous substances/materials which cause damage not only to the human life but also to the environment. Not much has been discussed about this because the impact of military activities and their effects are felt at over a limited area and for a limited duration of time. More importantly most of the adverse impacts get unnoticed in the 'fog of the war'. At times the contributions by military activities towards causing environmental damages are indirect hence people fail to take notice of it.

This chapter attempts to analyse the roles played by wars towards environmental degradation[2]. The chapter offers a brief narrative about how over the years various military campaigns have adversely impacted environment and then discusses international efforts undertaken to limit these damages and what could be done in future.

What Wars Can Do

War causes human suffering, disturbs peace and notably gives a long lasting blow to the environment. The damage is caused to human lives and

---

2 Author has worked on the similar subject earlier and that work was produced as a chapter in his book titled *Weather and Warfare*, Lancer Publications, New Delhi, 2006. Here author has expanded the concept further.

property in many ways with varying degree of intensity. It mostly depends on the overall geographical and political circumstances. Apart from this wars also cause a permanent damage to the ecosystem.

The impact on the minds of the people could get healed up with time and well managed reconstruction package. However, the impact on the environment is everlasting and at times gets worsened with time. It is not necessary that the environmental damage remains restricted to the war zone only. Topography and terrain of a region has a role to play towards the formation of various in situ weather systems. Sustained military campaigns over a limited geographical area at times bring some changes to the topographical features of the region and also leave an impact on vegetation of the place and this in turn could bring micro climatic changes and in certain cases even significant climatic changes.

Wars are fought in air, on ground and in water so naturally the destruction caused to the environment is all pervasive. Environmental consequences of the war are wide ranging. Air and water pollution takes place because of the oil and chemical leaks caused by the aerial bombardment and artillery firing. The movement of armed forces on the land (particularly armoured corps) destroys natural resources. The impact of pollution on water, biodiversity and other ecosystems lasts for years together and create health hazards for coming generations.

The weaponry, particularly the munitions used in any conflict always leave adverse impact on the adjoining environment. Such munitions come in types of varieties from land mines to laser guided munitions (LGBs). The TNT and/or RDX based munitions creates blasts of significant intensity. Such blasts create craters on the earth in turn causing damage to the natural landscape. Such munitions also mix its poisonous ingredients into the soil damaging its fertility. Apart from actual military campaigns the testing of various munitions and weaponries has also played some role towards environmental and ecological destruction.

Iconic images of the First World depict the landscape of black stumps of shattered trees and destruction carried out to topography and terrain of various places in the world. Since then all evolving twentieth century military technologies have played role in causing damage to the environment in some form or other. Particularly, landmines planted in various wars, amounting to millions in numbers could be said to be the real 'culprits'. No one realised during early days of war fighting that usage of such mines could be suicidal for the environment. For army commanders they were of greater significance as a Khmer Rouge (1975) general claimed them 'the perfect soldier': cheap, efficient, expendable, never hungry, never needing sleep. But, for environment they have done the maximum damage and in some parts of the world are still continuing doing it because nobody actually knows where they are planted in ground. Accidental explosion of such mines is causing damage to human life as well as to environment.

In terms of environmental impact, First World War I could be said to be most destructive. Major part of various campaigns during this period involved trench warfare. Digging a tranche causes direct damage to the 'earth'. It crushed grasslands tossed up huge amount of soil causing major erosion and altered soil structures significantly. This war is famous for the poisonous gases being used during various campaigns. These causes caused significant amount of deaths of the solders and polluted battlefields. End of war never ended the environmental misery. This is because change in landscape had impact on local weather conditions and to that the problem got aggravated because of unexploded ammunition.

Geographical coverage of Second World War was significant and naturally it damaged environment in various parts of the world. Again weapons used during this war also played a role towards degrading environment.

Nuclear attacks over Hiroshima and Nagasaki could be said to be the 'epitome' of environmental damages for a particular region in the shortest possible timeframe. Apart from significant human damage these blasts kicked up mushroom cloud constituting of sand, pebbles, dust particles and radioactive debris. The blasts subsequently caused many fires over the region. The blasts were responsible for killing many plants and animals over a longer duration of time because of continuing radioactive precipitation for some time. From water to sand everything was polluted causing damage to agriculture for years to come.

Subsequent Vietnam War lasted almost for two decades. Naturally, the extent of war itself was responsible for continual damage to the environment over a longer period of time. Apart from conventional weaponry particularly the usage of chemical spray (Agent Orange) for destroying forest cover used as a cover by the Viet Cong guerrillas has caused some permanent damages to the environment. The Americans had used herbicides for denuding the broad-leafed trees so that the US troops could better spot the enemy in the jungle. These herbicides have spoiled the ecosystems of many parts of Vietnam. Fires were put on by militaries for various purposes had said to be damaged a vast area of almost 15,000 sq km which mostly included tickly vegetated areas and forests.

The Cold War period was not totally void of military campaigns but what could have caused more damage to the environment during this time must be the 'power show' displayed by the two superpowers during this period by testing various types of new weapons and munitions.

The nuclear weapon testing carried out in yesteryears by major powers has also been responsible for some of the most profound and persistent environmental damage to life on earth.[3] Even the May 2009 underground nuclear test carried out by North Korea would have had some impact on the environment near the testing site. Nuclear radiations coming out of various nuclear tests have caused severe damage to lives of some people. Accidental nuclear disasters like the infamous Chernobyl disaster (on 26 April 1986 an accident took place at nuclear power plant in Ukraine killing few and spreading huge dosage of radiation into the atmosphere) has contaminated a large geographical area with radioactive fallout. Even the nuclear waste coming out of nuclear energy installations is damaging because of its poisonous and toxic chemical constituents. The race for supremacy during Cold War period demonstrated that even preparing for war causes widespread damage to the environment.

During eighties the war between Iran and Iraq had caused widespread damage to the local desert ecosystem. However, Persian Gulf War (1991) could be termed as the 'black spot' in the history of environmental degradation caused by any military campaign. Starting January 1991, this Operation Desert Storm meant for liberation Kuwait was also was aimed at destroying all Iraqi war waging assets like their air force, anti-aircraft facilities, and command and control facilities. In this war, the Iraqi President Saddam Husain had unleashed a new military tactic: deliberate environmental devastation. This battle was fought in Iraq, Kuwait and the Saudi-Arabian border region. The allied forces led by Americans had used both aerial and ground artillery. Hence, apart from Saddam Husain's

---

3 http://www.ppu.org.uk/war/environment/index_en.html, accessed on September 22, 2008

tactics of intentionally burning oil wells the allied forces have also played a significant role towards making this war as one of the most environmentally devastating wars ever fought.

The entire Persian Gulf region had witnessed an environmental catastrophe due to the intentional torching of Kuwaiti oil wells by Iraq and bombing of Iraq's civil, military and economic assets by the US led coalition forces. This war witnessed one of the largest intentional 'oil spill' in history. Also, crude oil was spilled into the desert, forming oil lakes covering 50 square kilometers. Eleven million barrels of oil were dumped, of which three million ended up on the beaches of Saudi Arabia, Qatar and Iran. Saddam also ignited 600 Kuwaiti oil wells, with the uncontrolled burning of unrefined crude oil creating clouds of toxic pollution and releasing half a ton of air pollutants into the atmosphere.[4] These actions took a toll on the environment as clouds of black smoke and soot lingered into the atmosphere for months together and helped smog formation and acid rain. This blanket of soot, gasses and chemicals, which hit marine life across the Gulf and helped to lower sea temperatures by as much as 10°C. Oil fires were of such intensity that it took nine months for them to get extinguished. Even the job of putting these fires off also played some role towards causing subsequent damages because seawater was used to extinguish the oil fires and this resulted in increasing salinity in areas close to oil wells.

Allied forces as a war policy had targeted many dams and sewage water treatment plants. This caused the sewage to flow directly into the rivers Tigris and Euphrates and polluting them severely[5]. The destruction of sewage works and industrial plants also led to rivers flowing with effluent, spreading pollution and disease. Subsequent research has suggested that the civilian population — including —Kuwaitis — was particularly badly hit by the air pollution, with increases in chronic respiratory diseases. Millions of barrels of oil were spilled into the gulf's fragile ecosystem. The oil slick clogged up bays and mudflats, killing tens of thousands of birds (probably around 25,000 migratory birds got killed) and ruining shrimp

---

4   Desk Study on the Environment in Iraq, *United Nations Environment Programme,*2003, http://www.unep.org/pdf/iraq_ds_lowres.pdf, accessed on November 14, 2008

5   Environmental effects of warfare, http://www.lenntech.com/environmental-effects-war. htm, accessed on September, 11, 2008

populations.[6] Plankton stocks were reduced to such an extent that it led to a fish famine and cannibalism among starving sea birds. The impact on marine life was most severe, because warm water sped up the natural breakdown of oil. Local prawn fisheries did experience problems for many months after the war.[7] In due time the oil percolated into groundwater aquifers. Pollutants leaked from bombed chemical plants into the rivers affected the drinking water supply too. Also, the drinking water extracted from the river was polluted. This resulted in widespread diseases like typhoid and few other diseases.

This particular war brought utmost damage to the environment because pollution prone oil wells, oil tankers and oil production facilities itself were the primary targets. Post 1991-1992 Gulf War a slow but definitive degradation of the ecosystem of this region has taken place. At least 1,000 people had lost their lives in 1991 as a direct result of breathing in the heavily polluted air.[8] Scientists are of the opinion that the burning oil fields would further accelerate the problem of climate change via greenhouse pollution and global warming over the region and adjoining areas in years to come. Damage to oil wells in 1991 have caused spills on dry land, and over 1,000 oil lakes and ponds dotted Kuwait, contaminating some 40 million tonnes of soil. In Kuwait this has poisoned 40 percent of its scarce underground water.

It is difficult to judge the exact damage caused to the environment during this war and how adversely it would affect the weather pattern of the region. In fact scientists are of the opinion that these environmental costs may have repercussions not only for the region, but also for other countries in central and south Asia. Some scientists have speculated that a 1994 cyclone in Bangladesh that killed 100,000 people was precipitated due to climactic changes from the Kuwait oil fires[9]. It would be very difficult to

---

6 **Anthony Browne, "Gulf scarred by environmental impact of war",** *World News,* **March 12, 2003 available at** www.timesonline.co.uk/article/0,,3-607612,00.html, accessed on January 11, 2009

7 Environmental effects of warfare, http://www.lenntech.com/environmental-effects-war. htm, accessed on September, 11, 2008

8 Environmental Impact of War in Iraq 2003 - A collection of related articles, **http://www. mongabay.com/external/iraq_war_new_scientist.htm**, accessed on February 11, 2009

9 Abdhesh Gangwar, Impact of War and Landmines on Environment, Centre for Environment Education, Himalaya, 2003, Conference proceedings available at **http:// www2.mtnforum.org/oldocs/1409.pdf**, accessed on March 12, 2009

prove this fact with certitude however, such possibilities cannot be totally ruled out. This is mainly because the weather systems react to various micro changes taking place in the environment. Weather could change its track even depending on what is commonly known as a Butterfly Effect. This effect is based on the famous mathematical theory called Chaos Theory. This theory describes behaviour of certain dynamical systems. These systems are highly sensitive to initial conditions. In short this means that weather of a particular location could get impacted even by the butterfly flapping its wings in some other part of the world.

During First Gulf War the Americans had used newly developed armour- piercing projectile weapons. These weapons were made from Depleted uranium (DU) which is a radioactive and chemically toxic nuclear waste product. Health and environmental consequences of DU are severe and enduring. These weapons may have given the allied forces a battlefield advantage but the environmental damage caused by their usage is irreversible. Breathing in DU dust is known to contribute to many health problems in humans. Such weapons may cause kidney and lung infections for highly exposed persons. Many civilians and soldiers involved in these operations are reported to be facing DU related health problems like lung cancer, kidney problems, birth defects etc. DU is extremely long-lived and at least 300,000 kilograms of DU and uranium dust was left around Iraq, Kuwait and Saudi Arabia by US and British forces during the Gulf War. There were unconfirmed reports that the Americans had used DU weapons even during 2001/2003 Afghanistan and Iraq conflicts. Currently there is a need to stop the rapid proliferation of depleted uranium weapons because they are likely to bring tremendous human and environmental devastation. The environmental cost of war inevitably translates to financial costs. In September 1995, Kuwait filed a $US385 million claim against Iraq for environmental damage due to Iraq's occupation of Kuwait. The claims made were for damages to health, coastal areas, maritime environment, water resources and desert environment.

The 2001 American military action over Afghanistan have left a long term impact on overall environment of the region. The Americans had used a very high volume of firepower over the region. It constituted Tomahawk cruise missiles, 500 pound laser guided bombs. Munitions like GUB 16 and GUB 28 and laser guided munitions weighing 1000 to 4700 pounds. All these munitions have caused damages due to blasts, fragmentation and heat created by them. According to experts, an explosion of a 240 kg bomb creates a crater 4 m deep and up to 50sq miles in area. In Afghanistan cities like Kabul, Khandhar, and Mazar-e-Sharif have borne the brunt of this bombing. Also hilly areas have suffered the most damage since Osama bin Laden was expected to be moving across those regions. This destruction of the fertile layers of soil would mean the destruction of associated flora and fauna. The process of restoring soil fertility and the natural biochemical cycles may now take several thousands of years. The conflict of March and April 2003 in Iraq has been markedly different from the 1991 Gulf War, having been focused on major urban areas in Iraq, especially Baghdad and Basra. As result, the environmental consequences have also been very different, with the most obvious problems being air pollution from oil-trench fires and the damage to essential services such as water and electricity supplies.

This American invasion and the subsequent Urban War in Iraq has brought forward different dimension of environmental problems. During this war the Americans had tried to avoid the collateral damage and hardly any oil wells were put on fire by the either side. Still some amount of pollution of Iraqi rivers has taken place compounded by destruction of water supply and sewage-treatment works. This has created many health related problems. Even in Yugoslavia more or less similar problems were faced during NATO operations. They also had faced problems of toxic gas leakage due to the bombing of pharmaceutical factories.

During 2003 war, the US Defence forces were deployed in Arabian Sea, Mediterranean Sea and Persian Gulf for many months. Wastewater and garbage (mainly the oil based products) from these unusually large numbers of ships in the area have contributed to the further pollution of coastal waters.

Large-scale aerial and naval bombardment targeting urban infrastructure, weapons facilities, petrochemical, and industrial storage plants is likely to affect the environment in long-term. Many environmentalists are concerned about the use of armaments that probably incorporate depleted uranium (particularly, the cluster bomb type munitions used by USAF). Even though The U.S. military has studied the health effects of DU extensively, and maintains that there are no serious long-term health consequences there are very few buyers to this theory.

The Iraqi forces themselves had littered many parts of their country with land mines. These mines along with unexploded ordnance of all sizes and types have caused few accidents and have contributed towards the damage to wildlife for years to come and also degrade the ecosystem. Presently approximately 33% of Iraq's total area is the desert, which is a living ecosystem. The march of heavy military equipment over these areas has probably done an extensive damage to this ecosystem that may take decades to heal.

The problems generated by the torching of the oil wells remain more entrenched, since the desert environment lacks the natural cleansing process (i.e., waves and abrasion) of the ocean. The past experience shows that the ecological landscape of Kuwait and the Persian Gulf were irrevocably damaged post 1992, due to the destruction unleashed by the burning oil wells. The damages caused during this war are not expected to reach to this extent (as compared to more than 700 oil wells on fire during 1991 this time it was hardly seven or so) but pollution problems do exist. Also intentional burning of oil kept in trenches close to Baghdad to deceive the enemy aircrafts has contributed a lot to the air pollution of that area. It has been scientifically proven that one gram of soot can block out two-thirds of the light falling over an area of eight to ten square meters. Hence temporarily the heat balance of the region may change.

It is expected that oil spilled into the Persian Gulf, contaminated water, pollution, oil well fires, bombing etc. might have killed several birds, fishes and animals. Also approximately 2 to 3 million birds regularly use the gulf as a resting area during the 'spring migration' to Europe and as a result of this war they may have died elsewhere due to various reasons like change of route, lack of food/water etc.

The more worrying factor is the destruction of sewage works and industrial plants. As a result of incessant American bombing fires, huge volumes of smoke, huge volumes of acid gasses were a common phenomenon for 20/25 days in many parts of Iraq. Bombing tends to allow water and sewage systems to get mixed together, and water contamination increase health related problems. The conflict on the soil of Iraq is likely to further damage Iraq's already highly stressed environment. Depending on the scale of contamination, the effects on the Tigris and Euphrates rivers, and the Mesopotamian marshes, farmlands, and aquatic ecosystems in southern Iraq could be severe, affecting weather systems, solar radiation, and food chains in long run.

Before the start war it was expected that this war might follow the similar course of 1990-1991 Gulf War. Also it was expected that Saddam Hussein might behave irrationally and burn most of the oilfields. The expected huge amount of soot in the atmosphere was the major cause of concern. Luckily no significant burning of oilfields took place hence the environment got saved from pollution. But in spite of one-sided victory of America with relatively less collateral damage and minimal visible damage to the environment, it is still expected that this war may lead to a major impact on the environment of Middle East in days to come. However, it must be understood that the impact on the environment of the 1992 Gulf War was neither as apocalyptic as first feared by some scientists, nor it has completely healed yet. The soot and plumes from the oil fires and bombardment would not wreak havoc on the monsoon patterns in southern and central Asia. However today Iraq faces many small-scale but long-term environment related crises. Critical environmental vulnerabilities and risks of Iraq are particularly associated with water resource management (including groundwater), ecosystem degradation, desertification and deforestation, and loss of biodiversity, waste management and damaged oil industry management. Over the years many war campaigns have shown the adverse impact on the environment ranging from destruction of rainforests to destruction of manmade dams. There exists a danger of long-term damage that may be caused by the use of weapons of mass destruction. There indiscriminate impact can lead to an environment hostile towards many forms of life.

As per the report titled "A Climate of War: The war in Iraq and global warming" published by Oil Change International, March 2008 the impact of this ongoing war on the environment is scary. The report states that:

This war is responsible for *at least* 141 million metric tonnes of carbon dioxide equivalent (MMTCO2e) since March 2003. To put this in perspective:

- CO_2 released by the war to date equals the emissions from putting 25 million more cars on the road in the US.

- If the war was ranked as a country in terms of emissions, it would emit more CO_2 each year than 139 of the world's nations do annually. Falling between New Zealand and Cuba, the war each year emits more than 60% of all countries Emissions from the Iraq War to date are nearly two and a half times greater than what would be avoided between 2009 and 2016 were California to implement the auto emission regulations it has proposed.

- In 2006, the US spent more on the war in Iraq than the whole world spent on investment in renewable energy.[10]

Above findings are somewhat US specific because that was what the mandate for this report was. However, at a broader scale they demonstrate how emissions stem from fuel-intensive combat, oil well fires and increased gas flaring, heavy use of explosives and chemicals actually contribute towards global warming.

Both the Gulf Wars (1991 and 2003) are much discussed and debated wars because of the global attention they received. However, one major conflict that had taken place in the post Cold War era also needs a mention from the point of view of environmental degradation. Yugoslavia conflict saw a series of violent conflicts in the region of the former Republic of Yugoslavia that took place almost for a full decade starting from 1991.

With respect to the environment, this conflict has had a strong impact, in particular in Kosovo, as a result of Yugoslav Army activities. All over Yugoslavia, the infrastructure suffered heavy damage. Based on the evidence gathered during this conflict it is concluded by scientists that following types of environmental damages have occurred because of the various military campaigns during a span of almost ten years.

- High levels of pollution around main military targets, in particular chemical industry.

- Soil pollution and associated food and drinking water contamination.

- Damage to ecosystems in particular to river ecosystems.

- Environmental disturbances resulting from the refugee situation

---

10A report titled "A Climate of War: The war in Iraq and global warming" published by Oil Change International, March 2008, available at http://priceofoil.org/wp content/uploads/2008/03/A%20Climate%20of%20War%20FINAL%20(March%2017%202008).pdf, accessed on May 18, 2009

in Kosovo, Albania and Former Yugoslav Republic (FYR) of Macedonia, but also from refugees coming home (e.g. use of wood for heating etc.) and refugees in Serbia and Montenegro.[11]

The above discussion has covered that how various military campaigns have contributed adversely towards damaging the environment. All the military campaigns covered over here were state versus state conflicts. However, particularly during last few decades the world is witnessing a new phenomenon of asymmetric warfare where a state is continuously been targeted by a non-state actor by using various unconventional methods of war fighting like suicide bombing and few other acts of terrorism like using IEDs etc. Such acts are usually isolated in nature and are not expected much to destroy/pollute the environment. However, during 2008-2009, Sri Lanka in its backyard almost for a year fought a significant battle to disintegrate one of the most dreaded terrorist organisations called the LTTE. Mostly this battle was fought in the jungles and with conventional weaponry. No scientific analysis is available about the impact this counterterrorism action would have had on the environment. However, it could be easily concluded that considerable amount of degradation of environment must have caused during this battle for taming the Tamil Tigers.

International Efforts

The scientific assessments of environmental impacts of various military campaigns have convinced the states that this issue is serious and demand separate attention. Currently efforts are being made at various levels from local NGOs to the United Nations to control this damage.

Particularly in the area of landmines much of organised work has been done. As per the 2000 report of International Campaign to Ban Landmines (ICBL), there are more than 250 million antipersonnel mines in the arsenals of 105 nations, with the biggest estimated to be China (110 million), Russia (60-70 million), Belarus (10-15 million), United States (11 million), Ukraine (10 million), Pakistan (6 million), and India (4-5

---

11 "Assessment of the Environmental Impact of Military Activities During the Yugoslavia Conflict", Preliminary Findings, June 1999, a report prepared by The Regional Environmental Center for Central and Eastern Europe for the European Commission DG-XI - Environment, Nuclear Safety and Civil Protection and available at www.rec.org/ REC/Publications/YugoConflictAssessment/contents.html, accessed on Jan 12, 2009

million).[12] The report mentions that people have understood the horrific human and environmental impacts of landmine usages and there is a positive change in the attitude of the states and the situation is improving, though lot more needs to be done. The report also observes that there has been reduced use of the weapon in recent years.

However, this is just the beginning and landmines caught the attention of many because of the various wartime and post war human casualties caused by them. Other weapons (apart from being an accidental explosion of the unexploded weapon) normally do not cause visible damages to the human health in a post war scenario. The after effects of poisonous chemical gases or radiations are slow on human body and more so, on the environment. Hence there is a need to look at environmental effects caused by munitions consisting of depleted uranium, bombing of factories and storage facilities by using conventional weaponry and other issues like the burning of oil refineries more seriously.

To diplomatically address all these problems many international conventions like Hague Convention, Geneva Convention, Environmental Modification Convention exists to mitigate the impact of war on the environment, agriculture, animals and other natural resources and many countries in the world subscribe them. The need of the hour is the thorough review of these conventions, with an eye towards strengthening them in light recent environmental devastations during Iraq, Kosovo, Afghanistan and Iraq conflicts.

The wars all over the world during last few decades have shown that environment is the most silent sufferer of the doings of the war. It had succeeded in getting attention of the few policy makers. Since 1999, the United Nations is monitoring and assessing the damages caused to the environment due to the armed conflicts. And since the year 2002, the United Nations has started observing 'November 6' as the 'International Day for Preventing the Exploitation of the Environment in War and Armed Conflict'. After the end of any war or armed conflict the UN looks for pollution and other collateral damages caused to the environment due to the bombing of factories, oil refineries and storage facilities. They also look for deliberate acts of environmental sabotage like draining of Mesopotamian wetlands, torching Kuwaiti oilfields, ruin of arable land by landmines etc.

12 "Landmine Monitor Report 2000: Towards a Mine-Free World", http://lm.icbl.org/index. php/publications/display?url=lm/2000/report.html, accessed on March 16, 2009

Hence, the 6ᵗʰ November of each year is observed as an International Day to fight against these "War made Environmental Disasters". In taking this action, it is considered that damage to the environment in times of armed conflict impairs ecosystems and natural resources long after the period of conflict, often extending beyond the limits of national territories and the present generation. However, the way the issue of environment is dealt over the years by the major powers raises a question about the future of this UN effort.

However, it could be said that observing a particular day is important but is more of a tokenism. Much more needs to be done in this field. Particularly, the major powers need to come together and accept the reality that in the global fight against climate change and global warming it is essential to address this issue also. There is a need to rethink about the way military campaigns and military exercises are undertaken globally. Even munitions manufacturers need to think about the damage their munitions are doing to the environment. A new thought process need to emerge where even munitions design and production could factor in the environmental issues.

Wars are inevitable in certain cases. Hence, it is important for global community to come together in the post war scenario not only for rebuilding the nation but also to see to it that certain measures are taken to repair the damage caused to the environment. This is possible only when there would be a wider recognition amongst the states that such problem exists and need a solution. This issue needs to be factored into various global environmental debates and provisions need to be made while devising treaties that would look into these matters in greater detail and would have some form of international legal structures.

Conclusion

Wars of yesteryears and recent military campaigns have demonstrated that there is a link between conflict and climate change. It has been found that wars affect environment in numerous ways. It affects land use, ecology, water supply, agriculture and biological resources. It also pollutes the air significantly. This impact in most of the cases is limited for a particular locality however in the long run it could adversely affect the weather patterns of the region in some form or other.

Military campaigns have a distinct lifecycle; they could last for few years or could get over within few days. Subsequently, the process of re-building starts. Various global powers come together to undo the undo the doings of the war and help the suffering population to cope up. But, the damage these campaigns cause to the environment are difficult to restore.

Some scientific studies have succeeded in quantifying the greenhouse gas emissions of the wars and the climate change. Such emissions associated with the wars normally go unreported. There is a need for states to understand that their every action on the battlefield or the preparation for waging a war adversely impacts environment. It is a known fact that warfare negatively impacts specific ecosystems. Hence, it is essential to incorporate ecological science into military planning and improved rehabilitation of post war ecosystem services[13].

Issues related to human rights have been at the centre stage of various debates related to modern day war fighting. It has become a global norm that the civilians should not be military targets. In the 21st century the states involved in war fighting fully understand their responsibility towards avoiding collateral damage. Now, there is a need for global community to factor in the issues related to environmental degradation due to war fighting in their pre and post war planning.

---

13 Gary E. Machlis and Thor Hanson, "Warfare Ecology" *BioScience* September 2008, Vol. 58 No. 8, p.729. http://www.eurekalert.org/images/release_graphics/pdf/Machlis%2009-08.pdf

IX

Indian Fishermen's Livelihood In The Palk Straits And The Kutch

- Adhuri Subrahmanyam Raju

Fishing is the key source of livelihood and employment for fishermen. Fishermen go in search of fish wherever they are available. In this pursuit, they hardly respect the maritime boundaries. This is the case everywhere and the fishermen in South Asia are no exception. For instance, the Indian fishermen are crossing maritime boundary and entering into the Pakistani, Sri Lankan and Bangladeshi waters. Similarly, Sri Lankan fishermen are entering into Indian and Maldives waters and Pakistani fishermen entering into Indian waters. The increasing depletion of fish in the traditional catchment zones further contributes to the fishermen crossing the neighbours' waters. Sometimes, the fishermen unwillingly and unknowingly cross other's territory owing to engine failures, no clear demarcation, tidal currents, cyclones and lack of navigational aids.

As crossing international maritime boundary is an offence, the fishermen are arrested/punished by authorities of the other side. In the process especially human rights are violated when the trespassers undergo trial. Worse still, the treatment given to them is justified in the name of nationalism. Any action against the so-called 'poaching' fishermen is a gross violation of all human rights. The paper discusses the livelihood of Indian fishermen, who fish in Indo-Sri Lankan and Indo-Pakistani waters.

Problems in Indo-Sri Lankan Waters

The short distance of 12 km between Rameswaram (India) and Talaimannar (Sri Lanka) makes it difficult to restrict the fishermen crossing neighbouring waters. In spite of the restrictions imposed by the Indian navy and attacks carried out by the Sri Lankan navy, the Indian fishermen enter into the Sri Lankan waters for fishing, as it is the only source of livelihood. The waters on the Indian side are overexploited and so more fertile fishing grounds are always vulnerable. However, the attacks on the fishermen have continued and are a major source of tension between India's central government and Tamilnadu state. Now, some demands of the Tamilnadu leaders include Human rights are violated when the trespassers undergo trial and worse still; the treatment given to them is justified in the name of nationalism. This is against the Article 73 of UNCLOS-III, which forbids the imprisonment of fishermen who are found poaching.

During the civil war, the Sri Lankan navy was not able to distinguish between the fishing boats and the boats involved in the nefarious activities. The navy, instead of identifying the boats engaged in illegal activities, treated all boats' activities as threat to its security. The navy personnel used to fire at boats, which resulted in killing of innocent fishermen. They argue that they suspect the sailors as LTTE forces and they couldn't come closer to them for identification because the LTTE cadres might attack them. However, the number of incidents has decreased since 1998. This is because of the Indian navy's persuasion not to kill the fishermen. However, recently when the Sri Lankan government lifted the ban on its fishermen fishing in their waters, it was reported that the LTTE and the Sri Lankan fishermen began attacking the Indian fishermen, who were crossing their waters.

Apart from these, the fishermen within the region also face problems. There is a conflict between the fishermen who are using mechanised boats and those who are using country boats. The mechanised boats are powerful and they are preventing the country boats to fish in the waters. There is a restriction on the mechanised boats not to fish in three nautical miles from the shore where as the country boats are allowed to fish in that area. However, the mechanised boats are often violating the existing norms and fish in the prohibited area. There has been fight between these two groups and the navy personnel are not able to sort out their differences.

Tamil Nadu government has initiated certain measures to help the fishermen which include: Marine Fishermen Free Housing Scheme; National Marine Fishermen Savings cum Relief Scheme; Fishermen Personal Accident Group Insurance Scheme; Marine Fishermen Accident

Group Insurance Scheme; Supply of Inboard/Outboard Motors to the traditional craft fishermen. However, the fishermen told the author that the welfare schemes are not reaching them and they are depending on fishing only. In the following section an attempt is made to see how the sea tigers are threatening the fishermen.

There are other three issues (Kachchativu island, threat from Sea Tigers and construction of Sethusamudram), which mainly determine the livelihood of the fishermen, who fish in the Palk Straits.

Kachchativu Island

Kachchativu Island had been used by the British since 1920 as a naval gunnery practice range. The island is one-mile long, 300 yards broad and has an area of 285.2 acres. It is a barren, uninhabited place and without drinking water. It is to be noted that the Indian fisherman built a Catholic Church dedicated to St.Anthony. The fishermen and pilgrims of both the countries used to visit the church in the month of March every year for religious festival. St.Anthony is considered as the guardian of the fishermen. The fishermen believe that St.Anthony would protect them from turbulent seas and inclement weather. People of both countries from northern Sri Lanka and Tamil Nadu used to share their culture and ideas. Historically fishermen communities of both countries have common similarities. They speak Tamil and continued to have relations for centuries. There was free movement of people before the independence and it continued till 1974. After the 1974 and 1976 agreements and the eruption of civil war in Sri Lanka in 1983 the situation entirely changed and the relations between the peoples of two countries has undergone transformation.

Though the island is a barren and uninhabited, its surroundings are possessing prawn in abundance. For the Indian government the island is not strategically important. But for the Indian fishermen it is very important place for their livelihood.

In his speech in the Rajya Sabha in September 1960, Jawahar Lal Nehru, the then Prime Minister of India, said: "There was a claim on one of the old principal Zamindaris and it was part of the Zamindari. The Zamindari has gone now and I do not know where the matter stands."[1] In

---

1 *Rajya Sabha Debates*, New Delhi: Parliament Secretariat, 1 September 1960, cols. 3049–50

the Rajya Sabha, to a question, he replied: " The Island is 18 miles east of Pamban. Where Pamban is I do not know." [2] One can understand that he did not have any interest in maintaining the island under the control of India. Later, Prime Minister, Indira Gandhi said that since both countries had cordial relations, it was not wise to raise voice over the island.[3] She felt that the island was a "sheer rock with no strategic significance." She did not even bother to consult the Tamil Nadu government regarding the island. In 1974 India and Sri Lanka had signed an agreement[4], which ensured the sovereign right of Sri Lanka over the island of Kachchativu.

According to the 1974 agreement the Indian fishermen and pilgrims would continue to enjoy their traditional rights. However, the Sri Lankan government did not subscribe to the Indian government's view. It argued that the agreement did not give any fishing rights but only the rights to dry their fishing nets, rest and the right of the pilgrims to visit the island for religious purposes. The nets would become wet only when fishermen fish in and around the island. However, now the fishermen are using nylon nets and they do not need to dry their nets. The agreement was drafted in such a way that it can lead to ambiguous understanding.

Later, India and Sri Lanka had another agreement on the boundary in the Bay of Bengal and the Gulf of Mannar in 1976. Unlike the earlier agreement, this agreement did not deal with any disputed island. However, this agreement deprived the fishing rights for India in the Palk Straits. Both India and Sri Lanka had agreed that "after the determination of the maritime boundaries, fishing vessels and fishermen of one country shall not engage in fishing in the waters of the other..."[5] Therefore, the problems of ownership of the island of Kachchativu and Indian fisherman's

---

2   *Ibid*, col.3050.

3   *Hindustan Times*, 2 March 1968, cited in V.Suryanarayan, *Kachchativu and the Problems of Indian Fishermen in the Palk Bay Region*, Madras: T.R.Publications, p.17.

4   The 1974 agreement has two clauses, which protect a few activities of the Indian fishermen. Article 5 maintains "Subject to the foregoing, the Indian fishermen and pilgrims will enjoy access to visit Kachchativu as *hitherto* and will not be required by Sri Lanka to obtain travel documents or Visas for these purposes." Article-6 of the agreement States "The vessels of Sri Lanka and India will enjoy each other's Waters such rights as they have enjoyed therein."

5   Cited V.Vivekanandan, "Crossing Maritime Borders: The Problem and Solution in the Indo-Sri Lankan Context", in K.G.Kumar (ed), *Forging Unity: Coastal Communities and the Indian Ocean's Future*, Chennai: International Collective in Support of Fishworkers, 2003, p.79.

fishing rights in and around Kachchativu were resolved once for all by the agreements of 1974 and 1976. This position was accepted by the central government of India. While demarcating the maritime boundary with Sri Lanka, India tried to have a trade off between Kachchativu and the Palk Straits. This resulted in the sacrificing of the Indian fishermen's fishing rights in both the areas.

The fact is that the Indian fishermen will not easily give up their livelihood as they have been enjoying that for centuries. The Indian fishermen are being not allowed to enter into the island by the Sri Lankan navy. The Sri Lankan government argued that the island was used for illegal activities and hence it has been preventing the entry of foreign elements on Kachchativu. The Indian government never raised its voice against the Sri Lankan move. The government in New Delhi could not take the problems of the fishermen of Tamil Nadu into considerations in its policy towards Sri Lanka. It adopted some sort of an accommodative attitude towards the neighbour. However, the fishermen in Rameswaram and Pamban, in an interview given to the author, told that they are not bothered about who is controlling the island but they are insisting about the restoration of their old rights to fish around the island. Now, with increasing attacks on Indian fishermen, the demand to bring back Katchthivu under the control of India has risen again. The voice has been bipartisan in the AIADMK-led government in Tamilnadu as well as the DMK have demanded for the same.[6]

Sethusamudram Ship Canal Project

The Indian Cabinet Committee on Economic Affairs approved a Rs.2,427 crore Sethusamudram Ship Canal project on 2 September 2004[7] and the construction would be completed soon. The project links the Palk Bay with the Gulf of Mannar on India's east coast by dredging a shipping canal through Rameswaram. The canal starts from the Tuticorin port on the

6 Jaya tells PM: Get back Katchatheevu for fishermen Hindustan Times, June 14, 2011 http://www.hindustantimes.com/India-news/NewDelhi/Jaya-tells-PM-Get-back-Katchatheevu-for-fishermen/Article1-709468.aspx and Bring Katchthivu back under India's control, *The Hindu*, August 22, 2012 http://www.thehindu.com/todays-paper/tp-national/tp-newdelhi/article3805677.ece

7 The Proposal was not of recent one and many proposals were considered since 1860 onwards. For more details see A.Subramanyam Raju, "Sethusamudram Ship Canal Project: Problems and Prospects", *Indian Ocean Survey,* vol.1, no.2, July-December 2005, pp.105-108.

west, extends north-east in a straight line up to Mansfield patch south of Pamban Island, cuts through the east of the Kodandaramaswamy temple and then turning further north-east joins the Bay of Bengal channel. Since the Palk Bay is narrower and the depth is not beyond fifty meters at any point, all the ships from Chennai to the west coast are currently sailing via Colombo harbour.

Though India will have advantages[8] through construction of the canal, the fishermen will be affected. The fishermen from Tamil Nadu opposed the project as it would deny their fishing rights. The livelihood of five lakh fishermen in 138 fishing stations along the five coastal districts will be severely affected. There is also concern for over the impact of the project on the environment. It involves extensive dredging of the Pamban channel where coral reef[9] is available in abundance leading to the depletion of the fish and the destruction of the marine ecology. The National Environmental Engineering Research Institute (NEERI), Nagpur, examined the viability of the project. The NEERI report stated that the project was environmentally safe. However, it was silent on the impact of the project on the lives of fishermen. Once the construction of the canal is completed, it would break the continuous lime stone formation. This would cause sudden tilting drift, gravitational pull on various other violent processes. It seems that the Indian government has taken only the economic benefits into consideration through the project, while ignoring the ramifications, consequences and calamities once the dredging of the sea is undertaken.

---

8 The canal will provide berthing facilities for many international vessels at Tuticorin port. It will promote economic development of the backward areas of Ramanathpuram and Tirunelveli districts of Tamil Nadu. It will also avoid circumnavigation of ships around Sri Lanka and save fuel costs and standing charges associated with extra period of voyages and improve operation of fishing vessels. Through this project Tuticorin will regain its old commercial glory. It will promote coastal shipping. It will also generate employment opportunities. The canal can be used in transporting coal from Haldia, Paradeep and Vishakapatnam ports for the thermal power plant in Tuticorin. This canal reduces the distance between the east and the west coasts: the distance between Tuticorin and Chennai from 769 to 335 nautical miles; Tuticorin to Vishakapatnam can be 652 as against 1028 nautical miles and Tuticorin to Calcutta (Kolkata) can be 1031 instead of 1371 nautical miles.

9 Coral Reef is the feeding and breeding ground for various marine organizations. It acts as carbon sink by absorbing carbon-di-oxide and converts it into calcium carbonate. It protects the seashore from tidal erosion. It provides people with living sea walls against tides, storm surges and hurricanes.

Problems in Indo-Pakistani Waters

There are more than seven million people in India and Pakistan, who depend on fishing for their livelihood. Indian (and Pakistani) fishermen are being arrested/ killed by authorities of the other side. Indian fishermen are suspected of collaboration with Research & Analysis Wing, (while Pakistani fishermen are suspected to be the agents of Inter-Service Intelligence). The fishermen of both the countries are often arrested for crossing borders and are becoming victims of undefined boundaries. They are being treated as prisoners of war. The arrests of fishermen started since 1987. The Pakistani fishermen go over to the Indian side to catch pomfret, grouper, prawns, shrimp, etc. and the Indian fishermen cross the Pakistani waters in search of squid, ribbon fish, red snapper, tiger prawn, etc.

Till date the fishermen of each nation have not been arrested on the ground that they were carrying arms and ammunitions on board. There are incidents where the fishermen were being arrested and kept in jails for years together on both sides. For instance, 180 Pakistani fishermen were kept in jail in India for more than five years and similarly 193 Indian fishermen were kept in jail in Pakistan by 1997. Their release always depends on the state of relations between the two countries. Often the fishermen are released in equal numbers on both sides. The arrested fishermen on both sides are suffering during their stay in jail. There are no proper sanitation facilities, lack of privacy and keep many of them in a crowded place.[10] The fishermen's mistake was to cross over into the neighbour's waters for their livelihood. They are socially and economically poor. Since both the states are not able to come to an agreement on demarcating their sea borders, it is better both the nations adopt a humanistic and sympathetic approach towards the fishermen who are crossing into each other's waters.

A breakthrough has been achieved by India and Pakistan to agree on a bilateral code of conduct minimizing the inter boundary cross over by the fishermen. Over the past five years, as part of the on going peace process the maritime dispute mechanism has been consciously incorporated into the negotiations agenda. Arresting the fishermen from both sides has been reduced significantly. On 4 September 2003, the Pakistani government

---

10 For the fishermen experience in jail, see Charu Gupta & Mukul Sharma, "Blurred Borders: Coastal Conflicts between India and Pakistan", *Economic & Political Weekly*, Vol.39, No.27 (3 July 2004), pp.3010-3013.

freed 269 Indian fishermen out of 343 lodged in various jails in Karachi.[11] Similarly India also released seventy four Pakistani fishermen lodged in the Jamnagar jail of Gujarat. This decision was taken by both the governments in response to the peace initiatives undertaken by the then Prime Minister Vajpayee. After the official talks in June and August 2004, in a joint statement, both the officials stated that all the arrested fishermen in each other's custody would be released.[12] In April 2005, 156 Pakistani fishermen were released.[13] In June of 2012, 311 Indian fishermen straying into Pakistani waters were released.[14] While the penalty for trespassing is only six months most of them spend long years of incarceration. The eve of the visit of Indian foreign minister S.M.Krishna to Pakistan in September 2012 saw the release of 48 Indian fishermen from the Malir jail in Sindh province.[15] Nevertheless, positive bilateral initiatives need to be concretised into long term plans to put an end to arrest the fishermen, who cross into each other's waters. Both the countries should establish Maritime Risk Reduction Centres (MRRCs), which could provide a ground to solve the fishermen problems if they were caught during poaching into each other's waters. Both the countries are in favour of creating a buffer zone, extending five nautical miles into each other's maritime boundary.[16]

Environmental Issues

Environmental issues are not the main concern for most of the countries in the Indian Ocean region. South Asia is no exception. In the long run, environmental degradation will have serious implications not only for marine ecology but also affect the livelihood of the fishing community. One of the reasons for fishermen crossing into others' waters is due to depletion of fish in their own waters. Apart from over fishing, the other factors that have serious effect on fish stocks and fisheries are: degradation of coral reefs-

11 *The Hindu*, 5 September 2003.

12 See Gupta and Sharma, n.11, p.83.

13 *Indian Express*, 14 April 2005.

14 Interpress service, June 4, 2012 http://www.ipsnews.net/2012/07/fishermen-caught-on-a-political-hook/

15 Pakistan releases 48 Indian fishermen, *The Express Tribune*, September 10, 2012 http://tribune.com.pk/story/434257/pakistan-releases-48-indian-fishermen/

16 Sandeep Dikshit, "Fishermen: India-Pakistan deal in sight", *The Hindu*, 30 November 2004, cited in www.thehindu.com/2004/12/01/stories/2004120105431200.htm.

resulting from climate change, discharge of fuel and emissions by ships and land based pollution. Fifty thousand tonnes of oil and fuel are routinely dumped daily in the Indian Ocean region by large tankers.[17] Mangroves are important to the livelihood of coastal fisherfolk. They provide nurseries for fish and supply food for various species. They also prevent intrusion and erosion of the sea. However, due to decrease in fresh water supply, the mangroves are being destroyed. It was reported that mangroves, which occupied 345,000 hectares along the Sindh coast, reduced to 160,000 to 205,000 hectares.[18] Apart from urbanisation of Karachi, oil refineries, coal and oil-fired power plants are other sources of pollution. "Dumping of industrial effluent and sewage water has seriously affected the small fishing business along the 350-kilometre coastline which stretches along three districts, Karachi, Thatta and Badin"[19] in Pakistan. Gujarat has the largest coastal area in India and has a rich heritage of live corals and coral islands in the Gulf of Kutch. The coral reefs[20] play an important role in marine life. But they are being dredged out due to various reasons. For instance, sand dunes and mudflats are being removed and that led to damage of marine life. Like Karachi, Gujarat state has also invested in chemical industries, fertilisers, textiles, chemical dyes and paints, insecticides, refineries, pharmaceuticals, soda ash, cement, salt etc.[21] Due to commercialisation, thousands of fishermen have been displaced from their livelihood through the destruction of the Indus Delta. Many of them left with no option but to migrate to other places.

Oil spills in the Arabian Sea, which were rare earlier, are now increasing. The MV Tasman Spirit, the Greek tanker carrying 67500 tonnes of crude, which broke in to two on 28 July 2004. It leaked nearly

---

17 *Meeting on Indian Ocean Maritime Security Issues* (Washington DC: Stimson Centre and Dubai: Gulf Research Center, 7-8 October 2008).

18 V.Suryanarayan, "Glimpses into Maldivian History", *Journal of Indian Ocean Studies*, vol.4, no.1, November 1996, p.25, cited in Gupta & Sharma, n.11, p.55.

19 Survival of 4m fishermen hangs in balance as fishing sites rapidly deteriorate, *The Express Tribune*, June 30, 2012, http://tribune.com.pk/story/401236/survival-of-4m-fishermen-hangs-in-balance-as-fishing-sites-rapidly-deteriorate/

20 Coral Reef is the feeding and breeding ground for various marine organizations. It acts as carbon sink by absorbing carbon-di-oxide and converts it into calcium carbonate. It protects the seashore from tidal erosion. It provides people with living sea walls against tides, storm surges and hurricanes.

21 Gupta & Sharma, n.11, p.59.

25000 tonnes of crude. As a result the entire marine life off the Karachi coast destroyed. In August 2010, two container ships, *MSC Chitra* and *MV Khalijia II*, collided[22] spilling 800 tonnes of oil near Mumbai. It affected the regeneration of 1273 hectares of mangroves in the Vashi area near Mumbai.[23] Another oil spill due to the bursting of an oil pipeline of the ONGC off the Mumbai coast occurred in January 2011 and was contained by the Coast Guard in *Operation Paryavaran Rakshak* but not before 55 tonnes of oil flowed out[24]. The supply to the pipe was cut and diverted to another duct. If such incidents occur in the Arabian Sea, India and Pakistan will the worst affected. In South Asia, Indian Coast Guard is the only agency that is capable of dealing with cleaning of marine oil spills. Cooperation between India and Pakistan (and other littorals) is needed to address if such incidents occur in future.[25] On the other hand, emission of carbon dioxide, sulphur and hexafluoride into the atmosphere is a matter of global concern. Due to the impact of climate change, it is expected that the sea level will grow up. Then people, who live in coastal areas, will be affected. It is estimated that by 2050, about 250 million people may migrate due to intensifying monsoon flooding, desertification and reduced food production.[26] India and other littoral states must work towards reducing green house emission.

Conclusion

For fishermen, survival is important and they do not believe in borders. For them, Ocean is their work place. They cross maritime boundaries and enter into the neighbour's waters. It is important that the governments of coastal states must take into account that the fishermen problems are to be understood on humanitarian grounds. There has to be a networking

22 Oil coats Arabian Sea after ships collide, *CBC News*, August 9, 2010 http://www.cbc.ca/news/world/story/2010/08/09/india-oil-slick.html

23 Oil spill damaged 1.2K ha mangroves, *The Times of India*, January 25, 2011 http://articles.timesofindia.indiatimes.com/2011-01-25/mumbai/28375756_1_mangroves-deepak-apte-oil-spill

24 Coast Guard ends op to control oil spill, *The Times of India*, January 23, 2011 http://articles.timesofindia.indiatimes.com/2011-01-23/mumbai/28361156_1_oil-spill-pollution-control-vessel-coast-guard

25 See Ghosh Prabal, "Confidence Building Measures in South Asia – The Maritime Angle", Discussion Paper-8, LNCV Workshop on South Asia, Como, Italy, 27 September 2004.

26 *The Hindu*, 7 March 2009, p.12.

among the fishermen of South Asian countries to bring them on a platform where they can discuss their problems and share their experiences and their ideas. The coastal states of South Asia have to think in terms of encoding a common maritime conduct and regional maritime law. In this manner, most of the problems of the fishermen can be addressed without much delay in case they enter into each other's waters. However, this problem will remain as long as political will for long-term solutions is lacking. The South Asian countries have to realise that they have to shift from the security of the borders to the security of the people.

X

Chinese Occupation of Tibet: Impact on Environmental Security of South Asia

- Sudhir Kumar Singh

Current Situation

In March 2008 despite all the tall claims of the Chinese rulers Tibet became restive with the sudden eruption of violent incidents. Although almost each year March remains turbulent in Tibet but 2008 March was extraordinary turbulent. The sustainability of the movement was extremely intense and despite all instruments of cruel suppression adopted by the Chinese authorities they could not control it for several weeks. The 2008 March appraisal had been embedded by the coincidence of Beijing Olympic and the Olympic torch had started by that time the dissent was blown in its full proportion. The new dimension of the Tibetan protest was that it was not confined within Tibet only but also equally protested into the streets of Europe and the United States despite abnormal security arrangements. The intensity of the protests could be gauged by the fact that despite all round security arrangements for the Olympic torch, its light was lit off by the protesters in many places in Europe. In few places the torch relay run was suspended and it was covered by plane. The entire world was witnessed the intensity of the movements and the Tibetan Diaspora have done tremendous hard work to raise the issue in an articulate manner. However the relationship between China and Tibet have had been extremely interesting.

Tibet-China Relations

Sino-Tibetan relations can be traced back as far as 7th century AD, when the once mighty Tibetan empire was a constant source of menace to the Tang court.[1] In the 13th century, when the Mongols ruled the Eurasian continent, Tibet, like other Inner Asian territory, also became a subjugated part of the Mongol empire.[2] Yet Tibetan relations with Mongols differed somewhat from those of the other conquered peoples in Eurasia. They were based on a special relationship called Cho-Yon [patron-priest], developed between the two nations. In 1254, Kublai accepted Phagspa, master of the Tibetan Sakya sect, as his religious mentor. This relationship required Kublai to accept the religious superiority of his teacher, and as a result, the status of Tibet, and the Sakya sect in particular, was elevated within the great Mongolian empire.[3] Even during the later period whenever the Han nationalism took root and tried for expansion, it took all possible efforts to control Tibet but that point of time China was extremely weak and vulnerable to external aggression and this particular situation of China prevented it to consolidate its position within Tibet. In the early period of the 20th century the Czarist Russia was advancing so was the case of the British Empire and both were dedicated to extend their influence over Tibet for the promotion and protection of their respective empires but finally they remain satisfied to keep Tibet under their power of influence. Czarist Russia was anxious about the apprehensions about the expanding nature of the British Empire, which had already rooted in India and trying to enhance its influence over Tibet. By the turn of the 19th century, the British government realised that China had no real power in Tibet. The Manchu authorities had not been able to enforce Tibetan compliance of both the Anglo-Chinese convention of 1890 and the regulations of 1893. The British government had also heard rumours of Russian influence in the counsels of Lhasa. Tsar Nicholas II [r. 1895-1917] had received Lama Agvan Dorjiev , one of the Buriyat subjects

---

1   Christopher L. Beckwith, *The Tibetan Empire in Central Asia,* Princeton University Press, Princeton, 1987.

2   It is not easy to give a clear definition of the terms "Central Asia" "Inner Asia", or "Eurasia ". Svat   Soucek,s work defines " Inner Asia" as the landlocked   core of the Eurasian continent , including Russian [western] Turkestan [present day Kazakhstan, Kyrgyzstan, Tajikistan, Turkmenistan , and Uzbekistan, the Republic of Mongolia, and the Xinjiang Autonomous Region of the People's Republic of China [PRC]. He further argues that "Inner Asia" designates the whole Eurasian area in its historical and geographical sense, whereas "Central Asia" basically indicates the "Western Portion of Inner Asia, that is western Turkestan, together with such adjacent areas as northeastern Iran and Northern Afghanistan. See for further elaboration Svat Soucek, A history of Inner Asia, Cambridge University Press, Cambridge, 2000,P-11.

3   Hsiao-Ting Lin, *Tibet and Nationalist China's Frontier,* UBC Press, Vancouver, 2006, P-3.

who had been a tutor of Dalia Lama Thubten Gyatso. Consequently, containment of Russian influence in Tibet became the preoccupation of the British Empire. The British government sent an expedition under Col. F.E. Younghusband to Tibet in 1903. When the Tibetan government refused to negotiate with Col. Younghusband, the British expedition continued its march to Lhasa in the summer of 1904. Dalia Lama, Thubten Gyatso left for Urga, the headquarters of the Jebtsundamba of Magnolia. Col. Younghusband and Thi Rinpochhe Lobzang Gyalzen, the Regent of Tibet in absence of Dalia Lama from the country, signed a convention at Lhasa on 7ᵗʰ September 1904, which secured for the British government among others, a guarantee to exclude any other power from influence in Tibet. The British government occupied the Chhumbi valley in lieu of the payment of reparations of Rs. 75,00,000. by the convention signed by the British and Chinese governments at Peking on 27ᵗʰ April 1906, confirming the convention of 1904, the British government recognised the suzerain, not sovereign , position of China in Tibet.

All those factors kept China away and the Chinese were never able to establish sovereignty over Tibet; however at some point of time which was not sustainable they were able to maintain their suzerainty over Tibet.

The ongoing unrest in Tibet and to a certain extent in Xingjiang has been embedded with the burden of history. With the restoration of communist regime in 1949 in Beijing, the communist China became extremely ambitious and hence consolidated its position in Tibet. India was on the strong wicket as far as Tibet is concerned due to variety of proximities with Tibet but Prime Minister; Nehru gave much of India's capacity to China through 1954 treaty. It was a Himalayan blunder and reflected in 1962 when China attacked on India. After 50 years of that attack, Chinese government has classified documents which revels that China was extremely apprehensive about Indian attitude towards Tibet and 1954 treaty gave an adequate space to China to strengthen its holds over Tibet.[4] When Prime Minister, Rajiv Gandhi visited Beijing in 1988 after many decades , according to Natwar Singh, who was part of Indian delegation, Chinese top dignitaries spent 40 minutes discussing Tibet and it was more than half of the entire dialogue between both top leaders which vindicates that still Chinese are not sure about the Indian attitude about

---

4 Krishnan, Anant, Behind the War, a genesis in Tibet, *The Hindu*, New Delhi, 20 October 2012.

Tibet. Tibet is not a simple territory but constitutes one third of Indian Territory and remains as the water tank of Asia. Ten big Trans national river of Asia originates from Tibet and right from the beginning, Chinese had an eye of these particular natural assets including others to sustain its growth.

This is one of the most visible aspects of China which we have witnessed since last several years. Much has been debated on this line but one thing which has not been adequately debated within Tibet debate has been environmental degradation of the plateau and its impact over the ecology of whole Asia in general and South Asia in particular. Since millennia, Tibet has been the hub for the preservation of environment for the surrounding regions. For South Asia it has been more exclusive. Right from the Brahmputra to the Indus, almost every important rivers of South Asia originates from the Tibetan plateau. The year 2009 had been celebrated by China as 50th year of its illegal occupation of Tibet therefore Chinese efforts of maximisation use of natural resources of Tibet must be taken into account. This paper is exclusively intended to debate over this matter. We are well aware about the fact that global warming has become an issue of international concern and right from Rio de Janeiro summit in early 1990s several international summits have been already held to resolve the matter but till now any consensus measures could not be evolved to resolve this impending danger on humanity.

Tibet's Ecology

Tibet is called the roof of the world because of its geological position. It is one of the direct conduit points of the environment and within this situation any tempering with its ecological status would be disastrous for the countries of South Asia, who depends on Tibet not only for river water but also for the preservation of their ecology. The Tibetan plateau happens to be the largest water reservoir in the world. All ten major rivers of Asia including Sutlej, Brahmputra, Irrawaddy, Salween, Indus and Mekong originate in the Tibet plateau. It constitutes the life line of world, nearly two billion people living in South Asia; from Afghanistan to the Ganga-Meghna basin, and in Southeast Asia.[5]

China has made rapid strides in development over the last six decades

---

5   Hari Bansh Jha " Tibetan Waters; A Source of Cooperation or Conflict'? *IDSA Comment,* New Delhi, September 2011.

and is ambitious to develop more in the foreseeable future. For that purpose they need more water and exploitation of natural resources for the larger interest of their mainland. China has already started exploitation of Tibetan natural resources but the growing pace of its mainland development requires more rapid exploitation of the natural resources of Tibet. Tibet is a land of less population due to its inhospitable weather. China has used Tibet in recent years for the promotion and protection of mainland. It is pertinent to mention here that this is the main purpose the ecological asset of Tibet has been widely exploited. Tibetan-originated rivers pass through India, Pakistan, Bangladesh, Bhutan, Nepal and additionally through Burma. In recent decades, thousands of ethnic Chinese have settled in the Tibetan territory and this has created a new pressure on Tibetan ecology. However the most important and dangerous factor is that China has decided to convert the flow of certain rivers' branches which flow throughout South Asia towards mainland China.[6] If this attempt will materialise the majority of the rivers of South Asia would be converted as the dry lanes and will devastate the ecology and forced millions of people in starvation.

The debate of global warming has taken a new lease of life since last several years. With the beginning of 21st century this debate has reached into new level because the global warming has challenged the survival of the human being on the planet earth. The ongoing ecological disaster in Tibet sponsored by China therefore has become a push factor for global warming and thus going to affect not only surroundings but the entire world. South Asia constitutes almost 22% of the global population and majority earns their bread from agriculture sector. In South Asia, nine out of every ten liters of water is used for farming –related activities. The region has the largest rural population in the world with about one billion people living in the countryside.[7] The ecological problems in Tibet will weaken the lone opportunity of bread for vast hapless people of South Asia therefore this issue has an international dimension too. Under the provisions of the international law, this ongoing disaster of Tibetan ecology therefore has not confined as Chinese internal issue and needs international attention too. Although China is assuring the riparian countries particularly India to not disturb the Tibetan ecology but it keep it going on and not allowing

---

6   Massive water diversion project nears completion in China, The Hindu, February 6, 2012 http://www.thehindu.com/news/international/article2866492.ece

7   *World Bank Report*, South Asia, World Water Day, 22 March 2007, <http;//web. worldbank.org/>.

CHINESE OCCUPATION OF TIBET: IMPACT ON ENVIRONMENTAL SECURITY OF SOUTH ASIA

any international agency to look into the matter in an impartial manner. China has deliberately not signed any bilateral or multi lateral treaty for water sharing with any of the riparian countries. China has also not signed the 1997 UN Convention on the Law of the Non Navigational Uses of International Waterways. China probably have understood what George Ginsburg wrote, "It could dominate the Himalayan piedmont by virtue of holding Tibet, and by doing so , it could even threaten the entire South-east Asia and so to say all of Asia.[8] It is due to the fact that the Chinese efforts of exploitation of Tibetan ecology for the larger development of mainland China is not only going to hamper Tibetan ecology but it is going to deliver devastating results for the agro-based economies of South Asia.

The plan includes diverting not only the Yangtze to the Yellow river but also "a number of rivers on the Qinghai-Tibet plateau, including the Brahmaputra and Mekong"[9]. The $80 billion project is expected to supply water to the arid northern region as early as next year. If this attempt diverts the majority of the rivers of South Asia would be converted into dry lanes and will devastate the ecology.

The debate of global warming has taken a new lease of life since last several years. With the beginning of 21st century it has reached a new level because the global warming has challenged the survival of the human being on the planet earth. The ongoing ecological disaster in Tibet sponsored by China therefore has become a push factor for global warming and thus going to affect not only surroundings but the entire world. South Asia constitutes almost 22% of the global population and majority earns their bread from agriculture sector. In South Asia, nine out of every ten litres of water is used for farming-related activities. The region has the largest rural population in the world with about one billion people living in the countryside.[10] The ecological problems in Tibet will weaken the opportunity of earning their livelihood for the hapless people of South Asia. Therefore, this issue has an international dimension too. Under the provisions of the international law, this ongoing disaster of Tibetan ecology therefore has

---

8 Vasudeva, P.K, Chinse Dam in Tibet and Diversion of Brahamputa; Implications for India , *Journal of United Service Institution of India*, Vol.CXLI, No-588, April-June 2012, P-274.

9 Ibid.,

10 *World Bank Report,*   South Asia, World Water Day, 22 March 2007, <http;//web. worldbank.org/>.

not confined as Chinese internal issue and needs international attention too. Although China is assuring the riparian countries particularly India to not disturb the Tibetan ecology but it keep it going on and not allowing any international agency to look into the matter in an impartial manner. China has deliberately not signed any bilateral or multi lateral treaty for water sharing with any of the riparian countries. China has also not signed the 1997 UN Convention on the Law of the Non Navigational Uses of International Waterways. China probably have understood what George Ginsburg wrote, "It could dominate the Himalayan piedmont by virtue of holding Tibet, and by doing so, it could even threaten the entire South-east Asia and so to say all of Asia.[11] It is due to the fact that the Chinese efforts of exploitation of Tibetan ecology for the larger development of mainland China is not only going to hamper Tibetan ecology but it is going to deliver devastating results for the agro-based economies of South Asia.

As geographical landmass, the Tibetan Plateau is the highest and largest plateau in the world, exposing its inhabitants to a challenging environment of living at an average elevation of roughly 4,000 meters above sea level. This prominent landmass in South Central Asia is roughly 2.5 million square kilometer in size; geologically, it is considered to be young and still growing in height. The Plateau is the predominant driver of South Asia's annual monsoon winds, which deliver summer rains from eastern Pakistan to Central China. The Plateau also derives the seasonal latitudinal position, duration, and intensity of jet stream, which in turn drive so-called regional climate "teleconnections" that influence seasonal weather trends and extreme events.[12]

The fresh water resources in Tibet constitute some 104,500 cubic meters per person, ranking the region fourth in the world after Iceland, New Zealand and Canada. An important hydrological attribute of Tibet's snowmelt water's is that they provide perennial base flow to many of Asia's major Trans boundary international rivers, the water sheds of which are the home of more than one quarter of the human population . Apart from the perennial base flow, Tibet's rivers and basins support a variety of unique flora(25 percent of which is endemic to Tibet) and fauna, much

---

11 Vasudeva, P.K, Chinse Dam in Tibet and Diversion of Brahamputa; Implications for India , *Journal of United Service Institution of India*, Vol.CXLI, No-588, April-June 2012, P-274.

12 Tsering, Tashi, Policy Implications of current dam projects on Drichu—the upper Yangtze river, *Tibetan Bulletin*, Vol-9, Issue-1, January-February 2005,P-17-18.

of which exists nowhere else in the world or is limited to the Himalayan region, which provide the matter and nutrient energy base for terrestrial and aquatic downstream ecosystems.

Here it is pertinent to mention that according to the United Nations 2006 report Asia has the minimum water after Antarctica. However, we know that two third of the world is water but at the same time we know it that much of this water is of no use. The entire water's only 2.5 % is for the drinking purposes but significantly its two third share lies in glaciers. The ongoing ecological disaster in the name of sustainable development in Tibet has posed a severe threat to the longevity of these glaciers therefore is a severe threat of the availability of drinking water for the mushrooming humanity. It is impending threat to Asia in particular and rest part of the globe in general.[13] India is an agriculture based economy despite the fact that service and technology sector is growing rapidly. Any diversion of the river's which enters Nepal from Tibet could be detrimental for India. It will directly affect the flow of water in the Ganges, the soul of the people living in the Indian sub-continent including in Nepal. The legendary river Ganga desperately needs fresh water from its tributaries. Nepal alone accounts for 46 % of the flow of the Ganga and its contribution grows to 71 % during the lean period.[14]

In Pakistan and Bangladesh too, scarcity of water has started triggering local level conflicts and slated to expand due to inherent fact that flow of water from upstream is declining. In rest part of Asia due to variety of negligence, the people are eliminating the minimum requirements for the sustainable environment and this has been emerged as the push factor for the growing tentacles of the global warming. The ongoing crises of water are going to boo merged in foreseeable future and this will pose a threat of conflict within Asia.

Tibet - Apple of discord for Sino-Indian conflict

Tibet is one of the important reasons where such kind of conflict could trigger if China will continuously pursue its policy of exploitation of Tibetan ecology for the sustainable development of mainland China. Chinese

13 Challni, Brahma, We have to escape from Asian Water War, *Japan Times*, Tokoyo, 2 October, 2008.

14 Dwarika N. Dhungel and Santa B Pun, Eds " *The Nepal –India Water Resources Relationships ; Challenges*" [Springer, 2009] , P-1.

and Indian economies are agro based economies and the future of these economies are based on nice monsoon, which has remained uncertain to predict. Both economies are growing very rapid ally and even in this era of global recession when almost all established economies are unable to sustain their pace. The growing economy of China and India requires more and more water and this demand is going to increase in geometrical way in foreseeable future. If water crisis erupts then China and India will become food importing countries instead of food exporting countries despite feeding their monstrously huge population. Despite all round of development China and India both remains agro dominant economies.

For South Asia, agriculture still remains the only way to earn bread particularly for the rural poorest of the poor. Agriculture roughly contributes to one- forth of the total gross product of South Asia. According to an estimate over 50 % of the total water of the region is consumed in agriculture. Quite naturally, with the rapid increase in population the use of water is also on rise whereas its resources are becoming scarce. This fact gives Malthusian supporters a chance to vindicate his views.[15] Thus the availability of water for irrigation has been reduced sharply in South Asia. This may adversely affect food production in the regional countries. In this situation the prices of food production are likely to rise. According to a latest research conducted by the World Bank, the prices of the food commodities overall have risen 83% whereas the prices of wheat have risen 120 % in 2007.[16] The worst sufferer will be the hapless masses of South Asia in general and India in particular. Of course, India has done excellently well in past couple of decades but still today around one third Indian masses are living under poverty line. It means that they are unable to fulfill their genuine requirements. Growing industrialisation and urbanisation in India has also consuming more water and slated to increase in future. Already many Indian states are contesting a pig war for major share of water.

Successive governments have taken certain majors to correct the situation but it could not create adequate results. The best example of this thesis is that during 1971 general election, Indira Gandhi gave the slogan of

---

15 Mastoor , Maryam, Environmental Degradation ;Focus on Water Scarcity in South Asia, *Regional Studies*, Vol- XXVII, No-1, Winter, 2008-09,P-100.

16 Iqbal, Anwar, " Food Crisis may lead to wars, riots; experts' *Dawn*, Islamabad, 14 April 2008.

Garibi Hatao [Elimination of poverty] but even at the outset of 21st century the same Congress party government has insisted that proper attention must be given towards common people [aam adami].[I and II Manmohan Singh Government 2004-2014] This fact itself vindicate that poor people are still suffering despite all efforts done by government machinery since last six decades. It is significant to mention here that majority of common people still live in villages and Indian Budget 2012 says that only 29 % people live in urban areas. This data vindicates the fact that agro sector has been extremely important for Indian economy and if India aspires to be a global power in the foreseeable future then it needs to provide basic amenities to all its poor people who still languish under the cruel wheel of acute poverty.

So, or some cases more acute, is the situation of Pakistan, Bangladesh and Nepal. Without upgrading agricultural sector these important countries of South Asia could not even dream to strengthen their nation building process. In 1985, South Asian Association of Regional Cooperation [SAARC] came into being for accelerating the pace of regional cooperation among South Asian countries. One of the most important agenda of the SAARC has been elimination of poverty and all kinds of misery of South Asian people. Despite several summits SAARC as a regional organisation has not been successful to yield adequate results due to gamut of factors. Poverty still remains an issue to be reckoned with in the South Asian context.

But the case of Pakistan, Bangladesh and Nepal, where poverty is so rampant that it has threatened the survival of democracy in these countries is also acute. Without upgrading agricultural sector these important countries of South Asia could not even dream to strengthen their nation building process. In 1985, South Asian Association of Regional Cooperation [SAARC] came into being for accelerating the pace of regional cooperation among South Asian countries. One of the most important agenda of the SAARC has been elimination of poverty and all kinds of misery of South Asian people. Despite 17th Summit [2011, Male Summit] SAARC as a regional organisation has not been successful to yield adequate results due to gamut of factors. Poverty still remains an issue to be reckoned with in the South Asian context. It has been established long back by all international agencies that water and poverty is inter related. Less availability of water is creating more poverty and due to ongoing development of mainland of

China and diversion of South Asian bound river's towards the mainland China will increase further poverty and lawlessness in South Asia and devastate the ecology of Tibet in general and accelerate the consequences of climate change at the global level.

The Tibetan plateau has been one of the most important source of fresh water for the countries of South Asia as well rest part of adjoining Asia too. Due to its appetite for more development China needs to provide more water towards their mainland and this they can do only while tempering the Tibetan ecology. Tibetan people have been natural guardian of Tibetan ecology since centuries but since Chinese illegal occupation in 1950,s they are struggling for their own existence therefore one should not hope from them to protect the Tibetan ecology. China is misusing the water resources of Tibet for the generation of hydro power and diversion towards mainland China and needless to say that it has devastated the ecology of Tibet in a massive way. There is ample proof which vindicates that China is making a big dam on Brahamputra. The flow of water to riparian Indian state of Assam and Arunachal is getting worse affected with this construction. One dam of such kind was demolished due to unknown reason in Tibet resulted into the flash flood killing 7 people in Pasighat, Arunachal Pradesh in June 2009. in following years the river Brahamputra which is several KM wide near Pasighat narrowed down in narrow channels.[17]

How it could be saved, is a big question and I think it is very tough to respond however in the concluding part of this debate I will try my level best to respond this significant question.

It is significant to mention here that India have more agricultural lands than China. India has 16-5 crore Hactare land in comparison with the Chinese 13.71 Crore Hactare.[18]

Both Chinese and Indian economies are water based economies. Maximisation of the utilisation of water resources could push both countries towards confrontation. Both countries have rated by gamut of estimates as the emerging super powers of 21st century. Their expanding economies need more water for all purposes of development and put them in a situation as the Middle East countries are confronting today.

17 River flowing from China dries up in India , Lawmaker, *Economic Times*, New Delhi, 1 March 2012.

18 Op. Cit, No-6, P-67.

Here lies the seed of the conflict. The year 2012 is the 50th anniversary of 1962 Sino-Indian war. Many secret Chinese documents are classified and it revels that water resources was one of the prominent factor of Chinese intrusion of Tibet in 1950,s and 1962 Sino-Indian war and must remain the major preventive factor for resolving 4000 KM thorny boundary disputes between India and China. China is contesting the legality of Mac Mohan line with India but has settled border disputes with Burma on the basis of Mac Mohan line. It revels that Chinese are hell bent that it will not allow India to keep its influence in Tibet at any cost and it is due to the fact that Tibet is the hub of natural resources particular fresh water and many pundits of the international system has already predicted that water could trigger third world war.

Minus the Ganges all important rivers which flown through India and Pakistan, Bangladesh and Nepal originates from the mountains of Tibet. Not only that due to it's geo-strategically location Tibet is important of course but it is equally important because of the fact that all important rivers of Asia originate from Tibet. By illegally occupying Tibet, China has captured this huge hub of water resources. Right now, China has continued with its south north water transfer plan. Through this plan, China is willing to bring water into its semi-arid northern areas. In the third phase of this plan, Tibetan plateau's water will be diverted towards that direction in a massive way. Former President of China, Hu Zintao [2002-2012] had been the administrator of Tibet and has been one of the core harbingers of this plan. During his regime in Tibet, oppression became part and parcel in Tibet with its ugliest way. His elevation as the President of China had been embedded with his brutal oppression of Tibetan movement. Being a water scientist he spent several years in Tibet and is well versed with the potential of Tibetan ecology. With his this practical experience of Tibet, he was hell bent to exploit Tibetan ecology for the larger development of mainland China. Being the President of China for ten years he had clear direction to implement his minds.

The natural status of Tibet has been granted by nature and China with these efforts, is trying to temper with this pristine Tibetan situation. This effort of China will devastate the ecology of Tibet and its consequences will be on large South Asian countries and elsewhere too. For example, the Brahmaputra River originates from Tibet and China aims to divert it towards north and thus weaken the flow of water towards India and

Bangladesh. India has protested this move but in the meanwhile the Chinese have identified a place from where Brahmaputra enters into India. The place is naturally unique with the fact that here lies the largest reservoir of water. In this place the Brahmaputra makes one of the largest water reservoirs on the planet and this has become a Chinese obsession. China plans to establish a hydro power electric plant at that point. If established the entire flow of water towards India and Bangladesh through Brahmaputra will be sizably reduced. Needless to say that if China will go ahead with this plan, the conflict between China and India is imminent. China has consolidated its position in Tibet due to variety of factors and one of the important among them has been Indian weakness to assert on Tibetan front as the bargaining chip against China.

The best example of this argument is Chinese Ambassador to India dared to question the visit of Indian Prime Minster into Arunachal Pradesh but government of India could not reply it properly. If China could claim on Arunachal then India must say that Chinese occupation on Tibet is illegal and if China will not provide adequate autonomy and restore proper respect for the Tibetan people then India could consider recognizing Tibet as an independent country under the rules of the international law. Like the US India could not appoint Tibetan coordinator within its foreign ministry. This weakness in Indian policy towards Tibet has been witnessed since the inception of India till date. This lukewarm Indian policy for Tibet has encouraged China to consolidate its holds over Tibet. China has dared to do so despite the fact that human right has become the focal attention of the international politics since the end of cold war. The US policy of China has been guided after the end of the cold war by three cardinal policies and human rights remains one of the cores among these three. The western world has been raising the destruction of ecology in Tibet since several years and they have created an understanding among all stake holders of the international system that China has violated the pristine beauty of the Tibetan plateau.

Recently China has constructed a railway link between Beijing and Lhasa and through this process devastated several aspects of ecology. This kind of construction is going on within Tibet but a new turn has come in Chinese, which has the potential to trigger fresh conflicts within Asia particularly between India and China. China has decided that they will exploit the natural resources of Tibet to ensure sustainable development of mainland China. Dilution of water resources is one of the most ambitious agenda of the Chinese plans in this direction. China has already started working on this dream plan and after conclusion this will devastate the trans–national rivers of South Asia.

Needless to say that South Asia still constitutes almost 40% of the global poor and represents around 22% of the global population. The majority of South Asian population earns their bread through agricultural products. The ongoing wave of globalisation even has not been able to change their traditional way of living. If China will divert all water resources towards mainland than the countries of South Asia will be under severe crisis and they have to defend their water resources. India constitutes 2/3 of South Asia therefore will be severely effected and this unrest could be converted into war also.

Impact on South Asian Environmental Security

The ongoing Chinese plan has posed a severe threat on Tibetan ecology, which has been the bedrock of South Asian ecology since millennia. The contemporary international situation has provided a new lease of life to the Chinese who plan to dominate Asia and become one of the important pillars in the chess board of the international politics too. In the prevailing situation, the Tibetan people with positive support of international civil-society are sustaining their struggle for self-determination. But given the grassroots' reality, it seems to be very tough that in the foreseeable future China would ease any control or provide even an iota of autonomy for the Tibetan people. In this situation it is almost certain that the Chinese are going to destabilise the ecology of Tibet and needless to say that its impact would be devastating for South Asia. It has already been stated that the entire river basins of South Asia originate from the Tibetan mountains. In this section it is argued that the extent to which the Chinese plan to exploit Tibetan ecology for the development of mainland China succeeds would impact on South Asia's environmental security. Before insisting on this point it would be proper to emphasise the concept of environmental security.

After the end of the cold war there has been an urge to redefine the national security and build up a comprehensive view of it.[19] The thrust of

---

19 Barry, Buzan, "*Rethinking Security after the Cold War*, Nordic Journal of International Studies , Vol-32,No-1, March 1997.

the comprehensive view of security has been to secure social, economic and environmental dimensions along with securing the boundaries of the state.[20] The traditional concept of security surrounded along defending territory and political integrity of a country.[21] The state was responsible for the securing its sovereignty and integrity and the armed forces were assigned this duty. The state alone had to perform this responsibility as there were no such other institutions which could share it.[22] With the end of the cold war and decreasing of geo-strategic considerations, the national security is being viewed in a comprehensive perspective. The comprehensive view of national security is based on the notion that it is not only the state alone which needs security but the people, the resources and socio- economic structures within the state also need to be secured. In fact, now it is strongly believed that the security of the state is meaningless unless the people are secure. Therefore, some scholars have tried to define national security in terms of human security. The concept of human security gives the impression that securing the human beings should not remain confines into boundaries of the state. The comprehensive view of national security obviously includes social, economic, environmental security along with the security of the state. Thus both the military and non-military dimensions are important in the changed framework of national security.

The environmental security has become an important dimension of the comprehensive national security. The environmental security as a concept was officially mentioned for the first time, in the General Assembly of the UN in 1987. [23] Since then, it has become an important aspect of security studies both in the theoretical and empirical contexts. It has been widely accepted that the indiscriminate attitude of the people and government towards the environment , the self interest , over the exploitation of the resources, etc, have ensured scarcity of resources and their fast depletion as well as degradation of the environment. This has caused conflict and violence among and between the states.[24] The scarcity

20 Barry, Buzan, "*The Logic of Anarchy,* Columbia University Press, New York, 1992, P-34.

21 Narottam Gann, " Environmental Security ; An Appendage to Geo-Political World Order of the United States , *BIIS Journal,* Vol-24,No-3, July 2003,P-428.

22 M.P Leffer, " The American conception of National Security and the Beginning of the Cold War, 1934-48, *American Historical Review* , Vol-89, 1984, P-247.

23 Our Common Future, *OUSD,* Oxford University Press, Oxford, 1987.

24 F. Thomas and Homer Dixon, *Environment, Security and Violence,* Princeton, NJ, 1999,P-48.

of resources may give rise to conflict for remaining resources. Therefore, there is a need to secure the environment. The security of environment needs a positive attitude towards it. Thus, environmental security may be defined as avoidance of negative linkages between human activities and the environment.

The notion of environmental security underlines the need to explore and propagate inter-linkage between resource use and environmental degradation. The environment can be properly protected and managed only when we understand urgency behind it. In this context environmental security can be viewed as an effective measure towards sustainable development.[25] Since environment can be a cause of conflict, violence and a threat to peace and security, securing the environment would mean, in a broader perspective, removing the causes of environmental conflicts, as well as , the causes of environmental scarcity.[26] This would require sustainability of the biotic resources of the world and it is possible through environmental security.[27] Thus, environmental security means ordering and managing the resources and biosphere activities. It is related to the establishment of a proper human -nature relationship.

After the end of the cold war there has been much debate on the comprehensive approach to national security. It is widely accepted that the national security has to be viewed in a wider perspective. The environmental security constitutes a significant dimension of the comprehensive national security. The environment has to be viewed in a wider perspective where human and non-human beings are also important along with the nature. The environment and the living beings are closely inter-related. Hence, environmental security must take into consideration a balanced and sustained inter-relationship between the two. In South Asia the environmental issues have become important in the overall framework of security due to high population growth, prominence of agriculture sector even in 21st century, excessive dependence on nature, uneven infra-structural development, poverty, underdevelopment and fragile ecology.

---

25 Homer, Dixon, Environmental Changes as the causes of acute conflict in Richard K Belts [ed] *Conflict After the Cold War; Agreements on the Causes of Conflict and Peace,* Macmillan, New York, 1994,p426.

26 Michael , Rinner , *National Security ; The Economic and Environmental Dimensions,* Washington, 1989.

27 B.C. Upreti, *Contemporary South Asia,* Kalinga Publications, New Delhi, 2004,p5.

In 2009 the Monsoon has not yielded adequate rain in India and elsewhere within South Asia, although the Monsoon has been extraordinarily good over the past several years. But if the Monsoon is bad for at least two consecutive years then its consequences will be devastating for the economies of South Asia. We are aware about the candid fact that out of every five citizen of the planet earth, one live in South Asia and their livelihood depends on agriculture, which interestingly depends on Monsoon. The agriculture sector is not only provides food materials for the huge population of South Asia but additionally it also provides income for the poorest of the poor in vastly stretched rural South Asia. Pakistan faced the consequences of unprecedented flood in 2010 and 2011 resulted into the deaths of around 2000 people and devastation of agriculture sector and infrastructure. Water scarcity is one of the most important burning problems of Pakistan. Unlike India, all four provinces in Pakistan have been fighting against each other for larger share of water. The decade old controversy over the construction of Kalabagh dam and its opposition by Sindh, Kyber Pakhtunwah and Baluchistan could be seen in this context. Pakistan is also an agriculture based economy and water is extremely important for the sustainable growth of Pakistan. All important rivers of Pakistan originate from Tibet and Chinese growing domination over water resources of Tibet will not only reduce the flow of water in Pakistan but may bring 2010-2011 like devastating floods frequently. Bangladesh is another extremely vulnerable country within South Asia for climate change. Its entire economy depends on Tibet Origin Rivers. By 2020 with the sea rise, there is a strong possibility of the submerging of low lands of Bangladesh. It will push the illegal migration towards India, which is active slowly till date. In lean period, Bangladesh is confronting with the paucity of water and share of river water with India remained major bone of contention between India and Bangladesh. The 1996 treaty has solved the sharing of Ganga water but Teesta water sharing remains a thorny issue between both countries till date. Prime Minister, Manmohan Singh September 2011, Dhaka visits even could not resolve the matter due to strong dissent by west Bengal government.

We have seen within this debate the relevance of the Tibetan ecology has been tremendous for a sustainable ideal ecology within South Asia. It is also candidly clear that the indigenous Tibetan people who worship nature as the direct god and has not been happy with the present status within Tibet but unable to do anything concrete for the protection of Tibetan ecology. The international civil-society has been raising the issue time and again but its level of protest has been modest. Given the entire framework in an empirical way it is absolutely clear that China is going to sustain its agenda of exploitation of Tibetan ecology for the larger benefit of the its mainland in foreseeable future also. In this situation what could be required from the South Asian fraternity for the prevention of the erosion of the Tibetan ecology.

Concluding Remarks

These are extremely serious issues and very tough to respond in an articulate manner. If South Asian region has to protect the ecology and sustain the welfare measures for their poorest of the poor then they have to do something concrete for the correction of the situation. As the first step, SAARC could appeal China in a boldest way that it should refrain exploiting Tibetan ecology because it is not their internal matter and has the potential to sabotage the economies of South Asian region therefore China should take any action in this regard after due consultation with the SAARC countries. We are at the same time aware about the fact that since last several decades, China has used Pakistan as a stooge within South Asia for the pursuance of their "Encircling India" policy within South Asia. Pakistan –China relationship has been termed as 'all weather friendship'. After the elimination of Osama Bin Laden from Abbotabad, Pakistan in May 2011, China-Pak relationship has been further strengthened. Pakistan has ceded an important part of its occupied lands in Jammu and Kashmir to China. Pakistan is also an important member of SAARC and probably will not allow this resolution to be passed in forthcoming SAARC summits. If it happens then India could take the lead and must issue an appeal to China of the same nature. Of course, China will not provide much heed on that Indian advice but in this situation India could take the help of the international community. In this direction as the next step, India must forge a consensus of like minded countries within South Asia and appeal to China and if again unheeded must approach international organisations. India must also convince Pakistan that declining ecological health of Tibet will be detrimental for the sustainable growth of Pakistan therefore it must support a consensus resolution of SAARC appealing China to stop unilateral use of water resources of Tibet and must keep SAARC countries particularly India and Pakistan also in loop.

These approaches seem to be funny at this juncture but given the enormity of the problem, it is required and changing contours of international politics would be push factor to create concrete pressure on China. The well being of the Tibetan ecology is not only required for the betterment of the countries of South Asia and within Tibet but it is equally required for a developed China and for many other countries of Asia . It is vindicated with the following statement of Chinese Prime Minister, Wen Jiabao, "Country's next five year economic plan would focus on "clean energy," writing that "[w]e can no longer sacrifice the environment for the sake of rapid development and reckless construction."[28]

If one could examine the number of natural calamities within last one decade in China, things could be vindicated. China has created many dams in recent past and planned to do so at large scale in near future Major Dam projects have other, less predictable consequences. With a reduced amount of sediment in downstream river flows, the river moves more rapidly below the dam. (The opposite is the case above the dam.) This can increase riverbank erosion and lead to devastating landslides. Because artificial reservoirs place new stresses on the shoreline's geology, landslides are also common around large dam reservoirs. Between 2004 and 2007, more than 13,000 people in Fengjie County alone were forced to relocate because of concerns about landslides caused by the Three Gorges Dam reservoir.[29]

Earthquakes may be another consequence of mega dam projects. The concentrated pressure of hundreds of millions of tons of water and the seeping of water into cracks in the earth's crust can weaken fault lines and make seismic activity more likely. Some scientists believe that the pressure of Zipingpu Dam's reservoir in central China may have contributed to the 7.9-magnitude earthquake in Sichuan that killed 80,000 people in 2008.[30]

This finding could exacerbate hostility between local residents and the central Chinese government. Tension was already high after grief-stricken parents accused officials of corruption and incompetence, leading to shoddy school construction. (Approximately 10,000 school children were killed in the Sichuan earthquake, most of them in schools that, citizens

---

28 Quoted in Peter Bosshard, "Dam Nation," *Foreign Policy* (8 Mar. 2011)

29 Jim Yardley, "Chinese Dam Projects Criticized for Their Human Costs," *New York Times* (19 Nov. 2007).

30 Richard A. Kerr and Richard Stone, "A Human Trigger for the Great Quake of Sichuan?" *Science*, vol. 323 (16 Jan. 2009): p. 322.

allege, did not meet building standards.)[31]

As the risks dams pose become better known, backlash against major hydro-projects by those who bear these risks looks to increase in the future. International water resource sharing is a difficult process anywhere. In Asia, one of the least-integrated regions in the world, this difficulty is compounded by increasing water stress, a history of distrust and conflict, and extreme power imbalances. China, which controls the territorial headwaters of most of the Himalayan Rivers, is not party to any bilateral or multilateral agreements regarding water resources. This may explain why more than half of the world's 45,000 dams are now located in Asia, and nearly all of them were built in the last 60 years.[32]

China considers hydroelectric power to be a key element of sustainable development, as do other countries in Asia. Combined with nuclear and other clean power sources, Beijing hopes to increase the portion of renewable power in its energy portfolio from the current 9.5 percent to 15 percent by 2020.[33]

India officially protested about the diversion of Brahamputra in November 2006 when Chinese President Hu Jintao visited India. China had decided to appease the legitimate Indian grievances. At that time, Chinese Foreign Ministry spokesman Liu Jianchao also confirmed " The Chinese government has no plans to build a dam on the Yarlung Tsangpo River [Brahamputra] to divert water to the Yellow river. Though , the Indian NRSA confirmed that construction was on at the Zangmu site on the Chinese side of the Brahamputra river , prompting the government of India to take up the matter with China at a political level.[34] It is also believed that the diverted waters from the river would irrigate the northwestern part of China,s Gobi desert in Xinjinag and Gansu, up to 650 KM,s away, and recharge the dying Yellow river , which now runs for much of the year. Prime Minister, Manmohan Singh raised the Indian concerns about the diversion of Bramputra and other rivers when he met Chinese President,

31 Edward Wong, "Chinese Stifle Grieving Parents' Protest of Shoddy School Construction," *New York Times* (4 June 2008).

32 World Commission on Dams, *Dams and Development: A New Framework for Decision-Making*, Earthscan Publications Ltd. (Nov. 2000): p. 9

33 Peter Fairley, "China Doubles Down," *IEEE Spectrum* (11. Nov. 2011): p. 46

34 http;//zeenews.india.com/news/nation/re-agency-spots-china-s-dam-on-brahmputra, 575946.html

Hu Jintao in 2011. He has also raised this issue with his latest meetings with the Chinese Prime Minister, Wen Jiabao. But the Chinese have kept their traditional appeasement policy to assure India that it is not diverting the rivers.

The ongoing Chinese tampering with the Tibetan ecology is not only disastrous for Tibet but it is more devastating for South Asia , South East Asia and China as well. It is high time to realise this impending danger, other wise severe conflicts could occur exclusively for this reason therefore all concerned parties needs to take it as a serious threat to their ecology as well as national security and needles to say that onus of this effort lies on Indian shoulder. In July 2009 G-8 conference held in Italy, both China and India has resolved that they are united to counter the challenges of global warming. The start of this endeavour must be from the preservation of Tibetan ecology if both countries are really serious about their pledge about containing global warming. India need to take lead from South Asian fraternity and convince China that its unilateral misuse of Tibetan ecology will put South Asia, South East Asia and China itself in serious trouble and climate change consequences could not be prevented at least in Asia. Protection and promotion of Tibetan ecology is in the larger interests of every concerned countries of Asia. The contemporary world politics in general and Asian politics in particular will be a push factor in this regard. Being an important nation of Asia and one of the most dependent countries on Tibetan ecology India must ensure the safety of Tibetan ecology with all possible measures.

XI

India's Marine Pollution As A Growing Environmental Threat

S.Utham Kumar Jamadhagni and C.S.Anuradha

Human existence has been afforded comfort through the major inventions and discoveries of the industrial and technological ages. However the age now is not just the information age but that of the environment as well. This is because of the realisation that preservation and extension of human survival rests on the bulwark of environment. Awareness of problems to the environment and need to seek possible solutions is increasing. Among the worst challenges to the environment is man-made pollution. It is posing a grave challenge in that it is affecting all spheres of economic and social activity of ocean-dependent countries like India. The issue is more complicated when the surrounding is the oceans we are looking at. In the first instance, population pressures are increasing on the coasts. Coastal mega cities and economic capitals have become migration hubs. Civic amenities and waste management practices are unable to keep pace with this expansion causing serious environmental and health problems. Another problem peculiar to the ocean is that the effect of external impacts like pollution is not immediately obvious. By sheer volume, oceans can take in much larger amounts of waste and other matter as compared to land and air. The issue here is that precisely this ability of the oceans could mean that manifestation of effects of pollution could occur at a late stage that could be too late for action. Hence the imperative is to focus greatly on marine pollution.

World has literally and figuratively moved around the oceans. Civilisational contact extended to far flung areas through the sea as it sustained trade and in due course, cultural contact since ancient times. Origins of a thriving maritime trade can be traced to as far back as the Bronze Age, some 5,000 years ago through archaeological evidence. Arabs and the ancient Indians too established long-lasting trade routes around Alexander's time (600 B.C.)[1]. Underwater resources like fish and treasures from the depths of the oceans like pearls, corals and minerals developed the aesthetic and economic life of mankind. We also use the oceans for our nourishment. People on an average obtain 16 percent of their animal protein from fish. As land-based food supplies reach their limits, fisheries will become even more vital to food supplies. Ocean floor deposits are the source of one fourth of the world's annual oil and gas production[2]. Direct proportion of increase in human population to that of the food from the oceans, energy and other resources is the basic issue. Not only is the rise in demand for additional resources but the greed to get the maximum benefit in a short span of time that has reached the brink of sustenance of the very source of unending provision of necessary products and services.

Throughout history, the oceans have been treated as inexhaustible both as source and destination. It was assumed that the tides that seemed to wash nearly everything away meant that human race could do anything that would only temporarily alter the coastal waters and not worry about the consequences. Hence there was room for the possibility of oceans being unable to bear the effect of human activities.

Since nearly half the world's population live within 200 km of the coast, the enormous demographic pressure has increased around the coasts though they are only a tenth of the total land available on earth. From 3 billion in 2003 (48 per cent of the total population) to 5 billion in 2030 – about 60 per cent of world population – would reside in cities around the coasts[3]. The projection is that all urban agglomerations that abound the coasts and the number of urban dwellers is bound to increase manifold. According to UN estimates, the worrying trend for India is that Mumbai, a coastal city, would become the fourth largest mega-city by 2025

---

1 Manoj Gupta, *Maritime Affairs – Integrated Management for India*, Manas Publications, New Delhi, 2005, p. 67

2 Anne Platt McGinn, Safeguarding the Health of the Oceans, Worldwatch paper 145, March 1999 p.20 http://worldwatch.org/worldwatchppr145Ocean health.pdf accessed July 18, 2005

3 UNFPA State of the World population 2004: Migration and Urbanization (Source: http://www.unfpa.org/swp/2004/english/ch4/index.htm)

with nearly 26 million inhabitants while Delhi and Calcutta would be 2nd and 12th respectively[4]. This mass of humanity on the coastlines naturally would augment the vast damage that pollution would wreak on the oceans. The most worrying factor is that degradation of the marine environment due to pollution is still to be totally realised.

Pollution effect

Oceans - the lifelines of earth have been severely affected by the dumping of materials especially in the form of man-made chemicals and their residues. The toxic chemicals mixing with ocean waters have resulted in the complete destruction and in some cases extinction of precious marine species of fish, sea weeds etc. Other Marine animals that have survived have been made inedible as they are afflicted by lesions and ulcers. Production processes like power generation give out a lot of heat which also reach the oceans. The thermal pollution results in increase in water temperature hampering reproduction and the very survival of marine life. Apart from this, the introduction of exotic species mussels, fish and other marine creatures by human activity like shipping destroys native species. Fishing industry in that area is affected severely. Sewage contains organic waste that produces algae and other micro organisms that multiply and take up all available oxygen starving the rest of the marine life in the region. When they sink to the ocean after attaining vast volumes the decaying process begins and takes the left over oxygen. This depletion of oxygen or 'hypoxia' renders entire stretches of coastlines "dead". No marine life can survive in this area. Marine ecosystems – unique environmental treasures – like the coral reefs are dying due to this ceaseless assault on the oceans. In short, the oceans are deeply affected by chemical pollution, algal blooms, thermal pollution, ballast water pollution and more frequently sewage pollution. These have been dealt in detail below.

A. Chemical chaos

The rapid industrialisation and mass production of a number of products like textiles, leather, chemicals and fertilisers and their associated processes of bleaching, dyeing, washing, cleaning and treating need water. The waste water or water that has been used and left over from these processes (termed effluent) contains colouring agents, acids, alkalis and other solid

---

4 http://www.geohive.com/earth/cy_agg2025.aspx based on World Urbanisation Prospects
 : the 2011 revision UN, Dept of Economic and Social Affairs, Population Division Report

materials and let into waterways and in many cases the ocean mostly untreated. Basic properties of water namely opacity, salinity and nutrient quality are drastically changed due to the presence of detergents, alkalis and other chemicals in these effluents and also making water toxic. The marine life experiences discolouration, poisoning or asphyxiation due to this depletion in the water quality.

The health of the marine environment is deeply impacted by the physical, chemical and biological changes in the water. For example, Lead and cadmium are found in high concentrations in the Thane creeks on the Bombay coast and these toxic substances are getting into the food chain. The indiscriminate use of fertilisers and pesticides for crop cultivation in India affects its marine environment through run off. Annually, at least one fourth of 55,000 metric tonnes of these chemicals end up in sea[5]. This pollution leads to the contamination of shell fish and finfish making them inedible to the local populace and could even prove fatal if consumed.

A.1 Rain forests of the sea

Coral reefs are vital to marine health as they contribute significantly to fishery production, medicine, and tourism. Coral reefs, arguably the richest of all the ecosystems in the sea, have been threatened by as much as 75% from local activities and thermal stress[6]. India is ranked 8th among countries with lowest adaptive capacity in the face of threats to the reefs. Some 27 per cent of the world's reefs are at high risk of degradation: this figure rises to 80 per cent in populous areas. There has been rampant destruction in the South East Asian, the Indian Ocean and to a lesser extent the Pacific oceans.

There are a variety of reasons for damage to coral reefs across different regions of the world's oceans be it the Caribbean or the Indian Ocean. These include sedimentation, eutrophication, ships' anchors and even trampling of marine resources by tourists. Coral reefs are blasted to make way for ports or navigation, and mined for building materials and lime. Overfishing reefs can profoundly disrupt their ecosystems, while fishing with dynamite and poisons does further damage. Collecting coral for the

---

5   UNEP Global State of the Environment Report 1997 Chapter 3- Policy Responses and Directions : Asia and the Pacific Regional Initiatives, www.unep.org/geo/geo1/ch/ch3_14.htm accessed July 29, 2005

6   http://pdf.wri.org/reefs_at_risk_revisited.pdf accessed September 8, 2012

curio trade has done great harm in some places, especially around the South Indian coast but is now increasingly being managed as a sustainable activity.

Some of the most dreadful instances of the enduring polluting effects of chemicals in marine environment have been the methyl mercury poisoning at the Minamata Bay, Japan in the late 1950s and again in the 80s. This incident led to a growing consciousness about the environment and the ill-effects of man's interference with it[7]. The fish-eating Japanese consumed contaminated fish to suffer from a peculiar disease with symptoms like severe convulsions, intermittent loss of consciousness, repeated lapses into crazed mental states, and then finally permanent coma. Then, after the onset of a very high fever, it would result in death.

A.2 Bad bloom

The exploding population growth of microscopic plankton is called Red Tide. The over growth of algae is due to the excessive enrichment of water by nutrients like nitrogen and phosphates. Nutrient enrichment may be in the form of pollution from sewage, fertiliser, car emissions and industrial waste. The microscopic plankton has severe affects on marine life and humans as these release toxins. These toxins are 'environmental chemicals' that can interfere with metabolism, nerve conduction, and the central nervous system. The blooms mainly take place in coastal, warm waters. As the plankton multiply and grow, they become dense and hence cause a discolouration in the water near the shoreline. Often it turns a reddish-brown colour, hence the name "red tide". There have been occurrences where the water has turned a yellow, brown, or even a purple shade[8] due to algal blooms.

The increased use of pesticides in some areas like the Bay of Bengal has resulted in contamination of shell-and finfish. An estimated 1,800 tons of pesticides are supposed to enter these waters every year. In September of 1998, a red algal bloom outbreak in Kerala, India, forced authorities

---

7 For a detailed study of this and other chemical pollution incidents see Jun Ui, ed., Industrial pollution in Japan, United Nations University Press, Tokyo 1992 (http://www.unu.edu/unupress/unupbooks/uu35ie/uu35ie02.htm#i.%20environmental%20pollution:%20basic%20precepts) access date Jul 24 2005

8 Red Tide Phenomenon http://jrscience.wcp.muohio.edu/fieldcourses05/Papers Marine EcologyArticles/RedTidePhenomenon.html

to shut down shellfish beds and ban sales, leaving nearly 1,000 families without work[9]. This is because the blooms result in PSP or Paralytic shellfish poisoning – a high health risk to people consuming them. Eighty algal blooms were recorded during the period 1998–2010 in the Indian Exclusive Economic Zone (EEZ).[10]

Many harmful algal blooms are linked to increasing quantities of nitrogen and phosphorus in coastal areas, largely from nutrient-rich wastewater and agricultural runoff. These two nutrients are necessary for life, and in proper quantities they help plants grow faster. But in areas with limited water flows, the waters can suffer from over enrichment (**Eutrophication**), which triggers the oxygen depletion that leads to algal blooms. This over enrichment is not only harmful for other creatures but man too. From nutrient-rich sediments, fertilisers, and human waste to toxic heavy metals and synthetic chemicals, the outfall from human society ends up circulating in oceans, often for over long periods of time. Once contaminants collect in zooplankton, larvae, and small fish (often by direct consumption), they work their way up the food chain and cause problems in the fish, marine mammals, and people who eat them. The amounts of such material increasing in concentration as we move up the food chain is called bio-magnification and since human beings are at the higher end of the food chain, they would be the worst affected due to this phenomena. Among the most visible signs of marine pollution are out-of-control blooms of algae that blanket coastal areas.

The incidence of paralytic shellfish poisoning doubled worldwide in the two decades between 1970 and 1990 due to the spread of the toxin carrying plankton from the northern to the southern hemisphere. Although they are a naturally occurring phenomenon, the frequency and severity of harmful algal blooms (HABs) has increased in the past three decades, as has the appearance of novel toxic species. More than 60 harmful algal toxins are known today, compared with just 22 in 1984.

The large biomass of some algae alone makes them harmful. Algal blooms covering broad areas of surface water at times, growing to nearly

9   Red tide bloom foxes scientists, *The Hindu*, Oct 7, 2004 (http://www.thehindu.com/2004/10/07/stories/2004100707480300.htm) accessed July 29, 2005

10 K.B.Padmakumar, N.R.Menon, V.N.Sanjeevan, Is Occurrence of Harmful Algal Blooms in the Exclusive Economic Zone of India on the Rise?, *International Journal of Oceanography*, Vol 2012, http://www.hindawi.com/journals/ijog/2012/263946/

a million cells per milliliter of seawater, can block sunlight and air from reaching the life in the waters below. The dying algae complicate the problem as the dead algae sink to the ocean bottom, where bacteria digest them, consuming more oxygen in the process. Eventually, the bacteria-laden waters become so depleted of oxygen (a condition known as hypoxia) that they suffocate marine animals, which either flee or die. So, floating dead fish over vast areas of the ocean are signs of the effects of dead algae blooms.

B. Choking waste

As mentioned earlier, urban agglomerations in most developing countries are situated along the coasts and most of these processes produce waste that is let into the sea. In India, Kolkatta and Mumbai alone dump some 765 million metric tons of raw sewage and other municipal wastes into coastal waters every year[11]. The sewage piles up sediment, bacteria and other disease causing organisms in the water. Untreated sewage also results in the oxygen blockade and leads to death of precious marine life. The solid and liquid wastes that are generated by these settlements reach the ocean ultimately and rise in population without any prevention activity would only worsen the situation.

C. Harm of the Heat

Development means along with rising population demands for enormous amounts of energy increases as well. Energy is now obtained from the various sources as thermal, hydro electric and more recently nuclear. Such factories along the coasts discharge heated water into the oceans. While the production of energy through the use of nuclear power is a meagre 3% of the world total, the consequent effect on the surroundings is much higher. While obtaining electricity from splitting the nuclei, water is used as coolant in nuclear plants to absorb the heat. This heated water needs to be released and mostly it is let out into the sea. Nuclear Power plants in India that are stationed near Chennai and Mumbai along the coasts directly dump this waste water into the sea. The temperature is around 37°, nearly 7° higher than normal sea temperature.[12] An estimation of the

---

11 Don Hinrichsen, Ocean planet in decline (http://www.peopleand planet.net/doc. php?id=429&section=6) accessed date July 29, 2005

12 T.S. Subramaian, Special feature: Koodangulam Nuclear Power Project, Setting standards, *Frontline* Vol. 21, issue 10, Aril 10-23, 2004. (Source: http://www.flonnet.com/

quantity of such a release will certainly indicate the gravity of the problem. Even if the water does not possess any radioactivity, the temperature of this water is unsuitable for marine species to live. Hence appropriate methods must be used to prevent fish from entering the disposal pipes and removed from warm waters.

D. Ballast bother

Other than energy sources and their manufacture, the other source of pressure on the oceans is the global economy. The movement of goods from one place to another that drives world economy also entails great environmental challenges. One of the most important sources of concern is the ballast water. Ships carry large volumes of goods and to keep the ships afloat have to balance the weight with counter called ballast. Mostly the material used as ballast, as it is required in large quantities, is water. While off loading freight, the ballast water is also released. Usually this water amounts to thousands of tons in each ship. On an average, ships hold up to 60% of the total weight as ballast water. Every year an estimated 3 to 10 billion tonnes of ballast water is carried round the globe. The following **Table 1** gives the amount of cargo traffic that has plied over the past 13 years in India. This allows us to make a fair estimate of the average amount of ballast water that could be released in India's coastal areas.

Table 1 : Year wise traffic handled at Major and Non-Major ports in India (in million Tonnes)

Year	Major Ports	Non Major Ports	Total
2001-2002	287.58	96.27	383.85
2002-2003	313.55	105.17	418.72
2003-2004	344.79	120.84	465.63
2004-2005	383.75	137.83	521.58
2005-2006	423.56	145.53	569.09
2006-2007	463.78	186.12	649.9
2007-2008	519.31	203.62	722.93
2008-2009	530.53	213.20	743.73
2009-2010	561.09	288.86	849.95

fl2108/stories/200423004310300.htm) accessed August 2, 2005

2010-2011	570.03	314.85	884.88
2011-2012	560.13	353.02	913.15
2012-2013	545.79	387.87	933.66

Source: Indian Ports Association November 2013, e-magazine, http://ipa. nic.in/e-magazine.pdf

This huge amount of water contains a variety of marine organisms including ones that when introduced in alien surroundings multiply prolifically affecting the food and very existence of local marine species. The marine organisms include viruses, bacteria, jellyfish, molluscs, shellfish, crabs and fish which are transported from port to port. The enormous ballast-water tanks of ships are a medium for the introduction of alien species into the waters. It is estimated that at least 7000 different species are being carried in ships' ballast tanks around the world. The damage they wreak on ecosystems and human health is devastating. The bigger the ships the more is the amount of ballast and in turn, the greater is its potential for damaging the marine environment.

Biological invasion is the main effect of discharge of ballast water. The entire ecosystem of a region is a direct victim of such "invasions". Biological invasions are a leading cause of species extinctions and biotic homogenisation worldwide. Invasions are difficult to quantify because organisms at low density are often overlooked. Furthermore, because invasions are commonly initiated during trade, quantification requires the integrated analysis of ecological factors and commercial pathways. Accounting for movements of 7000–10000 species simultaneously, it is found that ballast water is the principal source of invasive species in coastal freshwater and marine ecosystems[13]. Mytilopsis Sallei is a mussel species accumulates in large quantity (10-12 kgs/m) and creates several maintenance problems with regard to marine structures, equipment and machinery. This species is strong enough to survive in difficult marine climatic conditions and also in polluted and oxygen deficient water. The ballast water problem has affected Indian coasts as well. Mussels that are endemic to the areas have been found in the Bombay and Vishakhapatnam port regions. Through port baseline survey and research work, it has been

---

13 John M. Drake and David M. Lodge, Global hot spots of biological invasions: evaluating options for ballast-water management (http://oit.nd.edu/research_computing/ researchandawards/documents/drake.pdf) accessed date Jul 23, 2005

established that Mytilopsis Sallei – a native mussel of Sub tropical Atlantic is found in these Indian ports.

Indian coasts are falling prey to the malicious Marine Bio invasion through ballast water. Basic public awareness on this issue is almost non-existent in India. The mussels clog drains, pipes and other material. India's shipping industry is growing at a rapid pace and highlights the need for additional port facilities. Due to the introduction of exotic creatures, native species are completely destroyed due to lack of food and other favourable conditions. Some species that are unique to the region could even become extinct. India as a sea faring nation has more than 7500 kms long coast line with 12 major ports. With an average of 5000 ships calling at the Mumbai port alone, 1.8 m tonnes of ballast water needs to be handled by this port alone each year. Already the Indian Ocean is one of the most widely used routes accounting for about 40% of the world's total shipping volume.[14] India also plans to increase port capacities and develop new minor and major ports which in turn would mean increased shipping traffic in the Indian Ocean region. Ballast water release would also increase correspondingly.

The problem of the ballast water is now under research focus. The mapping of the main transportation routes of ballast water around the world for example, reveals some interesting facts. Firstly, most of the transfers are occurring from the Southern hemisphere into the northern hemisphere. The areas of Asia, Africa and South America that fall under these pathways possess less than adequate legal and technical measures that can ensure the safe release of ballast water. More importantly most of these countries are coastal economies with fishing being a prime earner. Such invasions could have disastrous effects on the local economies.

By 2020, the volume of all international trade is expected to triple, according to the U.S. National Oceanographic and Atmospheric Administration (NOAA)—and 90 percent of it is expected to move by ocean. This is comparable to the Indian situation where 97% of trading volumes travel by sea[15]. According to James Carlton Professor in Marine Sciences at the Williams' College, Massachusetts, USA, ballast water introduction is perhaps the most dangerous of all modes of introduction

14 LNG traffic in Indian Ocean set to increase, (http://thestar.com.my/maritime/story. asp?file=/2005/7/18/maritime/11481143&sec=maritime) accessed 19 Jul. 05

15 Ministry of Shipping, Govt., of India website (http:// www.shipping.nic.in accessed Jul 05, 2005)

of invasive species round the world.[16]

The devastating effects of biological invasion through the ballast water are already evident around the world. The American comb-jellyfish has entered the Black Sea completely ruining the traditionally rich fisheries of the Black Sea. It was introduced from America via ballast water. Reaching 10 times the year's total catch, it wreaked havoc[17]. Another rather infamous introduction via ballast water is that of the zebra mussel into the Great Lakes of North America. These thumb-nail sized creatures cling to all hard surfaces be they natural or man-made multiply in vast numbers effectively starving the native populations of infested lakes and rivers. The mussel pollutes local water supplies and damaged underwater infrastructure by accumulating and clogging. Studies have shown that zebra mussels can accumulate the pollutants in their tissues in concentrations 300,000 times greater than in the environment. Zebra mussels may also present a health hazard by increasing human and wildlife exposure to organic pollutants such as PCBs and PAHs.

E. Ship breaking

Another ship-related issue that deeply affects marine environment is the breaking of ships. Ships have a life span of 26 years after which they are not treated sea- worthy. Roughly six percent of all ships plying around the world are lead to ship breaking yards. They are usually dismantled for scrap. The method of extracting this scrap from ships which is 95% steel is called ship breaking. The process of ship breaking entails getting steel, removing the paint and other substances that require careful industrial and technical standards to be followed for safe dismantling and disposal. The South Asian region is the world's leading ship breaking region with more than 70% of the world's old ships heading here in India as well as Bangladesh[18].

Paints on ships pose another pollution problem. Ships are made

---

16 Interview with James Carlton, (www.actionbioscience.org/biodiversity/carlton.html) access date Jul 26, 2005

17 Ballast-water - Floating vendors of disease, *Samudra* April 1999 pp 10-11. (Source: http:// www.icsf.net/jsp/publication/samudra/pdf/english/issue_22/ALL.pdf)

18 Ship breaking : A Global Environmental, health and Labour challenge, *Greenpeace Report for IMO MEPC 44th Session, March 2000*, (http://www.greenpeaceweb.org/shipbreak/ imo_mepc44_mrt2000.pdf

not just of steel but also of paint containing lead, cadmium, organotins, arsenic, zinc and chromium all toxic chemicals that harm the health of humans and that of the surroundings too. Other hazardous wastes like sealants, oil are made of PCBs, asbestos are also found on ships which are directly harmful to all living systems. Asbestos is used for insulation of steam pipes and boiler, PCB and sludge is present in the tankers. The toxin Tributylin oxide (TBT) is an aggressive biocide that prevents the growth of algae, barnacles and other marine organisms. It is a water repellant coating. TBT also impairs the immune system of organisms and shellfish develop shell malformations after exposure to extremely low levels of TBT in the seawater. Recent studies conducted by the Dutch Institute for Marine Research and the Free University (VU) of Amsterdam reveal that sperm whales that live and feed in the deep ocean far from ports and shipping lanes have appreciable amounts of TBT and its breakdown products in their bodies.[19] This indicates that TBT may be widely dispersed in the marine environment, including the deep oceans. Researchers opine that whales hitting ships or beaching could also be due to TBT[20]. This chemical leaches into the ocean waters and upon ingestion is harmful to marine life. It is responsible for the disruption of the endocrine system of marine shellfish leading to the development of male sex characteristics in female marine snails.

Polychlorinated butylene or PCB is another toxic chemical used in ships. It is a Persistent Organic Pollutant (POP). It is so named as they remain in the environment long after their release. Polychlorinated butylenes are compounds that are resistant to biological and chemical degradation. Such persistent organic pollutants are neither water nor fat soluble. This leads to bio accumulation in tissues of animals and humans. The Arctic seals exposed to PCBs, developed impaired immune functions and poor reproductive rates. Aquatic birds' hatching was severely affected and those that survived exhibited developmental deformities[21]. In humans, ingesting PCBs acute liver damage that might even prove fatal has been observed. Acute exposure results in chlor acne – an acne form chemically induced eruption.

---

19 http://archive.greenpeace.org/toxics/reports/tbtfactsheet.html) accessed date Jul 23, 2005

20 ibid.,

21 http://pops.gpa.unep.org/19pcbs.htm

The environmental dangers include the improper disposal of oil be it engine oil, bilge or fuel that was transported. Ships at dry dock are first bound to treat the oil that is biologically broken down. However release of this untreated oil into the sea affects the water quality, opacity and oxygen content threatening precious marine life that thrives along the beaches. Removal of hazardous wastes like asbestos whose particles directly impinge the air and suspended particles are an acute health hazard. The dangerous substances that are released when cutting steel and other metals are highly toxic and cause air pollution. Indian port of Alang is the most important ship breaking yard in India. Around 300 ships are broken in a year at Alang alone[22]. The numbers will rise as more and more ships reach the end of their sea life and other countries imposing strict conditions for ship breaking that escalates costs and creates time delays. Developing countries like India do not impose strict guidelines in working conditions for this industry. Appalling working conditions and the effect on local environment has been widely reported and debated. With the phasing out of single-hull tankers by this year, it is expected that more than 2000 oil tankers will have to be decommissioned over the next five years. The Kolkata, Kakinada and Vallianokkam ports are slated to be either developed or newly built specifically for ship-breaking[23]. The ship breaking industry needs to plough back the huge profit margins to ensure the safety of workers and the marine environment that is irreplaceable.

F. Slippery problems

Connected to shipping and ship breaking is another worrying form of pollution – the effect of accidental or wanton spillage of crude oil – from ships that transport this vital energy source round the world. The effects of oil spills include complete destruction of entire biological communities like the kelp – a type of seaweed that nourishes animal life under the sea and long-term chronic conditions in mammals and amphibians. Since oil is insoluble in water it forms balls, slicks etc, that spread due to ocean currents, wind pattern and other climatic conditions polluting a wide area of the ocean. Tar balls are formed when oil that is dense emulsifies with water. Cleaning up an oil spill is a costly and environmentally monumental

22 Robert McGowan, Asian Draw For Ship-Breaking *BBC News*, 14, Dec 2003 (Source: http://news.bbc.co.uk/go/pr/fr/-/1/hi/sci/tech/3266963.stm)

23 Santanu Sanyal, Kolkata Dock to re-build ship-breaking potential, *The Hindu*, July 11, 2005, (http://www.thehindubusinessline.com/2005/07/11/stories/2005071100330600.htm)

task and the affected marine area can never be restored to its pristine beauty or purity. Very few countries the world over possess the financial, technical and human requirements to control an oil spill.

Marine mammals living in cold climates (seals, sea lions, polar bears and otters) are likely to be more vulnerable than those living in temperate or tropical waters. In animals too, the internal system, sensory faculties can be damaged. Effects of oil on marine mammals depend upon species may, in addition to hypothermia, include: toxic effects and secondary organ dysfunction due to ingestion of oil; congested lungs; damaged airways; interstitial emphysema due to inhalation of oil droplets and vapour; gastrointestinal ulceration and haemorrhaging due to ingestion of oil during grooming and feeding; eye and skin lesions from continuous exposure to oil; decreased body mass due to restricted diet; and stress due to oil exposure and behavioural changes. The digestion system could collapse due to cell damage of its intestines thereby reducing the ability to eat or absorb food taken in. Fish ingest large amounts of oil through their gills. Salmon eggs died by the thousands due to the Exxon Valdez spill. Shell fish taste and smell bad making them inedible when exposed to hydrocarbons[24]. Numerous biochemical and cellular changes might result in respiratory rate change, fin erosion, enlarged liver and negative effect fertility.

The result of oil spills on avian population is especially of concern. When the feathers of sea birds come into contact with oil, feathers lose their lightness and get clogged with oil. This hinders the bird from flying as also affecting its buoyancy or ability to float thereby making the bird heavy and finally sink under its own weight. The insulating character of the feathers is lost and the birds in cold weather might die out of freezing (hyperthermia). While preening or cleaning their feathers the birds might inhale oil vapours or even ingest it. The toxic substances in the oil affect almost every organ severely damaging them. The reproductive health of a bird is also affected as the oil passes through pores in the eggshells thus either killing the embryos or leading to malformation of the cherubs[25].

---

24 For a detailed review on oil spills and their impact on marine environment see (http://oils.gpa.unep.org/facts/wildlife.htm) accessed Jul 20, 2005

25 Effects of oil pollution on marine wildlife Global Programme of Action for the Protection of the Marine Environment from Land-based Activities, UNEP information gateway (http://oils.gpa.unep.org/facts/wildlife.htm) accessed July 18, 2005

The sources of marine pollution from sea-based activities include marine transportation and offshore mineral exploration and production activities. Accidental oil spills have been frequently reported along these routes. It has been reported that beach tar along the west coast of India is a severe problem, with total deposits of up to 1,000 tons per year. In the port of Chittagong in Bangladesh, an estimated 6,000 tons of crude oil is spilled annually, while crude oil residue and wastewater effluent from land-based refineries amount to about 50,000 tons per year. Approximately 5 million tonnes of oil enter the Arabian Sea each year, while the Bay of Bengal receives some 400,000 tonnes from similar sources. Similarly, oil pollution from shipping and offshore oil rigs is a concern in East Asian seas. In the Straits of Malacca alone, 490 shipping accidents were reported in 1988-92, resulting in a considerable amount of oil spillage.

F.1 Hit or miss

The cases of oil pollution in the Arabian Sea (called north Indian Ocean) are well-documented by the oceanographers[26]. In 1974 the oil tanker *Transhuron* ran aground near Kilton islands of the Lakshwadeep atolls severely damaging the environment and even fishing was banned in the area. *Cosmos Pioneer* broke up near Porbunder in Gujarat and some 18,000 tonnes of oil were released into the sea[27]. The Japan Oceanographic Centre has reported that during 1975-80, on 495 out of 611 occasions, oil slicks were sighted in a sample quadrant close to Goa. This is highest frequency of oil slicks in the Indian Ocean. It is higher than even the transects surrounding Sri Lanka which is close to the super tanker lanes[28].

In June 1993 when the oil carrying vessel, *Sea Transporter* drifted close to Sinquerim beach, disaster was averted by the careful and laborious pumping out of hundreds of tonnes of thick, viscous furnace oil despite heavy monsoon showers. India has witnessed oil spills in 1974 and 1994. In March and July 2005, there have been oil slicks near the coast of Goa. So far, no major tanker disaster has been reported. About 35 per cent of global marine transport of oil from the Middle East takes place along the

---

26 Dr.Sengupta & S.Z.Qasim ed., The Indian Ocean, Volume 1, Oxford and IBH, 2001

27 Prabhas Chandra, *India's Coast And Ocean Management*, Part2, Kanishka Publishers, New Delhi, 2005 p.659

28 **Nandkumar Kamat ,Goa: Marine Pollution Management Needed,** *The Navhind Times,* **March 28, 2005,** http://www.navhindtimes.com/stories.php?part=news&Story_ ID=03283

Arabian Sea tanker routes. Annually, oil cargo of one billion metric tonnes is transported within just a few kilometres from the coastline of Goa. The probability of a major oil spill near the coast of Goa is very high because of the heavy super tanker traffic close to the coast. The entry of oil in the Arabian Sea from operational discharges has been about a million tonnes annually resulting in an estimated formation of 3700 tonnes of tar balls, annually. Due to currents, these are deposited on the beaches during the monsoon.

Cleaning oil tankers at high seas[29] also results in drastic effects on the marine life. There are also instances of wanton leakage of oil that has caused devastating damage to the marine environment. The cases of the Iran-Iraq war and the I Gulf war of 1990 had not only resulted in the spillage of about 8 million barrels of oil in the Persian Gulf but also severely damaged the littoral areas in the southern and northern regions, even affecting their soil and air[30]. But by the end of 1992, researchers reported that many of the worst hit beaches in Saudi Arabia were almost clean of oil. It is believed that this may have been the result of the warm water of the Gulf and the fact that its bacterial populations were able to degrade and weather the oil much more quickly than previously believed to be possible.

Yet another and perhaps more important source of pollution to the marine environment is the extraction of oil from coastal areas and the continental shelf of the Persian Gulf, coupled with its export and the passage of oil tankers along the waterway. At present, an estimated 100 ships enter and leave the Persian Gulf every day. This indicates that 40 percent of the world's total oil transportation passes through the region. Therefore, it is only natural that such an extensive transit volume will have negative repercussions on the marine environment. The oil sludge, released by the aggregate of tankers traversing the Persian Gulf, is estimated to be around 8 million metric tonnes per year. This kind of pollution represents some 60 percent of the pollution plaguing the Persian Gulf. Studies have shown that the major part of the pollution is caused by ships sailing from the Strait of Hormuz to oil terminals in regional countries. The resulting sludge brings with it a particularly foul smell too.

---

29 Oily beaches leave Goa vexed, *The Hindu*, July 28, 2005. p 24.

30 Water Pollution in the Persian Gulf and the Caspian Sea, *Payam-e-darya*, No.32, May 1995, pp.13-20. (http://www.netiran.com/?fn=artd(2369)) accessed August 24, 2005.

Other parts of the world like the East Asian seas are also subject to effects of pollution. Between 1973 and 2003, more than 2,350 oil spills occurred along the China's coast. On April 4 of 2005, the Portuguese oil tanker Arteaga, carrying about 120,000 tons of crude oil from the Yemen, struck a rock and became stranded off Dalian Port in north-east China's Liaoning Province. On July 2, a Chinese oil tanker collided with a Malaysian-registered 9,000-ton ship at Dalian Port while carrying 3,800 tons of diesel fuel to Guangzhou in South China's Guangdong Province, causing an oil spill. For days, tens of boats and helicopters have had to work ceaselessly to minimise the impact on the environment. Last December, two container ships from Panama and Yemen collided off the estuary of the Pearl River, just south of Hong Kong, leading to the leakage of 1,200 tons of oil into the sea[31]. More than half of Japan's annual total of about 700-900 reported marine pollution incidents in the coastal areas are oil-related incidents and these occur mostly along the coast between Hokkaido and Kyushu[32].

The Southern African waters are also notorious for oil spills. The effect particularly on the African Penguins has been disastrous. During the 20th century, there were six spills in which more that 1000 penguins were oiled: the *Esso Essen* spill in 1968, the *Wafra* in 1971, a slick of unknown origins which came ashore onto Dassen Island in 1972, the *Oriental Pioneer* in 1974, the *Apollo Sea* in 1994, and a spill of unknown origins in the sea off Danger Point in 1995. Besides the acute crises in which a large number of penguins are oiled simultaneously, there is a chronic, ongoing problem of small spillages that result in about 1000 oiled penguins every year[33]. The famous *Exxon Valdez* oil spill off the Alaskan waters in 1989 oiled an estimated 30,000 birds. This spill witnessed one of the largest cleanup efforts in global shipping history and garnered international action against this man-made environmental disaster.

---

31 Unprecedented pollution in China's seas *Asia news* 7, July 2005 http://www.asianews.it/view.php?l=en&art=3661

32 Ministry of the Environment, Govt. of Japan website: http://www.env.go.jp/en/pol/wemj/marine.html

33 For a detailed chronological study see, Avian Demography Unit Department of Statistical Sciences University of Cape Town website Les Underhill, *A brief history of penguin oiling in South African waters*, (http://web.uct.ac.za/depts/stats/adu/oilspill/oilhist.htm) accessed August 25, 2005.

G. Attempts at Prevention

The Basel convention dealing with transboundary movement of hazardous wastes of 1989 adopted an amendment that treats out-of-use ships containing hazardous chemicals as waste[34] directly dealing with ship breaking and the resultant pollution. The 1989 Basel Convention and its 1995 Basel Ban Amendment prevents export of the waste vessel if they are not decontaminated and stripped of toxic substances such as asbestos and PCBs under the responsibility of ship owners/exporting states. Whereas the Basel Convention places responsibility on industry and rich nations to prevent and even prohibit the export of hazardous wastes to developing countries, the new IMO Convention now being discussed will place almost all responsibility on the ship breaking countries and their facilities[35].

Individual developed countries have also unilaterally initiated strict guidelines and laws for controlling and preventing marine pollution. Australia has introduced new procedures for ballast water management in 1998 including a standardised ballast water reporting form for international shipping also include mandatory reporting on ballast management and mandatory access to on-board ballast sampling points. Verification of furnished information and penalties for false reporting characterise Australian guidelines[36]. They also recommend ships develop and keep on board a ballast water management plan. The Norwegian Pollution Control Authority has taken information-gathering tools one step further by setting up a warning system. The Authority is using radar satellite imaging to detect oil spills, establishing the world's first pollution alarm system. Since 1993, Norway has worked with Danish and other North Sea officials to install the detection network. Eventually, sea waters from Greenland to Estonia will be under their watch. The Basel Convention on transport of hazardous wastes stipulates the non-transfer of polluting materials to

---

34 'Basel Convention Decision VII/26 - Environmentally sound management of Ship Dismantling', Obligations and Opportunities for a Mandatory Alternate or Additional Instrument to the Basel Convention for End-of-Life Ships, Annex 1, Submitted by Greenpeace and the Basel Action Network (BAN) *26 May 2005*, pp.15-16. http://www.greenpeaceweb.org/shipbreak/mepclong.pdf

35 Proposed Ship Scrap Treaty Called "Too Little, Too Slow", July 22, 2005 http://Greenpeaceweb.Org/Shipbreak/News113.Asp

36 For a full review of Australian ballast water requirements see, Australian Quarantine and Immigration Service website http://www.affa.gov.au/corporate_docs/publications/pdf/quarantine/border/ausbwreq.pdf accessed August 5, 2005

developing countries[37]. The ships that are to be dismantled have only recently been added in the waste list.

Ballast water pollution has been attempted to be addressed internationally. The adoption of a global ballast water management plan by the International Convention for the Control and Management of Ships' Ballast Water and Sediments of February 2004, obligated both the shipping companies and the countries that allow ships to enter its ports. Starting in 2009 ships will have to ensure that ballast discharges contain fewer than 10 viable organisms larger than 50 $\mu m/m^3$[38]. Ratification of the treaty by nearly 30 of the 74 conference attendee countries makes enforcement problematic.

In November 1997, the International Maritime Organisation (IMO) adopted revised International Guidelines for Minimising the Risk of Introduction of Unwanted Aquatic Organisms and Pathogens from Ships Ballast Water and Sediment Discharges (IMO Resolution A.868(20)). The single hull tanker ships built before 1982 are to be phased out by 2005 and for post MARPOL the deadline was 2010[39]. The 2004 International Convention for the Control and Management of Ships' Ballast Water and Sediments places obligations on both the ships and the receiving ports regarding the transfer of ballast water. Survey, certification and verification of ballast water safety can be carried out by port state control officers to prevent any "threat to environment, health, property or resources" (Article 9)[40]. Countries like Canada and USA are working over regulations that warrant release of ballast water in the open seas before entering the ports[41].

The states that have suffered pollution damages in territory, territorial sea or EEZ can claim compensation under the international Oil pollution

---

37 For complete text of the convention see, http://www.basel.int/text/con-e-rev.doc accessed August 5, 2005

38 *UNEP Geo Year book 2004-5* (http://www.unep.org/geo/yearbook/yb2004/115.htm#b4) accessed Jul 23, 2005

39 Regulation 13G of Annex I of MARPOL (International Convention for the Prevention of Pollution from Ships, 1973, as modified by the Protocol of 1978 relating thereto (MARPOL 73/78)). Source: http://www.imo.org/Conventions/contents.asp?doc_id=678&topic_id=258 Accessed July 20, 2005

40 International Convention for the control and management of ships' ballast water and sediments, IMO 2004, http:// www.imo.org/Conventions/mainframe.asp?topic_id=867

41 Interim Report, National Ballast information Clearinghouse, October 2000 Source: http://invasions.si.edu/nbic/reports/NBASAnnRp1.pdf accessed August 4, 2005

compensation fund set up in 1992[42]. For pollution damage due to oil spills by tankers an International Maritime Organization (IMO) assisted international regime, looks at compensation. Marine environmental problems are gaining priority on the legislative agenda and strict adherence to newly made laws can enable curbing and, even in some cases, prevention of problems of pollution of our marine environment.

In the case of India too, there have been attempts to deal with marine pollution at least in part. The Ministry of Environment and Forests, Government of India has issued clear guidelines in 1989 on how to deal with oil pollution. Section 8 deals with routine monitoring of petroleum hydrocarbon inputs entering into harbours. Sub-section 8.3 asks for contingency plan for major oil spillage at sea. Sub-section 8.5 suggests a co-ordination authority for pollution abatement in case of oil spillage. Section 10 deals with accidents. If the state government were to have the previous record of accidents, collisions on the sea then contingency plan could have been put in action[43].

Conclusion

Polluting agents that affect the marine world have increased in volume and variety. The industries are the main sources of these agents in the way of wastes from processing activities and discharges resulting from manufacturing. Nearly two-thirds of the total input of marine environment contaminants is land-based and from atmospheric sources. They constitute 44% and 33% respectively of the entire polluting gamut[44]. They are outside the regular monitoring systems in place.

Principal regions of the ocean that are greatly affected by marine based pollution are the continental shelves and the coasts. Water pollution can be identified from several symptoms. Drastic decline in availability of one or several species of fish, and prevalence of a variety of diseases and pathologies among fish and other organisms, resulting increase in

---

42 THE INTERNATIONAL OIL POLLUTION COMPENSATION FUND 1992 Explanatory note prepared by the 1992 Fund Secretariat, http://www.iopcfund.org/npdf/mar05E.pdf

43 Nandakumar Kamat ibid.,

44 Anthropogenic impact in the sea and marine pollution by Stanislav Patin, translation by Elena Cascio based on "Environmental Impact of the Offshore Oil and Gas Industry" Source: www.offshore-environment.com/anthropogenicimpact.html July 11, 2005

poisoning or diseases transmitted to people who consume fish, significant degradation of healthy coastal ecosystems, spurt in algae blooms, and such others are some notable ones.

The adverse effects of human induced pollution have manifested in unimaginable ways and have resulted in even disturbing global climatic processes. We are yet to realise the enormous role oceans play in being a global "waste dump" that take in polluting agents and the resulting impact on our life on this planet. When India by the middle of this century becomes the most populated nation on earth, she must take up the indomitable task of balancing development with conservation. Of all forms of pollution, India's Marine pollution has been the most unnoticed and could spell disaster for this potential world power. Continuing challenges to our marine health include pressures of sustaining a huge population, unsustainable developmental activities and further increase in trade and in turn, shipping. All these will set off a chain of events beginning with pollution of fish populations, and other sea growing animals and plants, and need to be addressed urgently as they can pose a greater threat than other environmental challenges India is already facing.

India and such other emerging economies depend largely on the oceans for progress and hence have a selfish interest in preserving and protecting ocean wealth thought to be virtually an unending source provider. The ill effects of uncontrolled industrialisation, massive shipping activities, and energy extraction processes occurring the world over should be taken as important lessons. With advanced scientific and technical expertise looming crises like invasion of exotic species, pollution caused by breaking of ships and purpoted or accidental spillage of oil need to be controlled and mitigated. In India, the Coast Guard has specialised in combating oil spills at sea. Ships specially equipped with skimmers, booms, oil-water separators, spraying arms and chemical dispersants are being pressed into service[45]. Due to their transboundary nature all the above issues require concerted cooperation among members of the international community and far greater enhanced international regulations.

Oceans need to be stabilised by adopting age-old methods of sustainable fishing techniques, multi-level imposition and enforcement of severe rules regarding management of industrial and domestic wastes

---

45 Prabhas, p.652

at the national, regional and global levels and the pooling of human and financial resources to find novel ways to restore the health of the oceans. Man can break faster than he can make. As Henry Havelock Ellis puts it, "The sun, the moon and the stars would have disappeared long ago... had they happened to be within the reach of predatory human hands"[46]. There is thus a need to protect marine life from indiscriminate destruction before it is too late. In the words of Rachel Carson, in her famous book the Silent Spring, *"The most alarming of all man's assaults upon the environment is the contamination of air, earth, rivers, and sea with dangerous and even lethal materials. This pollution is for the most part irrecoverable; the chain of evil it initiates not only in the world that must support life but in living tissues is for the most part irreversible. In this now universal contamination of the environment, chemicals are the sinister and little-recognised partners of radiation in changing the very nature of the world--the very nature of its life."*[47] We need to pay heed to this warning.

---

46   http://www.linkgrinder.com/wisdom/Full_List_Of_Famous_Quotes_From_HENRY_ HAVELOCK_ ELLIS.html

47 http://www.uky.edu/Classes/NRC/381/carson_spring.pdf

XII

India's Energy Need And Its Repercussion on Environment Security - A Case Study of Sardar Sarovar Dam on Narmada River

- O Nirmala

Introduction

The modern world today is highly dependent on energy. The universe is made up of energy - this is what the scientist says. The sun, the moon, the stars, and the planets everything is made up of energy. But today, Planet Earth faces a serious of risk due to the excessive use of different forms of energy. All action is possible because of energy. Energy is necessary for every state in the country for its overall development, but what kind of energy has to be used and how it has been utilised is more important. This is because human inventions and discoveries have promoted human survival. However, unfortunately, our planet is currently facing a problem because of excess use of non-renewable energy which has resulted in climate change, rise in sea water level, global warming, and other serious environmental issues, which undoubtedly affect all life.

In my opinion, man has disturbed the environment for his own pleasure. Man, who has the capability to think, started discovering and inventing so many things. But he has forgotten that he cannot create new energy for energy can neither be created nor destroyed, but it can change from one form to the other. Somehow today the whole earth is in danger due to the excess use of non-renewable energy for survival of human beings; this is the right time to take pre-emptive measures so that we can at least save the world for our future.

The detrimental change in environment today is due to pollution caused by the extreme use of natural resources, industrial and chemical wastes, deforestation, excessive use of automobiles, burning of fossil fuels, etc. This pollution may affect the productivity of natural resources, such as land, water, and forest areas in the future. Therefore, it is of vital importance to prevent environmental pollution and protect the environment.

Since the environment has no limitation it is hard to analyse every situation all over the world and even for a state like India it is very hard to find out any one issue because India faces so many energy security challenges such as gas pipeline from Iran, nuclear issue in Kudankulam, gas pipeline from Turkmenistan through Pakistan, hydro-electric dam at Narmada constrained by environmental problems.[1]

It is indeed necessary to know the current energy situation in India so that it is possible to find a possible alternative solution to the current energy and environment situation. India is considered as the one of the most rapidly developing economies in the world. It is a known fact that natural resources are plenty, but it is not available in all places and in all times. It is true in the case of non-renewable energy resources particularly oil, natural gas and coal. India, in order to meet its energy requirement, is dependent heavily on foreign sources especially from the Middle East[2] because India is a home of the world's largest population. By knowing all the threats, India started to shift its focus from non-renewable to renewable energy technologies in order to secure its citizens and its environment.

Renewable sources of energy such as solar, wind, biogas and nuclear are in use today, but hydro source will be more appropriate to produce electricity as India is a peninsular state, covered on three sides by water and is filled with rivers like the Ganges, Brahmaputra, Cauvery and their tributaries. No neighbouring state can claim rights over rivers that flow through the country. It is thus possible to have several major and small hydro projects. These projects have their own advantages and disadvantages, but this article mainly focuses on the Narmada river issue. In India major cities are located in the banks of the river. The chapter particularly focuses on the Sardar Sarovar Dam situated on the Narmada River. It tries to analyse how energy issues are themselves a threat to environmental security and how this situation is handled by the Indian Government.

---

1 http://www.isas.nus.edu.sg/Attachments/PresentationMaterial/20070709%20-%20 Dr%20Manjusha%20Gupte_23102009175123.pdf

2 *www.icrier.org/page.asp?MenuID=24&SubCatId=177...341*

Energy from Water

The energy in the flow of water can be used to produce electricity. Waves result from the interaction of the wind with the surface of the sea and represent a transfer of energy from the wind to the sea. Energy can be extracted from tides by creating a reservoir or basin behind a barrage and then passing tidal waters through turbines in the barrage to generate electricity.[3]

There may be many environmental and social problems, but hydro power is still considered to be the best, cheapest as well as the cleanest source of energy. Smaller hydro plants can be utilised to meet the energy requirements of rural areas because smaller plants do not affect the environment. Only big projects affect the thousands of people living along the banks of the river due to displacement. Such projects also divert the flow of rivers, destroying large forest areas that are home for thousands of animals and birds and other creatures.[4]

No country can guarantee its security and prosperity by only thinking about peace and rapid economic growth. Today the environment along with energy is the centre of gravity for all nations in order to have stability and sustainability in their growth.

India's Energy Need

According to statistics as given in 2011 India Energy Handbook, the total energy consumption of the country was as given n the table below.

Commercial Energy Consumption			
Source	Unit	2007-08	2008-09*
Petroleum Products	MMT	140.7	145.3
Natural Gas	BCM	31.5	31.8
Coal	MMT	457.1	493.3
Lignite	MMT	34.0	NA
Electricity	Billion kWh	813.1	842.8

(*estimate)
Source: Basic Statistics on Indian Petroleum and Natural Gas, 2008-09, Ministry of Petroleum & Natural Gas, New Delhi

---

3 *edugreen.teri.res.in/explore/renew/hydel.htm*

4 *www.ieahydro.org/reports/**Hydrofut**.pdf*

The table above clearly depicts the amount of commercial energy that India is using. According to this estimate the use of coal and the electricity increases when compare to the other products. India is the home to nearly 1.2 billion people; therefore the use of energy would increase proportionally to the growth of the economy. It is therefore essential to have an estimate on total energy that is required to meet the India's energy demand.

Total Energy Requirement

Total Energy Requirements (MTOE)						
Year	Hydro	Nuclear	coal	oil	natural gas	total
2011-12	12	17	283	186	48	546
2016-17	18	31	375	241	64	729
2021-22	23	45	521	311	97	997
2026-27	29	71	706	410	135	1,351
2031-32	35	98	937	548	197	1,815

Source: IEP Report, Page 28, Table 2.10

The table given above shows that despite of environmental issues, the use of coal is more predominant when compared to hydro energy. The order of use is - coal, oil, natural gas, nuclear and finally hydro. As per the data, the coal is used more than any other source of energy. However, this should not be the order of use as it is necessary to think not only about industrial production or the development of economy, but the environment in each state should be protected in order to have a clean, hygiene and healthy life for each and every person.[5]

India's Energy Mix

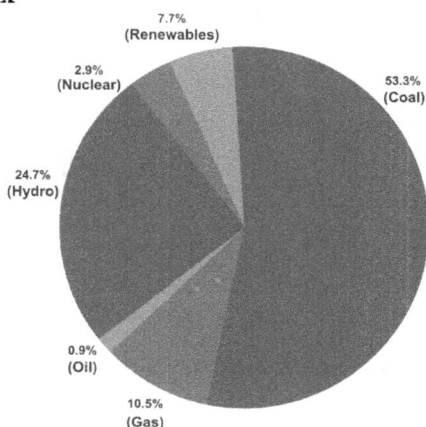

Source: Ministry of Power

---

5 *www.psimedia.info/**handbook/India_Energy_Handbook**.pdf*

By production source, India's electricity generation is derived from: coal (53.3%), Hydro (24.7%), gas (10.5%), oil (0.9%), nuclear (2.9%), and other renewable sources (7.7%). Compared to other forms of renewable energy Hydro ranks second (after coal) for generating electricity. Although renewables (other than hydropower) only contribute 7.7 percent to India's energy mix as of now, India is currently the fourth largest producer of wind energy.[6]

Hydro power in India

Hydropower is the key to the Government of India's plans of providing all its citizens with reliable access to electricity by 2012.[7]

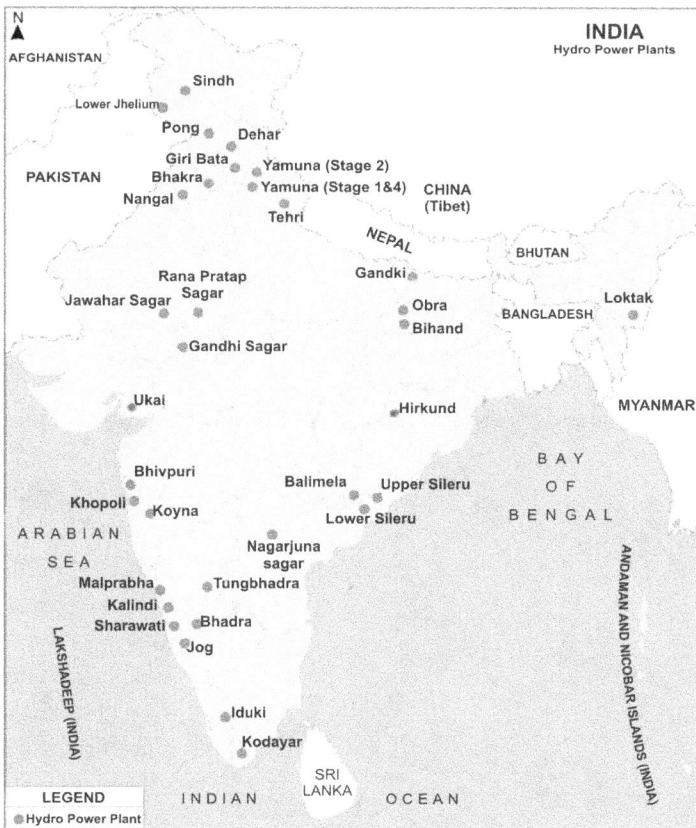

Source: http://www.mapsofindia.com/maps/india/hydropowerproject.htm

6   http://www.indiaclimateportal.org/India-s-Changing-Energy-Mix

7   http://www.worldbank.org.in/WBSITE/EXTERNAL/COUNTRIES/SOUTHASIAEXT/INDI
AEXTN/0,,contentMDK:20660353~pagePK:141137~piPK:141127~theSitePK:295584,00.html

The potential for hydro-electric potential in terms of installed capacity in India is estimated to be about 148,700 MW out of which a capacity of 30,164 MW (20.3%) has been developed so far and 13,616 MW (9.2 %) of capacity is under construction. [8]

Major Hydro Power Plants in India

Name	Location	Operator	Configu-ration	Important Facts
Babail	Uttar Pradesh	Uttar Pradesh Jal Vidyut Nigam Ltd	2 X 1.5 MW tube	The Babail mini-hydel project was approved in Sep 1986 and was awarded to PGM in Sep 1988 as a Rs 6.22cr turnkey project.
Bhandar-dara-1	Mahara-shtra	Dodson-Lindblom Hydro Power Pvt Ltd	1 X 14.4 MW Francis	This plant was acquired in 1996 from Maharashtra Water Resources Dept and overhauled in 1997/98 with assistance from AHEC.
Belka	Uttar Pradesh	Uttar Pradesh Jal Vidyut Nigam Ltd	2 X 1.5 MW tube	The Belka and Babail mini-hydel projects were approved in Sep 1986 and Belka was awarded to FCC and PGM in Jul 1988 as a total Rs 5.66cr project. Construction on Belka did not start until Dec 1996 after delays in securing forest clearance and land acquisition.

Name	Location	Operator	Configuration	Important Facts
Chenani-1	Jammu & Kashmir	Jammu & Kashmir Power Development Corp	5 X 4.66 MW Pelton	The Chenani I&II projects in Udhampur district were inaugurated in 1971 by Prime Minister Indira Gandhi. They were closed on 25 Feb 2005 following a landslide that damaged a 700m diversion tunnel. Repairs were completed at a cost of Rs 8cr and the plants put back in service in Jun 2008.
Bhatgar	Maharashtra	Maharashtra State Power Generation Co Ltd	1 X 16 MW Kaplan	The dam was part of the world's largest irrigation project, known as Lloyd Barrage. This was a multipurpose scheme which was initiated in 1923 by Sir George Ambrose Lloyd, then Governor of Bombay. The project was opened in Jan 1932.
Indira Sagar	Madhya Pradesh	Narmada Hydroelectric Development Corp Ltd	8 X 125 MW Francis	NHDC is a joint venture of NHPC and the MP government set up on 1 Aug 2000.
Little Ranjit	West Bengal	West Bengal State Electricity Distribution Co Ltd	2 X 1 MW Pelton	Operations commenced in 1970

Name	Location	Operator	Configu-ration	Important Facts
Jammu Canal	Jammu & Kashmir	Jammu & Kashmir Power Development Corp	2 X 500 kW Francis	This power station has been out of service since 1995
Matatila	Uttar Pradesh	Uttar Pradesh Jal Vidyut Nigam Ltd	3 X 10 MW Kaplan	This dam was built between 1952 and 1964 on the Betwa River in the Ganga Basin.
Salal	Jammu & Kashmir	National Hydro Power Corp Ltd	6 X 115 MW Kaplan	Built on the Chenab River this power station has a 118m high, 630m long rock-fill dam and a 113m high, 450m long concrete dam plus an 11m, 2,46km tailrace tunnel. The reservoir is 33km long. Project development started in 1970.
Omkare-shwar	Madhya Pradesh	Narmada Hydroelectric Development Corp Ltd	8 X 65 MW Francis	This 949m long concrete gravity dam reaches a maximum height of 53m. The Annual production is expected to be 1.1 TWh.
Samal	Orissa	Orissa Power Consortium Ltd	5 X 4 MW S-Turbine	OPCL is a power company promoted by VBC Ferro Alloys Ltd. Samal uses releases from Samal Barrage reservoir on the Brahmani River.

Source: http://www.mapsofindia.com/maps/india/hydropowerproject.htm

Hydropower is a renewable energy resource. It uses the Earth's water cycle to generate electricity. Water in its liquid form evaporates (gaseous form) from the Earth's surface, forms clouds, precipitates back to Earth (rain), and flows toward the ocean. The movement of water as it flows downstream creates kinetic energy that can be converted into electricity.[9] 2700 TWH is generated every year. Hydropower supplies at least 50% of electricity production in 66 countries and at least 90% in 24 countries. Out of the total power generation installed capacity in India of 1,76,990 MW (June, 2011), hydro power contributes about 21.5% i.e. 38,106 MW. A capacity addition of 78,700 MW is envisaged from different conventional sources during 2007-2012 (the 11th Plan), which includes 15,627 MW from large hydro projects. In addition to this, a capacity addition of 1400 MW was envisaged from small hydro up to 25 MW station capacity. The total hydroelectric power potential in the country is assessed at about 150,000 MW, equivalent to 84,000 MW at 60% load factor. The potential of small hydro power projects is estimated at about 15,000 MW.[10]

Small Hydro Power Projects in India:

Hydro power projects with a station capacity of up to 25 megawatt (MW) each fall under the category of small hydro power (SHP) in India. It is estimated that the SHP potential is about 15, 000 MW.

Details of the potential and installed/under installation projects in India:-

S. No	State	Potential		Projects Installed		Projects Under implementation	
		No.	Capacity	No.	Capacity	No.	Capacity
1	Andhra Pradesh	497	560.18	62	189.83	18	61.75
2	Arunachal Pradesh	550	1328.68	101	78.835	28	38.71
3	Assam	119	238.69	4	27.11	4	15
4	Bihar	95	213.25	18	58.3	11	36.31
5	Chhattisgarh	184	993.11	6	19.05	1	1.2
6	Goa	6	6.5	1	0.05	-	-
7	Gujarat	292	196.97	4	12.6	-	-
8	Haryana	33	110.05	7	70.1	2	3.4

9 www.epa.gov/cleanenergy/energy-and-you/affect/hydro.html

10 http://www.mapsofindia.com/maps/india/hydropowerproject.htm

S No	State	Potential		Projects Installed		Projects Under implementation	
		No.	Capacity	No.	Capacity	No.	Capacity
9	Himachal Pradesh	536	2267.81	112	375.385	40	132.2
10	Jammu & Kashmir	246	1417.80	34	129.33	5	5.91
11	Jharkhand	103	208.95	6	4.05	8	34.85
12	Karnataka	138	747.95	111	725.05	18	107.5
13	Kerala	245	704.1	20	136.87	7	23.8
14	Madhya Pradesh	299	803.64	11	86.16	4	19.9
15	Maharashtra	255	732.63	39	263.825	15	51.7
16	Manipur	114	109.13	8	5.45	3	2.75
17	Meghalaya	101	229.8	4	31.03	3	1.7
18	Mizoram	75	166.93	18	36.47	1	0.5
19	Nagaland	99	188.98	10	28.67	4	4.2
20	Orissa	222	295.47	10	79.625	5	3.93
21	Punjab	237	393.23	43	153.2	15	21.4
22	Rajasthan	66	57.17	10	23.85	-	-
23	Sikkim	91	265.55	16	47.11	2	5.2
24	Tamil Nadu	197	659.51	16	94.05	6	33
25	Tripura	13	46.86	3	16.01	-	-
26	Uttar Pradesh	251	460.75	7	23.3	-	-
27	Uttarakhand	444	1577.44	95	134.12	55	230.65
28	West Bengal	203	396.11	24	98.9	16	79.25
29	Andaman & Nicobar Islands	7	7.27	1	5.25	-	-
Total		5718	15384.15	801	2953.58	271	914.81

SHP projects installed in Private Sector (as on 31.03.2009)

S.No	State	Total Number	Total Capacity
1	Andhra Pradesh	43	104.43

2	Assam	1	0.10
3	Gujarat	2	5.6
4	Himachal Pradesh	63	271.25
5	Haryana	2	7.4
6	Jammu & Kashmir	2	17.5
7	Karnataka	95	694.90
8	Kerala	3	36.00
9	Madhya Pradesh	1	2.20
10	Maharashtra	13	74.00
11	Orissa	2	32.00
12	Punjab	18	26.20
13	Tamil Nadu	1	0.35
14	Uttaranchal	10	48.30
15	West Bengal	5	6.45
Total		261	1326.68

Source: http://www.indianpowermarket.com/2012/02/small-hydro-potential-in-india.html

Obstacles in building dams:

Building of dam alters the character of the river. Building a dam across a river floods the land where the local community lived and worked for years. It prevents the free movement of fish. Diverting a river affects the nature of the countryside and does not lend itself to use on a large scale. Permanent complete or partial blockage of a river for energy conversion is adversely affected by variations in flow. Building large-scale hydro power plants can be polluting and damaging to surrounding ecosystems. Changing the course of waterways can also have a detrimental effect on human communities, agriculture and ecosystems further downstream. Hydro projects can also be unreliable during prolonged droughts and dry seasons when rivers dry up or reduce in volume. [11]

---

11 www.eai.in/ref/ae/hyd/hyd.html

Hydro Power in India:

Hydropower, being an indigenously-available, clean and renewable source of energy, is keenly looked into by the Government of India. Currently only 23% of India's hydro potential is being utilised to provide the additional generating capacity it needs.

Additional hydropower capacity is desirable in India's generation mix, as it provides the system operator with technically vital flexibility to meet the changes in demand which typically affect a power network like that of India. The high density of household demand in India means that the system can experience a peaking load of anything between 20,000 to 30,000 Mega Watts. This sudden burst in demand can be best met by hydropower plants which have the ability to start up and shut down quickly.

The Government of India is committed to developing world-class companies that are able to design, construct, and maintain hydropower projects to international standards, and has requested the World Bank's support in this endeavour. In addition to helping with financing, the Bank brings extensive experience in developing such projects across the world.[12]

Advantages of Hydro Power

Water is a renewable source of energy as it saves scarce fuel reserves. It is non-polluting and hence is environment friendly. Cost of generation, operation and maintenance is lower than the other sources of energy. The ability to start and stop quickly and instantaneous load acceptance/rejection makes it suitable to meet peak demand and for enhancing system reliability and stability. It has higher efficiency compared to thermal and gas. The cost of generation is free from inflationary effects after the initial installation. Storage is based hydro schemes often provide attendant benefits of irrigation, flood control, drinking water supply, navigation, recreation, tourism, etc. It is being located in remote regions leads to development of interior backward areas (education, medical, road communication, telecommunication, etc.)

Hydro takes a back seat

The favourable economics of developing thermal generation coupled with

---

12 http://www.worldbank.org.in/WBSITE/EXTERNAL/COUNTRIES/SOUTHASIAEXT/
INDIAEXTN/0,,contentMDK:21388440~pagePK:141137~piPK:141127~theSite
PK:295584,00.html

difficulty in securing long-term financing presents a substantial roadblock for large-scale hydro development.[13]

Case Study of Sardar Sarovar project on Narmada River:

In India, Narmada and Tapti are the only long rivers that flow west and create estuaries.[14]Narmada River, also known as Rewa, is the fifth largest river in the Indian subcontinent and the third largest river that flows entirely within India after the Ganges and the Godavari. It flows through the states of Madhya Pradesh (1,077 km (669.2 mi)), and Maharashtra, (74 km (46.0 mi)) – (35 km (21.7 mi)) then along the border between Madhya Pradesh and Maharashtra and (39 km (24.2 mi)) and the border between Madhya Pradesh and Gujarat and in Gujarat (161 km (100.0 mi)).

The Narmada River forms the traditional boundary between North India and South India and flows westwards over a length of 1,312 km (815.2 mi) before draining through the Gulf of Cambay (Khambat) into the Arabian Sea, 30 km (18.6 mi) west of Bharuch city of Gujarat. It is one of only three major rivers in peninsular India that run from east to west (largest west flowing river), along with the Tapti river and the Mahi river. It is the only river in India that flows in a rift valley, flowing west between the Satpura and Vindhya ranges. [15]

History of hydro electric project in Narmada waters:

The project took form in 1979 as part of a development scheme to increase irrigation and produce hydroelectricity. India's Narmada Valley Project - a series of 3,200 dams to be built over a century on the Narmada River in the western part of the country - is the country's biggest irrigation scheme. And, according to many environmentalists, it is also India's most controversial. At a cost of Rs. 135 billion, the project will displace more than a million people and submerge 350,000 hectares of forest and 200,000 hectares of cultivated land in exchange for providing irrigation, electricity and the economic opportunities both will bring. As always, development comes with a price; the Narmada Valley Project is under worldwide scrutiny to determine how big its human and environmental price will be.[16]

---

13 *www.sardarprojects.com/sardar_power.html*

14 http://en.wikipedia.org/wiki/Major_rivers_of_India,

15 http://en.wikipedia.org/wiki/Narmada_River

16 http://www.veenago.com/nonfiction/Narmada_dam.pdf

After India's independence in 1947, the river became the inevitable source of inter-state water disputes, with each of the three states proposing their own schemes to harness its irrigation and power potential. The Narmada Water Dispute Tribunal was set up in 1969 to distribute these river resources equitably among the states.

Of these, the largest and most important are the Sardar Sarovar and Narmada Sagar dams, approved by the Indian federal government in April 1987. To assist the project, the World Bank came forward with a loan of Rs. 7 billion, of which the sum of Rs. 650 million has already been given to the government.[17] The rest is stalled because of the outcry from environmentalists and social workers. This is not the first controversy over major development works in India; the 1980s saw a number of people's movements protesting against the building of big dams and hydroelectric projects. Despite the opposition and stalemate on the loan, work on the dam sites continues.

Issues over Sardar Sarovar Dam:

The Supreme Court of India gave a green signal for the dam's height to be raised to 88m (289ft) from the initial of 80m (260) in February 2009.In October 2000 again, in a 2 to 1 majority judgment in the Supreme Court, the government was allowed to construct the dam up to 90m (300 ft).In May 2002, the Narmada Control Authority approved increasing the height of the dam to 95m (312 ft). In March 2004, the authority allowed a 15m (49 ft) height increase to 110m (360 ft). In March 2006, the Narmada Control Authority gave clearance for the height of the dam to increase from 110.64m (363.0 ft) to 121.92m (400.0 ft). This came after 2003 when the Supreme Court of India refused to enlarge the height of the dam again.[18]

The Supreme Court decision

The Supreme Court gave clearance for the height to be increased to 121.92m (400 ft), but in the same judgment Mr. Justice Bharucha gave directions to Madhya Pradesh and Maharashtra (the Grievance Redressal Authorities of Gujarat) that before further construction begins, they should certify (after inspection) that all those displaced by the raise in height of 5 metres have already been satisfactorily rehabilitated, and also that suitable vacant land

---

17 ibid

18 http://en.wikipedia.org/wiki/Sardar_Sarovar_Dam

for rehabilitating them is already in the possession of the respective states. This process shall be repeated for every successive five metre increase in height.[19]

Gains from Sardar Sarovar Project [20]

Irrigation:

The project will provide irrigation facilities to 18.45 lac ha. of land, covering 3112 villages of 73 talukas in 15 districts of Gujarat. It will also irrigate 75,000 ha. of land in the strategic desert districts of Barmer and Jallore in Rajasthan and 37,500 ha. in the tribal hilly tract of Maharashtra through lift. About 75% of the command area in Gujarat is drought prone while entire command (75,000 ha.) in Rajasthan is drought prone. Assured water supply will soon make this area drought proof.

Drinking water supply

A special allocation of 0.86 MAF of water has been made to provide drinking water to 135 urban centres and 8215 villages (45% of total 18144 villages of Gujarat) within and out-side command in Gujarat for present population of 18 million and prospective population of over 40 million by the year 2021. All the villages and urban centres of arid region of Saurashtra and Kachchh and all "no source" villages and the villages affected by salinity and fluoride in North Gujarat will be benefited. Water supply requirement of several industries will also be met from the project giving a boost to all-round production

Power

There will be two power houses viz. river bed power house and canal head power house with an installed capacity of 1200 MW and 250 MW respectively. The power would be shared by three states - Madhya Pradesh - 57%, Maharashtra - 27% and Gujarat 16%. This will provide useful peaking power to the western grid of the country which has very limited hydel power production at present. A series of micro hydel power stations are also planned on the branch canals where convenient falls are available.

---

19 *dictionary.sensagent.com/narmada+dam.../en-en/ - United States*

20 http://www.sardarsarovardam.org/Client/ContentPage.aspx

Flood Protection

It will also provide flood protection to riverine reaches measuring 30,000 ha. covering 210 villages and Bharuch city and a population of 4.0 lakh in Gujarat.

Wild Life

It is also proposed to develop wild life sanctuaries viz. "Shoolpaneshewar wild life sanctuary" on left Bank, Wild Ass Sanctuary in little Rann of Kutch, Black Buck National Park at Velavadar, Great Indian Bustard Sanctuary in Kutch, Nal Sarovar Bird Sanctuary and Alia Bet at the mouth of the river.

Additional Production

SSP would generate 5,000 million units of electricity. On completion, annual additional agricultural production would be Rs. 1600 crores, power generation Rs. 400 crores and water supply Rs. 175 crores, aggregating about Rs. 2175 crores every year equivalent to about Rs. 6.0 crores a day.

Environmental concerns:

Satellite data show that India is losing 1.3 million hectares of forest land every year. Sardar Sarovar dam will submerge 13,744 hectares of forest land; it does not include the thousands of hectares needed to build housing for the staff and other construction facilities. The federal Department of Environment and Forests originally stated that for every hectare of forest destroyed for dam construction, an equivalent amount of non-forest land had to be afforested. Replanting on degraded forest land was decided due to the scarcity of land for cultivation. But in the environmentalist opinion they were not satisfy because they say that reforestation cannot replace a natural forest and its values. They also claim that it will affect the wildlife and the tribal population living over those areas.

The environmentalists were more worried about the fate of the existing ecosystem which is already facing serious issues like climate change, rise in sea water level, ozone layer depletion etc., With the submerging of forest land, a wealth of flora and fauna will simply disappear. There are no forest corridors enabling wildlife to cross over from the submerged areas to other forested regions since the patches of forest are surrounded by agricultural and barren land.

Once the dams flood the land, the animals will either drown or be driven into the fields where they could destroy crops. The Sardar Sarovar and Narmada Sagar areas now shelter Panthers, Tigers, Sloth Bears, Antelopes, Barking and Spotted Deer, Sambars, Black Buck, Wild Boar, Porcupines, Wildcats, Foxes, Hyenas, Wolves, Black Langurs, Flying Squirrels, Rare Reptiles, Marsh Crocodiles and Freshwater Turtles. Their future is in question, along with that of large numbers of birds, including the Indian Parakeet, the Rose-Ringed Parakeet, the Grey Partridge, Jungle Fowls, Quails, Eagles, Babblers, Green Pigeons, Common Mynahs, Paradise Flycatchers, Bulbuls, Kingfishers, Vultures, Cattle Egrets, Herons and Woodpeckers.[21] There is a possibility of earth quakes, increased siltation, water logging and salinity, and a higher increase of disease.

There is a major geological fault at the Sardar Sarovar site according to Dr. Herbert Tiedemann, a Swiss engineering consultant who has studied the Narmada Valley Project. Contrary to project authorities, he believes the fault cannot be plugged with cement and so remains a permanent threat. Another expert at the National Geological Research Institute, who wishes to remain anonymous, says that an earthquake of Magnitude 6 could occur in the Narmada River basin. Both arguments receive support in a report issued by the fourth meeting of the Dam Review Panel. The report says, 'An earthquake of the magnitude of 6.5 could occur anywhere in the Narmada-Sone-Damodar... [and] filling the reservoir might cause the earthquake to occur sooner.' The annual rate of siltation per 100 km of catchment area of the Narmada Sagar dam is estimated at 5.62 hectometres. Siltation will shorten the dam's life span and limit its economic viability. A study by the Bangalore-based Indian Institute of Science concludes that at least 100,000 hectares of the irrigated land will be affected by severe water logging as well as salinisation of the soil.[22]

Alternative plan:

The environmentalist suggests that if the height of the Sardar Sarovar dam is reduced from 140 to 129 meters, 90 per cent of the population need not be relocated and 80 per cent of the agricultural land would not be submerged. Thousands of hectares of forest and agricultural land would

21 http://www.scribd.com/doc/48497966/Major-Differences-Between-Small-amp-Large-Hydro

22 *www.veenago.com/nonfiction/**Narmada**_dam.pdf*

be saved. The other two options that environmentalists suggest are lift irrigation and small scale reservoirs. It is estimated that the average cost of lift irrigation is less than Rs.10,000 per hectare, while canal building for reservoirs averages Rs. 25,850 for the same area.[23] In terms of water conservation and efficiency, single purpose reservoirs are by far the best option because they are connected to each other and to diversions from rivers and streams.

Suggestions by World Bank:

The World Bank has been engaged in hydropower project in India since the 1950s. Hydropower projects had some complex challenges. Therefore, the bank along with the Indian government and the international community experienced certain lessons about what works and what doesn't work in such projects. These include:

- Careful selection of the site and appropriate engineering design

- Solid initial investigation, especially regarding geological conditions

- Strong and competent implementing agencies

- Continued and substantive consultations with stakeholders

- Early attention to social and environmental aspects of projects, in particular mitigating the negative social and environmental impacts of the project

- Appropriate financing and tariff design that is critical to the financial sustainability of projects with long gestation periods

These lessons have now been incorporated into the Bank's operational policies and implementation practices in the sector.[24]

Conclusion

Although the project has environmental concerns the whole project cannot be stopped. The project is still under construction due to the cry

---

23 ibid

24 http://www.worldbank.org.in/WBSITE/EXTERNAL/COUNTRIES/SOUTHASIAEXT/
INDIAEXTN/0,,contentMDK:21388713~pagePK:141137~piPK:141127~theSite
PK:295584,00.html

of several environmentalists. If we see the energy requirement of India it is clear that the India is starving for energy in order to meet the requirements and hence, the bigger projects are more vulnerable to environmental security. Therefore it is better to shift proposals to a smaller scale because the smaller projects too can used to meet the energy requirement of rural areas. Both Energy security and Environment security are like two sides of the same coin - therefore no one can ignore one so it is better to go with the environment and at the same time the energy should not be wasted. Therefore the Sardar Sarover project issue should be critically examined and all the factors which were decided by the Supreme Court should satisfy the environmentalists' view because the environment has a much higher position when compared to the country's energy security issue, even though energy issues cannot be neglected.

XIII

Gulf of Mannar - A Case of Marine Environmental Degradation

- Udhaya Kumar

Introduction

The earth is mostly covered with water giving it the name, the Blue Planet. This vast expanse also consists of a variety of plants, animals and other organisms making it the most bio diverse area in the world. Not only do the oceans play an important role in regulating the earth's climate, but they also support human sustenance. The demographic map of the world shows much of the world's population living "within 60 km of the coastline and use of the coastline for their livelihood. [1] This dependency has resulted in extreme anthropogenic intervention in the ocean's health. Pollution, in particular, has increased the salinity of soil along the coasts, raised the temperature of water in some areas resulting in warmer surroundings unfit for most marine life and drastically changed even the deep sea environment.

India's case is interesting. It is listed as one of the 12 mega biodiversity countries in the world making it one of the richest in terms of variety of life within its borders. However, it also contains several "hotspots" or highly endangered eco-regions of the world. An ecological hotspot is an area which has atleast 1500 plant species as endemic and has lost more than 70% of its primary vegetation. With one of the longest coastlines and nearly 2.172 million sq kms of Exclusive Economic Zone, it boasts of a very wide range of coastal ecosystems such as estuaries, lagoons, mangroves, backwaters, salt marshes, rocky coasts, sandy stretches and coral reefs[2].

---

1   http://www.oceansatlas.org/servlet/CDSServlet?status=ND0zNTE4JjY9ZW4mMzM9MK
    iYzNz1rb3M~

2   http://www.mangrovesforthefuture.org/countries/members/india/

The Value of Marine Ecosystem

Apart from supplying nourishment, the oceans of the world are a source of transport and a rich untapped resource of hydrocarbons like oil and gas and other minerals, a climate regulator and recreation. Marine fisheries account for 85% of the total fish caught around the world. "Maritime shipping moves over 80% of the world's merchandise trade around the world."[3] The marine ecosystem includes oceans, salt marsh and intertidal ecology, estuaries and lagoons, mangroves and coral reefs, the deep sea and the sea floor. It is called an ecosystem as the plant and animal life support each other.

The marine environment is facing a number of pressures, arising out of the needs of people, and the multiple uses that coastal and marine areas can be put to. These pressures contribute to the depletion of marine resources and degradation of the marine environment. Increased loss of coastal and marine biodiversity components over the last few decades has been of great marine environment concern. Environmental changes, overexploitation and habitat loss are among the main causes of species loss.[4]

Gulf of Mannar - An Overview

The coastline of Tamil Nadu has a length of about 1076 km and constitutes about 15% of the total coastal length of India. It stretches along the Bay of Bengal, Indian Ocean and Arabian Sea[5]. Tamil Nadu's coast consists of three biosphere reserves - the focus in this article is on the Gulf of Mannar.

The Gulf of Mannar is a marine ecosystem, which includes coral reefs, salt marshes, algae communities, mangroves, and sea grasses, among many others. Forests of dry broadleaves can also be found throughout the buffer zones. The climate of the region is that of a tropical one, with high temperatures and heavy rainfall. The tides of the region are also considered to be rapid. The oceans have periods of calm in the fall, but are often

---

3   Prof. AN. Subramanian, Introduction: Marine environment, p.29 http://ocw.unu. edu/international-network-on-water-environment-and-health/unu-inweh-course-1- mangroves/Marine-Environment.pdf

4   http://envfor.nic.in/divisions/ic/wssd/doc2/ch11.pdf

5   State of the Environment Report 2005, Government of Tamil Nadu, Department of the Environment, p.40 http://www.environment.tn.nic.in/SoE/images/CoastalandMarine. pdf

choppy in late spring and through summer due to storms. Inland on the coastal plains, the wind velocity is usually high, which causes the tides to occasionally be irregular.

The Gulf of Mannar is made up of about 21 islands lying off the coast of Tamil Nadu along the 140 km stretch between Tuticorin and Rameswaram and spread over an area of 10,500sq km teeming with marine life. The Gulf of Mannar Biosphere Reserve is located on the south eastern tip of India and is near Sri Lanka. It was declared a biosphere reserve in 1989.

The Gulf of Mannar Biosphere Reserve is known for its vast coral reefs, mangroves, and lagoons. The majority of the ecosystem is aquatic, but there is a small portion based on land. Most of the land based ecosystem is found on the small islets littered throughout the gulf. There are many dry deciduous plants and forests found on land. The mangroves house many different species. The mangroves along the swampy islets and creeks between islands are ideal feeding grounds mullets, prawns, marine reptiles and nesting grounds for several species of terns.[6] The coastal lagoons making up the biosphere serve as nurseries for shellfish and other fish.

The Gulf of Mannar has a rich coral reef ecosystem. Coral reefs are considered as one of the most productive ecosystem resources on earth. It also provides shelter to many plants and animals. The coral provides crevices for fish, plants, and other animals to make their homes, breed, or find protection within. The reefs here are fringing reefs that grow in shallower water where they get lots of sunlight. They can be found directly off the shoreline and are extraordinarily diverse in colour and build. These reefs are delicate and grow slowly. Much of the fringe reef is made up of coral called "Hermatypes". The rest are non-reef-building coral called "Ahermatypes" which weaken the reef. There are over 117 species of coral found in these reefs, and is home to more than 3,600 species of plants and animals.

Some of the animals that can be found on the islands and coastal areas, found are Jungle Cat, Indian Tree Shrew, Spotted Deer, Grey Heron, Black Ibis, Spotted Crane, Common Kingfisher, Pied Kingfisher, Swallow,

---

6   V.K.Dhargalkar, A.G.Untawale, Marine biosphere reserves- Need of the 21st century, *Journal of Environmental Biology*, 1991, p.171 http://drs.nio.org/drs/ bitstream/2264/3181/2/J_Environ_Biol_1991_169.pdf

Common Indian Crocodile, and the Common Sand Boa. Many other animals like Smooth Indian Otter, Honey Badger, Blue Whale, Finner Whale, Sei Whale, Common Dolphin, Little Indian Porpoise, Sea Cow, five different types of tortoise, salmon, and heckle reside in the gulf itself. Unique organisms called "balanoglossus" also known as the "Living Fossil" are also found here. They serve as a link between invertebrates and vertebrates live here. Living among these creatures one can also find sea grasses. The Gulf of Mannar is home to one of the highest concentrations of sea grass species in India. These sea grass beds are some of the largest remaining in the area. They act as feeding grounds to many sea dwelling creatures like Dugongs, Sea Turtles, Dolphins, and Sharks. Different sea turtle species make these sea grasses their homes and breeding grounds. Whales have been sighted swimming through the area. Two different species of dolphin, Spinner and Bottlenose, have been known to frolic through the sea grass, and have even been caught in fishing nets on various occasions. The rich variety of resources of these ecosystems is now threatened due to human intervention and other factors.

Constituent Islands

The 21 islands (see figure-1) of Gulf of Mannar are divided into four groups namely Mandapam, Keezhakarai, Vembar and Tuticorin due to the proximity of islands to these locations.

	Island	Area
Mandapam Group	Shingle	12.69 ha
	Krusadai	65.80 ha
	Pullivasal	9.95 ha
	Poomarichan	16.58 ha
	Manoli	25.90 ha
	Manoliputti	2.34 ha
	Musal	129.04 ha

	Island	Area
Keezhakarai Group	Mulli	10.20 ha
	Valai	10.15 ha
	Talairi	75.15 ha
	Appa	8.63 ha
	Poovarasanpatti	0.25 ha
	Valimunai	6.72 ha
	Anaipar	1.00 ha
Vembar Group	Island	Area
	Nallathanni	110.00 ha
	Pulivinichalli	6.12 ha
	Upputhanni	29.94 ha
Tuticorin Group	Island	Area
	Karaichalli	16.46 ha
	Vilanguchalli	0.95 ha
	Kasuwar	19.50 ha
	Van	16.00 ha

Figure 1: The Islands of Gulf of Mannar

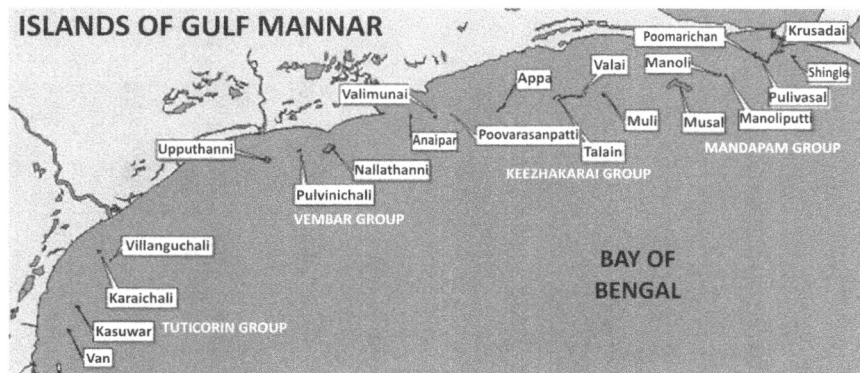

Source:http://www.indiancoastguard.nic.in/Indiancoastguard/NOSDCP/
Marine% 20Environment%20Security/gom.pdf

Major Ecosystems

The Gulf of Mannar is endowed with three distinct Marine ecosystems namely Coral ecosystem, Seagrass ecosystem and Mangrove ecosystem. Most of the islands have luxuriant growth of mangroves on their shorelines and wet regions. The sea bottom of the inshore area around the islands is carpeted with Seagrass beds. Highly productive fringing and patch coral reefs surround the islands and are often referred to as underwater hot rainforest and treasure house for marine ornamental fishes. All these ecosystems make Gulf of Mannar a unique large marine ecosystem in the Indian subcontinent[7].

Coral Reefs

In the Gulf of Mannar both fringing and patch coral reefs occur. While the Hermatypic corals build primary reef formation with the help of calcareous algae in shallow sea, secondary reefs are found in deeper water. A greater expanse of living coral reefs is found in the eastern side of the islands of the Gulf of Mannar Islands. The northern and western sides have been corroded by human exploitation. The Government of Tamil Nadu, for instance, has banned the quarrying of massive corals; only dead corals

---

7   E Kumaraguru.A. K. Sundaramahalingam.A, 2001, Socioeconomic Status of Coral Reefs Resources Users of Pamban Region. Gulf of Mannar, South India (1&2).

on landward sides can be extracted under a lease.[8]

Figure 2: Coral reef and Seagrass areas around the islands of Gulf of Mannar

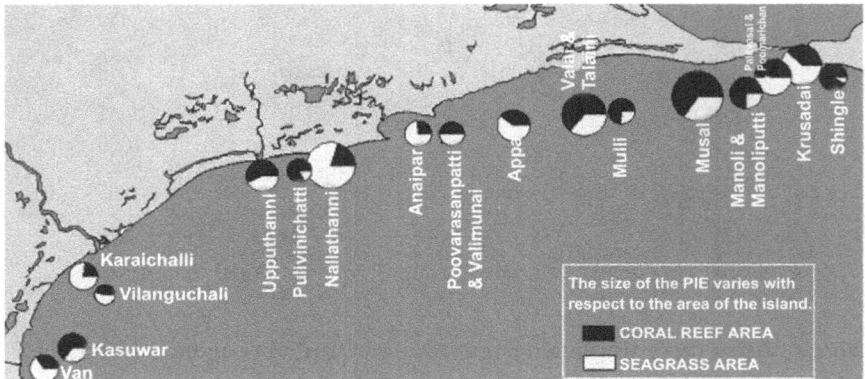

Source: http://www.indiancoastguard.nic.in/Indiancoastguard/NOSDCP/Marine
%20Environment%20Security/gom.pdf

Seagrass Ecosystem

Seagrasses are marine plants that act as breeding and nursery grounds for many epiphytic fauna and feeding grounds for sea cow (*Dugong dugong*). Seagrass roots bind sediments and prevent erosion. Of the 52 species of Seagrasses recorded worldwide, 12 species are found in Gulf of Mannar.

Mangrove Ecosystem

Mangroves are salt tolerant "forest ecosystem" that supports marine fisheries and protect the coastal zones, thus helping the marine coastal economy and environment. The mangrove ecosystems are biologically productive and ecologically sensitive.

The dominant genera were Avicennia, Rhizophora, Bruguiera, Lumnitzera, Ceriops and Pemphis. Pemphis acidula is found in all the islands.

---

8 Anuradha Sawhney, Underworld, Juanuary 30, 2012 http://wrd.mydigitalfc.com/ knowledge/underworld-427

Pearl Banks

The pearl banks are concentrated in the Pandiyan thivu, Van thivu, Upputhanni tivu and Nallathanni tivu. Normally they occur in depths between 10 - 20 m. The pearl culture industry for artificial propagation of pearls has been established. Other molluscs are also found in abundance.

Other Fauna

A variety of marine invertebrates are found in abundance in this area. The Krusadai Island in this region is commonly known as "The Paradise of Biologists". The seacow *Dugong dugong* is found in this area. It is an endangered species and has to be conserved.

Fishery Resources

Marine Capture fisheries are the major economic activity in Gulf of Mannar. In a total area of 15000 sq.km of EEZ in the Gulf of Mannar commercial fishing is done in about 5500 sq.km within 50m depth[9]. Some 441 species have so far been recorded in Gulf of Mannar. Gulf of Mannar is one of the best regions in the Indian subcontinent in fish biodiversity richness.

The chief fisheries are the Pelagic Sardines, Seer Fish, Tunas, Mackerel, Sharks, Carangids, Barracudas, Wolf Herring, Full and Half Beaks, the Demersal Perches such as Sweetlips, Groupers, Rock-Cods, Snappers, Goat Fishes, Croakers, Sharks, Rays, Skates, Coral Fishes, Threadfin, Breams, Silverbellies, the shell fishes like shanks, Squids, Cuttlefish, Shrimps, Crabs and Lobsters. Most of these resources are commercially exploited by mechanised trawlers. Shore seines, boat seines, trawl nets and hooks and lines are the principal gear operated.

Different types of nets and traps are used for a variety of fish. For example, Chala Valai is used for small pelagic fishes, Paru Valai for perches and tunas, Thirukkai Valai for rays, Nandu Valai for Crabs and Lobster, etc. Traps are used to catch reef dwellers such as Groupers, Snappers, Lobsters, etc. Shrimp and fish trawl nets are operated to capture a variety of Demersal fishes such as Silverbellies, Carangids, Perches, Pomfrets, Goatfishes, Rays, Prawns, etc. Among hooks and lines, longlines are used

---

9   Tune Usha, T.Shunmugaraj and S.Sundaramoorthy, , ICMAM, Project Directorate, Dept. Of Ocean Development Anna University, Chennai P.19 http://www.indiancoastguard. nic.in/Indiancoastguard/NOSDCP/Marine%20Environment%20Security/gom.pdf

for hooking Perches, Catfish, Sharks, etc and troll lines for Scombroids, fishes, sharks, carangids, etc. Depending on the tide and fishing season, Kalamkatti Valai is operated during night times on the shores of the islands for catching shore fishes and Mullets.

Only about 200 out of 441 species are of commercial importance. They are used either as food for human consumption or as fishery by-products like fish oils from sardines, liver oil from sharks and skates, isinglass from catfish, eels, threadfins, processed fish skin from sharks, rays and bigger groupers and fish meal from small-sized low-value fish for use in cattle and poultry farms.

Dependence Demographics

There could be as many as 125 fishing villages dependent on the fishery resources in the Gulf of Mannar area. There are 35,000 active fishers who depend on the resources in the Gulf of Mannar area, especially on fishing, and collection of seaweed and other marine resources. There are 5,000 fisherwomen who are dependent on seaweed collection in and around the 21 islands, besides 25,000 fishermen who dive to collect sea cucumbers.

Major threats to Biodiversity

The use of mechanised boats and trawlers, the mining of corals, using dynamite to fish and commercial fishing of special fauna like sea fans, shanks, sea cucumbers, sea horses, and endangered species like dugongs and turtles have led to marine degradation or a significant decrease in the quality of marine life in the region.

The quarrying of live and dead coral boulders is the main issue. Coral reefs off the Tuticorin group of islands have been obliterated with 15,000 tons of boulders and 10,000 tons of coral remains being removed every year. Coral mining for lime, fishing, pollution, and shell collecting for commercial sale are human activities that have impacted the reefs and continued their deterioration. Coral diseases caused by bacteria, viruses, protozoa, and fungi cause lesions and tissue loss in the coral. Stress on the environment is the main reason for these disease-causing bacteria. The proposed Sethu Samudram channel is feared to lead to further deterioration of coral reefs. The traditional activity of Trap fishing in the Gulf has damaged the reefs that act as breeding grounds for species such as groupers, breams and grunters. The over fishing is now leading to decreasing amount of fish being harvested. With so many relying on these fish to make a living, they have been far over harvested, and the waterways have had no time to replenish themselves. This biosphere reserve is also a popular region for pearl fisheries. "As a direct result of the great demand for pearls, the abundance of pearl oysters has declined as well"[10]. The Olive Ridley turtle eggs which are laid seasonally on the sandy beaches have suffered heavy destruction due to island based stake-net operations. The turtles that come for breeding are also caught in the drift nets. Besides, this area also has been identified as an important feeding ground for Green turtle and Hawks Bill turtle.

Environmental Concerns

Let us now see some of the environmental concerns which affect the bio reserve in this region.

Sewage Disposal

Sewage is discharged into the oceans all over the world mostly from urban settlements. The raw sewage contains higher concentrations of organic particulate matter, toxic and heavy metals. The main sources of sewage are the coastal outfall located near the cities. Also the increasing shipping activities also add higher concentration of sewage to the harbours and shipping routes. Many rivers transport sewage from the inner regions of the land. This sewage disposal near the Gulf of Mannar region creates a major threat to the ecosystem of this region.

Industrial Pollution

The location of industrial chemical industries, the Tuticorin Thermal Power Station and other lime based units along the coast has led to discharge mostly untreated ending in the Gulf has polluted the area. In fact, there is complete absence of flora and fauna in areas near the point of discharge.[11] Seafood processing plants produce effluents containing

---

10 E. G. Silas, S. Mahadevan and K. N. Nayar, Marine parks, Sanctuaries, Reserves, Zoos and Oceanariums, in B.G.Silas ed., Proceedings of the symposium on endangered marine animals and parks, Cochin 12-16 Jan 1985 http://eprints.cmfri.org.in/2361/2/article_67.pdf

11 J.K.P. Edward, G. Mathews, K.D. Raj, T. Thinesh, J. Patterson, J. Tamelander, D.Wilhelmsson, Coral reefs of Gulf of Mannar, India - signs of resilience, *Proceedings of the 12th International Coral Reef Symposium, Cairns, Australia,*

poisonous hydrogen sulphide and antibacterial agents like Cuttle Fish ink which affect the waters.[12]

Oil

Oil in the form of crude oil and other substances enter the oceans. The transportation of crude by waterways, offshore drilling for oil, presence of oil terminals, refineries, discharge of oil on land and its runoff and accidental spilling of oil from tankers and ships are the main causes. These have long-term and widespread effect on marine life. The birds and other animals are affected by the oil which smears on their feathers and skin. The sea currents might drag the oil spill to other areas and affect places that are not otherwise affected.[13]

Shipbuilding and related pollution

Ship building, ship breaking and repairs done on ships can also cause pollution. The antifouling paint on a ship is a major polluter[14]. When ships are dismantled due to aging or being unfit to be used it is called ship breaking. This is an environmentally dangerous activity. It releases harmful compounds like asbestos that are harmful for humans and fragile marine life. Direct dumping of hazardous waste into oceans is another polluter. In the event of the Sethu Samudram project being completed, the increased shipping traffic would also mean possibility of spillage, accidents and more pollution.

Conclusion

The marine ecosystem in the Gulf of Mannar region needs to be protected by declaring areas of coral reefs, mangroves and sea grass that are closed for fishing. Strict implementation of rules and laws already in place should

---

9-13 July 2012, http://www.icrs2012.com/proceedings/manuscripts/ICRS2012_18F_3.pdf

12 Arvind Kumar, C.P.Bohra and L.K.Singh, *Environment, Pollution and management*, APH Publishing Corp., New Delhi, 2003, p. 480

13 For a detailed discussion on the types of pollutants and their effects on marine life see, N.V.Vinithkumar, Marine Pollution - A perspective, montoring and control in india, http://www.niot.res.in/m5/mbic/me/data/me.pdf

14 Marina Valentukevičienė, Evelina Brannvall, Marine pollution: An overview, *Geologija*, 2008, no.1(61), p.19 www.lmaleidykla.lt/ojs/index.php/geologija/article/download/.../535

also be followed. Continuous monitoring of the levels of pollution along the coast needs to be spruced up. The creation of awareness among stakeholders specifically the coastal communities will go a long way in mitigating the problem. These activities must involve the local community, schools and other educational institutions and NGOs. The Department of Forests and the Department of Fisheries may take steps to stop anchoring of vessels on coral reefs, pair trawling, and dynamite fishing.[15] Already there has been an increase in the live coral cover mainly due to the halting of coral mining in 2005. There have also been efforts at coral reef monitoring[16]. The crossing of the International maritime border line is often cited as the reason for Sri Lankan Navy firing on Indian fishermen. While there is assurance from the central government that no attack occurred in the Indian territory, the fact that there has been loss of lives is a point of concern.[17] The basic issue perhaps is that there is no availability of fish in Indian waters due to over fishing forcing the fishermen to venture into neighbouring territory. The security implications of such a scenario need to be looked in very seriously.

15 Girija Phadke and Khaimesh Saigal, Management of Coral Reefs in Gulf of Mannar, http://aquafind.com/articles/Coral_Reef_Mannar.php

16 V.K.Melkani, *Status of Coral Reefs in the Gulf of Mannar Region, Tamilnadu, Southeast Asia,* Gulf of Mannar Biosphere Reserve Trust, Publication No.18, December 2008, p.11 p. http://www.gombrt.org/publications/154-status-of-coral-reefs-in-the-gulf-of-mannar-region.html

17 85 fishermen killed by Sri Lanka in 10 years: Govt, *The Times of India,* August 18, 2012 http://articles.timesofindia.indiatimes.com/2012-08-18/madurai/33260802_1_international-maritime-boundary-line-indian-fishermen-imbl

XIV

Resource Conflict - A Case Study of The Cauvery Water Issue

- R Sudhakar

Water, water everywhere, all the boards did shrink,

Water, water everywhere, not a drop to drink[1]

(The Rime of the Ancient Mariner – Samuel Taylor Coleridge)

Introduction

The fast depletion of natural resources, resulting in the scarcity of resources and the degradation of the environment and the increasing conflict over resources within and between the states has meant a growing concern for environmental security all over the world. Also, in recent years it has been widely accepted that environmental security is an important aspect of the national security[2]. It may be understood that man has been imposing his needs and demands on the environment since the time of evolution. Therefore, the relationship between human beings and the environment has always been significant and delicate.

The indiscriminate attitudes of individuals and even the governments of various countries towards the environment, the self-interest, over utilisation of resources, etc., have caused scarcity of resources and their fast depletion as well as degradation of the environment. This has caused

---

1   http://www.hartenshield.com/water_water.html

2   B.C. Upreti, *Environmental Security in South Asia: Dimensions, Issues and Problems*, pp.1

conflicts and violence among and between the states[3]. The scarcity of resources may give rise to a conflict over the remaining resources. There are many evidences in the world history of resource conflicts and the perfect example of resource conflict within a country is the Cauvery river water dispute.

Water as a Source of Conflict

The most important or vital resource for the human beings all over the world is water. There are lots of evidences of conflict over water especially the sharing of river waters. Water covers more than 70% of the earth. It fills the ocean and the rivers; it resides underground and is also present in the air which we breathe. Great civilisations have risen where water was plentiful and have fallen when the supply of water failed. Hence, this is proved by the fact that most of the big cities in the world are situated near the seashore or by the riverbed. Today, more than ever, water is both slave and master to the people[4]. Though population and economies grow exponentially, the amount of freshwater in the world remains roughly the same as it has been throughout history. While the total quantity of water in the world is immense, the vast majority is either saltwater (97.5 percent) or locked up in ice caps (1.75 percent). The amount available for human use is only 0.007 percent of the total, or about 13,500 km^3. It is used extensively in almost all activities of civilised man and it is important to remember that even though our demand for water may increase it is not really possible to easily increase supply.

Water scarcity can and will lead directly to violence or even warfare between and within states; throughout this chapter, it is emphasised that shared water does lead to tensions, threats, and even to some localised violence. Water resources continue to attract considerable attention and have increasingly become a significant feature of the world security environment. In order to locate water in the security continuum, it is necessary to revisit the debate on the traditional and non-traditional aspects of security.

Water scarcity due to ground water depletion is already a major problem. For example, 80% of the 14 perennial rivers in India are

---

3 B.C. Uperti, pp. 3.

4 River Water Sharing and Cauvery Water Dispute, http://legalsutra.org/1452/river-water-sharing-and-cauvery-water-dispute

polluted. Organic pollutants from industrial activities are a major cause of degradation of water quality throughout the region. India, for instance, is the third biggest emitter of organic water pollutants with 1, 651, 250 kg/day[5]. In terms of internal security, river-water issues have, over the last decade or so, become a law and order problem with aggressive protests and threats of violence. In India alone there is lots of river water sharing dispute have come to affect almost all states. Some of the major river water disputes in India include the following:

- Cauvery river water dispute among the Southern states of India

- Krishna river water dispute between Tamil Nadu and Andhra Pradesh

- Mullai Pereyar Dam issues between Tamil Nadu and Kerala

- Narmada river water dispute among Gujarat, Madhya Pradesh and Maharashtra

- Tungabhadra/Almatti water dispute between Karnataka and Andhra Pradesh

- Ravi-Beas water dispute among Punjab, Rajasthan and Jammu and Kashmir

- Godavari water dispute among Maharashtra, Andhra Pradesh, Chhattisgarh and Orissa[6]

It is clear that for India water security is less of inter-state problem. The evaluation, therefore, requires an intra-state perspective (within). The topic is very extensive and there have been multiple cases of inter-state river water disputes in India. Since, Cauvery River water rights have been a source of tension leading to violent expression and instability between Tamil Nadu and Karnataka. The attempt here is to analyse these issues in the context of Cauvery river water dispute between the Southern states of India. It is proposed to deal extensively only with the Cauvery Dispute as it is the most recent one and is the most appropriate dispute to study.

---

5 Utham Kumar Sinha, Water Security: A Discursive Analysis, *Strategic Analysis*, April-June 2005, pp. 325.

6 Bharat Jain, *Waters of Woe-The Fountains of Scared Rivers Flow Upwards*, April 2007, p.3

Brief History of Cauvery River Water Dispute

Before looking the dispute it is essential to see the outline of the River Cauvery, its importance to both the states, historic background of sharing of waters, etc.

Cauvery River Basin

The Cauvery River considered the lifeline of peninsular India is a trans-boundary river. Karnataka, Tamil Nadu, Kerala and Pondicherry are the four riparian states staking claim on the Cauvery waters and of these Karnataka and Tamil Nadu are the major riparian and contending states. The Cauvery Basin extends over an area of 87,900 km^2 which is nearly 2.7% of total geographical area of the country. The basin lies in the states of Tamil Nadu (48,730 km^2), Karnataka (36,240 km^2) and Kerala (2,930 km^2) (See Fig. 1). The Cauvery River rises at Talakaveri on the Brahmagiri range in the Western Ghats in Karnataka at an elevation of about 1341m and flows for about 800 km before its outfall into the Bay of Bengal. The important tributaries joining the Cauvery are the Harangi, Hemavati, Shimsha, Arkavathi, Lakshmanathirtha and Honnuhole are the major tributaries joining the river Cauvery in Karnataka and Amaravathi, Noyyal, Bhavani and Kodganaru are the major tributaries of Cauvery in Tamil Nadu. Kabini is from Kerala. The basin can be divided into three parts - the Western Ghats, the Plateau of Mysore and the Delta.

Fig. 1: Cauvery River Basin*

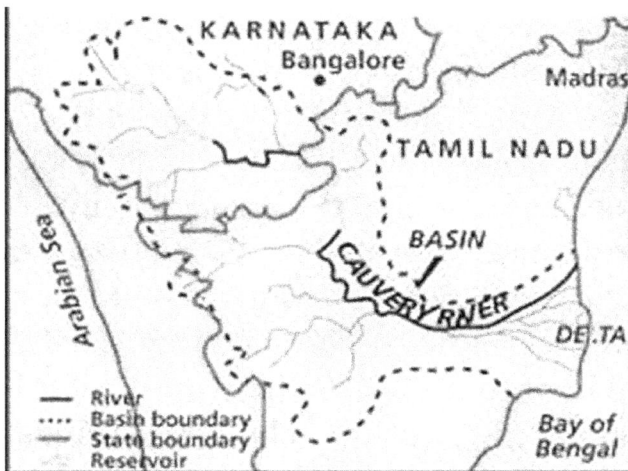

*Source: http://nabinadas13.wordpress.com/category/urbanisation

The main structures and projects on the river include:

➢ Krishnarajasagar dam of Mysore in Karnataka

➢ Hydro-electric project near the island of Sivasmudram in Karnataka

➢ Mettur reservoir and Grand Anicut in Tamil Nadu

The delta area is the most fertile region in the basin. The principal soil types found in the basin are black soil, red soil, laterite, alluvial soil, forest soil and mixed soil. Red soil occupies large areas in the basin. Alluvial soils are found in the delta areas. An average annual surface water potential of 21.4 km^3 has been assessed in this basin. Out of this, only 19.0 km^3 of water can be utilised.

Cultivable area in the basin is about 5.8 million ha, which is 3.0% of the total cultivable area of the country. Present use of surface water in the basin is 18.0 km^3. Live storage capacity in the basin has increased significantly since independence. From just about 4.1 km^3 in the pre-plan period, the total live storage capacity of the completed projects has increased to 7.4 km^3. In addition, a storage quantity of over 0.3 km^3 would be created on completion of projects under construction. An additional storage to the tune of over 0.3 km^3 would become available on execution of projects under consideration. The hydropower potential of the basin has been assessed as 1359 MW at 60% load factor.[7]

Importance of Cauvery to Karnataka

This state is one of the important economies of southern India. Bangalore, its capital city and it is one of the fastest growing cities in India. Growing high tech sectors are centred in Bangalore such as pharmaceutical and chemical industries. Due to the 'industry friendly' atmosphere in Karnataka, major international firms are finding it a beneficial location for business. International firms in Karnataka include Hewlett-Packard, IBM, Kentucky Fried Chicken, and Cargill Corporation.

This industrialisation is not without consequence for Karnataka. These firms and industry sectors require a large amount of water, a scare resource

---

7 K.Lenin Babu, K.L. Prakash, S.K. Pattanayak, E.T. Puttaiah, R.K. Somashekar, *Possible enhanced conflict situations on account of climate change on account of water sharing: A case study of three States of India,* International Workshop on Human Security and Climate Change, Oslo, 21-23 June 2005,

in this region. In times of weak monsoons, the fragile water situation in Southern India is exposed. In order to preserve the industrial growth and protect commercial use in Karnataka, local officials ration water to citizens on a rotational basis.

Importance of Cauvery to Tamil Nadu

While temples are the main attraction to Tamil Nadu, agriculture is the primary means of sustenance. Chennai is the capital of Tamil Nadu and it is one of the metro cities in India. Tamil Nadu relies on the Cauvery River to sustain its agricultural needs. Beyond the Cauvery, Tamil Nadu has very few resources for complex irrigation systems to maintain its water supply. Cauvery is the lifeblood of Tamil Nadu's agriculture. The state asserts that water sharing is a national issue that requires the intervention of the Government of India. Hence Cauvery is very important to Tamil Nadu.

Cauvery Water Dispute: A Brief History

Historical Background

The erstwhile state of Mysore was constituted under Article 4 of the Mysore Partition Treaty of 1799, which came about after British-led forces defeated Tippu Sultan at Srirangapatnam, (near Mysore city). Afterwards, it came to the notice of the British officials then that irrigation in the entire Cauvery region was confined to the tank system that needed repairs. However, efforts to repair them were met with protests in Tanjore district of Madras presidency, even though there was no major obstruction to the flow of Cauvery. This led to the first discord over sharing Cauvery water which took place in 1807.

Later the Mysore and the Madras governments entered into the 1892 Agreement which relates to all the main and minor rivers in the basin, and it was a general agreement related to the irrigation development in the basin of the interstate river Cauvery alone. The 1924 agreement was then framed and agreed by both Mysore and Madras governments in order to define the terms under which the Mysore government was to construct the Krishnarajasagar dam and to provide for extension of irrigation in both the states utilizing the flows in the river. The basic tenet enshrined in both these agreements is that no injury could be caused to existing irrigation downstream by the construction of new works upstream. It also stipulates that when upstream works are planned, the prior consent of the state government of the lower down area is to be obtained and the rules of regulation so framed as not to make any reduction in supplies to the established irrigation downstream.[8]

The Cauvery Dispute

The core of the Cauvery dispute relates to the re-sharing of waters that are already being fully utilised. Here the two parties to the dispute are Karnataka (old Mysore) and Tamil Nadu (the old Madras Presidency). Between 1968 and 1990, many meetings were held at the ministerial level but no consensus could be reached. The Cauvery Water Dispute tribunal was constituted on June 2, 1990 under the Inter State Water Disputes Act, 1956.[9]

There has been a basic difference between Tamil Nadu on the one hand and the central government and Karnataka on the other in their approach towards sharing of Cauvery waters. The government of Tamil Nadu argued that since Karnataka was constructing the Kabini, Hemavathi, Harangi, and Swarnavathi dams on the river Cauvery and was expanding the irrigation works, Karnataka was unilaterally diminishing the supply of waters to Tamil Nadu, and adversely affecting the prescriptive rights of the already acquired and existing irrigation works in Tamil Nadu. This is essentially because Tamil Nadu has rapidly developed irrigation compared to Karnataka.

The government of Tamil Nadu also maintained that the Karnataka government had failed to implement the terms of the 1892 and 1924 Agreements relating to the use, distribution and control of the Cauvery waters. Tamil Nadu asserts that the entitlements of the 1924 Agreement are permanent. Only those clauses that deal with utilisation of surplus water for further extension of irrigation in Karnataka and Tamil Nadu, beyond what was contemplated in the 1924 Agreement can be changed.

In April 1991, the Supreme Court of the Government of India reassigned a tribunal to settle the dispute as mandated in the Inter-State River Water Disputes Act. Almost 17 years after it was set up, the Cauvery

---

8 Case Study, *Inter-State Water Disputes among the Riparian States: The Case of Peninsular India*, PILDAT Publishers, Islamabad, Pakistan, January 2011, pp.12 (www.pildat.org)

9 Alan Richards & Nirvikar Singh, **Inter State Water Disputes in India: Institutions and Policies**, USA, October 2001 pp. 9. (http://people.ucsc.edu/~boxjenk/indiawater.pdf)

Water Disputes Tribunal in February 2007, gave its final verdict. The following are the highlights of the historic verdict:

- The total availability of water in the Cauvery Basin has been estimated at 740 thousand million cubic feet (tmc).

- Tamil Nadu will get 419 tmcf. This is against its demand of 512 tmcf.

- Karnataka gets 270 tmcf, as against its demand of 465 tmcf.

- Kerala gets 30 tmcf, while Pondicherry has been apportioned 7 tmcf.[10]

Figure-II

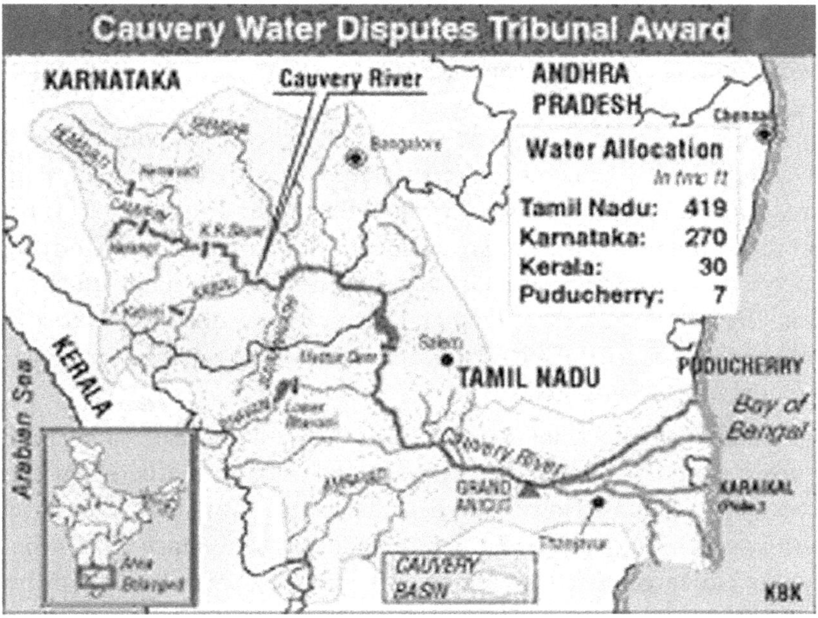

Source: http://www.indianetzone.com/30/water_sharing_river_kaveri_indian_river.htm

---

10 The Report of The Cauvery Water Disputes Tribunal with the decision, volume-V, New Delhi, 2007, pp.202.

Karnataka declined to accept the ruling of the Tribunal. The Government of Karnataka argued that the Tribunal issued a decision that was not implementable. Due to failed monsoons, many parts of Karnataka were left without adequate water supplies. If the government were to release more than 100 tmcf of water to Tamil Nadu, it would be disadvantageous to its own people. Karnataka then went ahead and promulgated an ordinance called the Karnataka Cauvery Basin Irrigation (Protection) Ordinance by means of which it tried to override the interim order of the tribunal which according to Karnataka, the Tribunal had no power to pass.

The rejection of the Tribunal's decision pushed the negotiations back on a downward spiralling path that eventually led to aborted talks. However, water issues seem to only erupt when there is a lack of adequate rain. In 1992, 1993, and 1994, the rain was sufficient to pacify the dispute between Tamil Nadu and Karnataka.

Immediate Cause of the problem

Apparently the immediate context of the conflict is the violation of the 1892 and 1924 agreements by Karnataka by constructing four new dams across the tributaries of Cauvery without the prior permission of the water commission and the central government. The government of Karnataka proceeded with these projects in stages from their own funds under non-plan. The four projects are Harangi, Kabini, Hemavathi and Suvamavathy with the total capacity of total storage capacity of 59.1 tmcf and an irrigation potential of 13.25 lakh acres.[11]

Tamil Nadu does not control any of the Cauvery headwaters, yet it is in possession of the tributaries Bhavana and the Moyar. There is peace in times of good rains. However, when the monsoons fail, violence erupts, from streets of Karnataka and Tamil Nadu to Delhi. Since 1974, when a 50 year-old agreement between the Madras presidency and the princely Mysore state collapsed, the Cauvery River Dispute has been a serious issue. However the immediate cause of the problem is the failure of monsoon and the violation of the verdict by the Karnataka has triggered the problem.

11 www.pildat.org

Conflict Dynamics

*THE CONFLICT DYNAMICS (SCARCITY) MODEL

Population pressure, resource depletion, uneven distribution

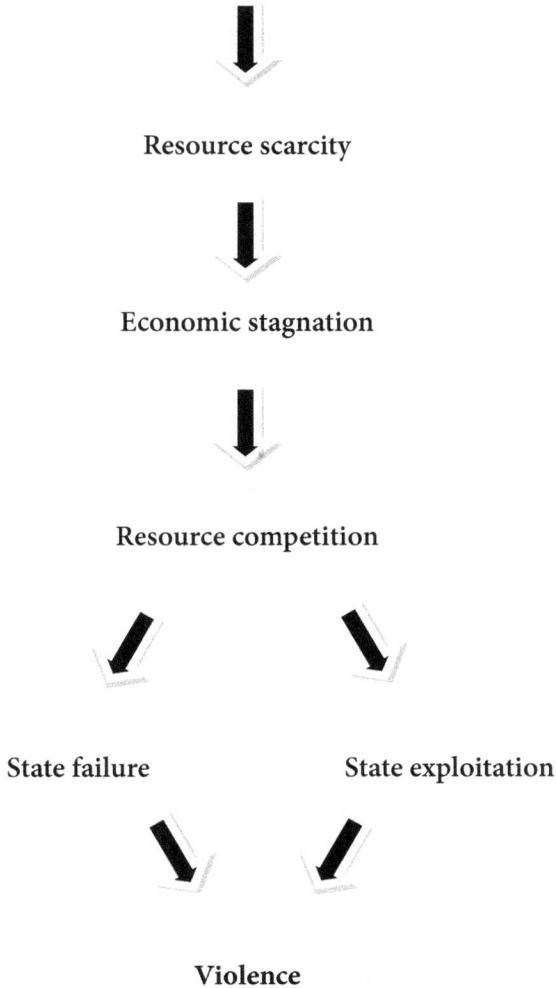

↓

Resource scarcity

↓

Economic stagnation

↓

Resource competition

↙ ↘

State failure   State exploitation

↘ ↙

Violence

*Source: Interpreted from **Henrik Urdal,** *Demographic Aspects of Climate Change, Environmental Degradation and Armed Conflict,* presented to the United Nations Expert Group Meeting on Population, Distribution, Urbanisation, Internal Migration and Development, New York 21-23 January 2008.

Transboundary water disputes have emerged as an increasingly important factor in various spatial levels. They relate to politics and conflicts at the level of a village as much to the economic development of nations and regions sharing common waters. In terms of internal security, river-water issues have, over the last decade or so, become a law and order problem with aggressive protests and threats of violence. The Cauvery River water rights have been a source of tension leading to violent expression and instability between Tamil Nadu and Karnataka. Hence the theoretical analysis of transboundary water disputes conflicts, accordingly, has become an essential part of security studies. Let us see the conflict dynamics in the Cauvery issue between the states of Tamil Nadu and Karnataka.

Since the beginning, human beings are dependent on the natural resources to live and hence the bondage between the human and the environment is obvious. Out of all natural resources the most important and the inevitable thing in human life is water. Sharing Cauvery River water is one of the most important issues in India, the fast increasing of population in the two states results in the more demand of water which leads to rapid depletion of natural resources, as a consequence, the scarcity of resources gives way to the economic stagnation.

Economic stagnation is an important factor behind conflicts for three reasons. First, when the nature of the disputes over water is looked at in depth, it is found that in a majority of cases, the contribution of water to competing economies has been the prime cause of disputes.[12] In the case of Tamil Nadu, agriculture being the largest consumer of water, the majority of trans-boundary water conflicts occur because of the conflicting agricultural water needs of co-riparians. The scarcity of resources leads to unequal distribution and resource completion, Karnataka's unilateral position not to abide by the Supreme Court's decision over the equitable distribution of water and to annul all inter-state river sharing agreements poses a serious threat to the federal nature of the Indian polity and raises an intense debate over the control of resources. Clearly, such noncompliance sets a dangerous trend and creates a retaliatory situation. For example, if Karnataka prevents water from flowing to Tamil Nadu, then the latter can cut the supply of electricity to the former.

---

12 Nilanjan Goash and Jayanta Bandyopadhyay, *A Scarcity value based explanation of trans-boundary water disputes: the case of the Cauvery River Basin in India*, Water Policy 11, 2009, pp.143.

Again in 2002, the rains failed and Karnataka refused to release water to Tamil Nadu. The Chief Minister of Tamil Nadu then began boycotting the meetings of the Cauvery River Water Authority (C.R.A), calling it a toothless body and simultaneously approached the Supreme Court to make Karnataka release the river water. In the C.R.A meeting, the amount of water to be released to Tamil Nadu by Karnataka was reduced. Karnataka then proceeded to begin releasing water to Tamil Nadu but this was once again put to a stop when four farmers jumped into the waters near Kabini to protest Karnataka's decision to release water to Tamil Nadu. It clearly showed Tamil Nadu's failure and the other state's exploitation. In turn, this has created violence between the states. Had this been an issue between countries, it could have resulted in a potential war.

The violence and the issues caused by Cauvery river water dispute between the two riparian states is as follows:

- ➤ In 1991, rioting took place in Karnataka as the leaders of both the states took a confrontationist posture. In 1995-96, poor monsoon heightened tensions and in 2002 curfew was imposed in the town of Mandya as the agitation turned violent.

- ➤ Karnataka refused to release water to Tamil Nadu. Tamil Nadu in turn cut off power to Karnataka from the Neyveli power plant. This motion was supported by some rather prominent members of the Tamil film community who obviously had their own political agenda.

- ➤ An important fact that was not realised was that the grid from Neyveli after entering Karnataka returned to Tamil Nadu and if power to Karnataka were cut then Tamil Nadu would also be affected – infact much more adversely.

- ➤ Even Tamil film super star Rajinikant observed a day's hunger strike in Chennai and called for an amicable solution between the two states.

- ➤ Apart from the delta farmers and different political parties and the state government, have also been quite vocal in protests.

- ➤ The centre of the agitation, this time, was not so much Bangalore as Mysore and Mandya. Not a single day passed without any demonstration, at K.R.Circle in Mysore.

➢ Right from the workers of BEL and Vikrant Tyres to doctors and engineers, from platform vendors to Brahamana Sangha, people from all walks of life have taken to the streets in support of the agitating farmers and it has been spontaneous.[13]

➢ Be it Deve Gowda or S.M.Krishna, the leaders had to jump in to capture the mass sentiments and retain their grip on mass politics in their strongholds of Mandya and Mysore districts. Both these leaders undertook padyatras on the issue, but both had to abandon their 'yatras' mid way fearing the fury of farmers.[14]

➢ There were riots in the city of Bangalore and the people from Tamil Nadu were assaulted and their properties ruined. Tamilians had to return to their state in fear.

➢ The situation in Tamil Nadu has been no less explosive. As a result of this Tamil people retaliated by burning the buses of the Karnataka and damaging the properties of Kannada people. These incidences instigated violence and tension between the two state borders.

➢ Finally, after nearly a month of stalling S.M Krishna tendered an unconditional apology to the Supreme Court and agreed to release the water, simultaneously however the monsoons began and the problem was temporarily solved.

There are several reasons why the negotiations between the two riparian states failed to bring about a consensus:

1) There was a divergence of interest between Karnataka and Tamil Nadu on the question of pursuing negotiations. Karnataka was interested in prolonging the negotiations and upsetting the reference to a tribunal, in order to gain time to complete its new projects.

2) The Cauvery issue became intensely politicised in the 1970s and 1980s. The respective Governments in the two states were run by different political parties and hence this made an ultimate solution more difficult.

3) Ministerial meetings were held at regular intervals, but no attempt

---

13 K.Lenin Babu, K.L. Prakash, S.K. Pattanayak, E.T. Puttaiah, R.K. Somashekar,pp.12
14 Ibid.

was made to generate technical options to share Cauvery water. Expert engineers were not able to work together for a common solution; rather they got involved in party politics.[15]

From the above, it emerges that at the intra-state level, water issues are about better resource management, a need for decentralised approach involving local population and active participation by civil society in the implementation of water sharing projects. One can, from the context of the security debate, place water issues (intra-state level) as one of 'securitisation'.[16]

Conclusion

River water disputes are a problem that India will have to continue to deal with in the near future. As states develop, their needs for river water will increase while the quantity of river water will remain approximately the same. It is important for all states to understand this, so that these disputes do not become a cause of enmity between them. It is important for each state to understand that the objective of other states is to secure water for their needs and not to deprive other states of it. If all states think in this way then it will be possible for them to solve the dispute through a process of negotiation.

The river water dispute clearly outlines that the issue can create a violent conflict and, in times, it may also escalate into a conflict between countries. Conflict is becoming less traditional, increasingly being driven by internal or local pressures, or more subtle issues of poverty and stability. The combination of changes, in water resources and in conflict, suggests that tomorrow's water disputes may look very different from today. Hence this resource issue must be viewed from a more comprehensive environmental security context.

15 http://legalsutra.org/1452/river-water-sharing-and-cauvery-water-dispute
16 Utham Kumar Sinha, pp. 326.

XV

The Dangers of Nuclear Powered Military Vessels In The Indian Ocean Region

- Ramakrishnan Ramani

The Indian Ocean

No country is as fortunate as India to have an 'ocean' named after it. Ever since its independence from the colonial yolk of the British, India has been trying to assert its influence militarily, diplomatically and culturally on the littoral states of the ocean with varying success. Perhaps it is because this country is centrally located among littoral states, probably it has the longest coast line, or maybe due to its ancient reputation as a key trading hub - a source of exotic spices and immense wealth. But

Quick Facts…

- It covers 20% of the Earth's main water surface, which is total of one-fifth of the world's ocean area.

- Zambezi, Shatt al-Arab, Indus, Ganges, Brahmaputra, Jubba and Ayeyarwady River are the major rivers flowing into the Indian Ocean.

- It is the warmest ocean in the world, which is why it has limited marine animal life.

- Beach sands of Indian Ocean are rich in heavy minerals and the offshore deposits are vigorously exploited by bordering nations.

- Suez Canal (Egypt), Bab el Mandeb (Djibouti-Yemen), Strait of Hormuz (Iran-Oman), and Strait of Malacca (Indonesia-Malaysia) are the four main access points to the Indian Ocean.

- Approximately 40% of the world's offshore oil production comes from the Indian Ocean. The Northern Indian Ocean also is the most important transport route for oil as it connects the oil-rich countries of the Middle East Each with Asia. Tankers carry cargo of 17 million barrels of crude oil from the Persian Gulf every day.

- The Indian Ocean gets 20 cm wider every year.

whatever the reason, the name has stuck and continues to be called the Indian Ocean.

This huge expanse of water, covering approximately 20% of the planet's surface is the third largest ocean in the world.[1] It is fenced by Asia on the north, by Arica on the west, by Australia on the East and by Antarctica to the south. Consequently, coastal countries on these continents form the littoral states of the ocean. Continent-wise, these 'Indian Ocean Rim' states are as follows[2]:

Africa: South Africa, Mozambique, Madagascar, French Southern and Antarctic Lands, France (Réunion, Mayotte), Mauritius, Comoros, Tanzania, Seychelles, Kenya, Somalia, Djibouti, Eritrea, Sudan, Egypt

Asia: Egypt (Sinai Peninsula), Israel, Jordan, Saudi Arabia, Yemen, Oman, United Arab Emirates, Qatar, Bahrain, Kuwait, Iraq, Iran, Pakistan, India, Maldives, British Indian Ocean Territory, Sri Lanka, Bangladesh, Burma , Thailand, Malaysia, Singapore Indonesia, Cocos (Keeling) Islands, Christmas Island

Australasia: Ashmore and Cartier Islands, Indonesia, Timor-Leste, Australia

Southern Indian Ocean: Australia Heard Island and McDonald Islands, French Southern and Antarctic Lands

---

1   http://seawifs.gsfc.nasa.gov/OCEAN_PLANET/HTML/oceanography_geography_Indian.html

2   http://en.wikipedia.org/wiki/Indian_Ocean#Bordering_countries_and_territories

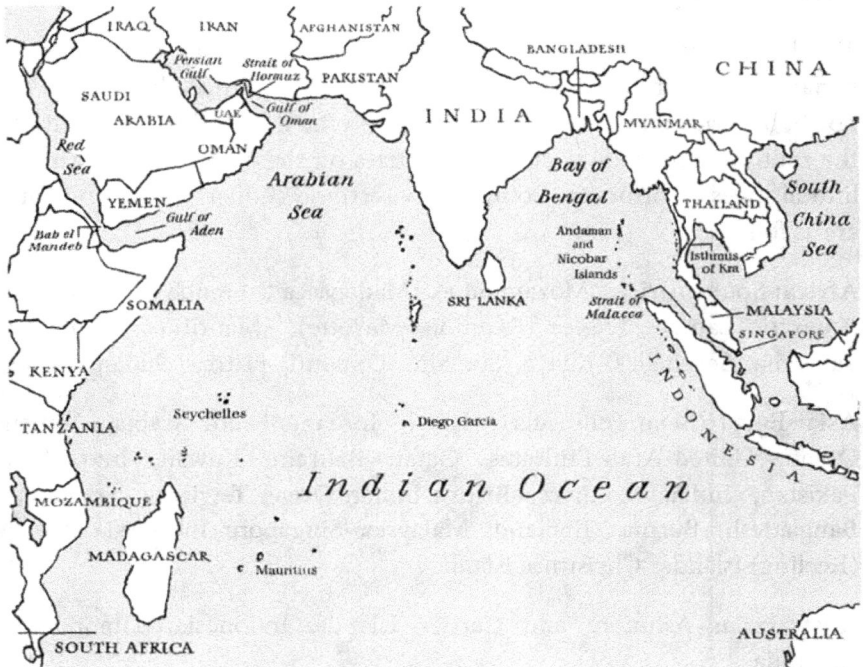

Figure caption: Map of the Indian Ocean

Source: http://www.foreignaffairs.com/files/images/Kaplan_Map_v2Small.jpg

Trade and Commerce

Maritime Trade

Since the days of Eudoxus of Cyzicus (circa 2nd–1st century BC), this massive expanse of water has been the major trade route for voracious trading countries from Europe as the ocean provides major sea routes connecting the Middle East, Africa, and East Asia with Europe, and later with America.[3] India and its neighbours have always been a favoured destination for adventurers and seafaring traders. European nobles, princes and kings have always found the spices, precious gems, fine silk cloth, and scented wood exotic, drawing repeated attempts to trade, control and even

---

3 http://en.wikipedia.org/wiki/Indian_Ocean#Trade

conquer this region. The ancient Tamil port of Poompuhar in present-day Tamil Nadu have seen trade with Malaysia, Arabia, Egypt, Rome and Greece.[4],[5] The items that were traded across the Indian Ocean were Silk and porcelain from China, Spices from southeast Asia, Pepper, gems, pearls, and cotton from India, Incense and horses from Arabia and southwest Asia, Gold, ivory, and slaves from east Africa.

The post Cold War period has witnessed the resurgence of Asia's cultural, political, and economic strength, which has manifested itself in varied events such as the rise of the Chinese economy, the growing influence of India's IT industry and the rise of Dubai as a global financial hub. The Indian Ocean is strategically located making it a major highway of the world's most pivotal shipping lanes. It is a critical waterway for international trade and commerce. This primary sea lane links the Orient with the Occident. This crucial Sea Line of Communication (SLOC) hosts approximately half of the world's containerized cargo and one third of its bulk cargo.[6],[7]

The Indian Ocean is focal in international trade that is facilitated by maritime transport[8]:

- Inter-state trade in the Indian Ocean region facilitates two-way logistics of cargo and within the subregions of the ocean.

- Inter-oceanic trade connecting the Pacific and the Atlantic, which has grown tremendously over the years with the economic boom in China, India and other developing economies in Asia.

---

4 http://mobiletoi.timesofindia.com/mobile.aspx?article=yes&pageid=30&sectid=edid=& edlabel=TOICH& mydateHid=24-06-2010&pubname=Times+of+India+-+Chennai&e dname=&articleid=Ar03000&publabel=TOI

5 http://drs.nio.org/drs/bitstream/2264/3087/2/New_Trend_Indian_Art_Archaeol_ 1992_2_493.pdf

6 Sakhuja V. (2003). 'Indian Ocean and the Safety of Sea Lines of Communications'. Institute for Defense Studies and Analyses, India., 18 July 2003. From www.idsa-india. org

7 Cozens, P. (date undetermined). 'Maritime Security in the Indian Ocean'. Overview prepared for a research project planned in cooperation with the South Asia Institute of the University of Heidelberg, Germany. From http://www.apri.ac.nz/maritime.html

8 http://www.mima.gov.my/mima/wp-content/themes/twentyeleven/cms/uploads/ presentation/93.Karachi%20_Mar07_.pdf

- The energy route connecting the world's major oilfields in Western Asia with major energy-importing countries in East Asia such as China, South Korea and Japan.

Being at the heart of Asian development, the Indian Ocean is today one of the busiest routes for the international mercantile marine. Almost half of the world's goods, tankers, container and other merchant ships navigate through these waters annually.[9]

Natural Resources

The ocean carries a particularly heavy traffic of petroleum and petroleum products from the oil fields of the Persian Gulf and Indonesia. In fact, the ocean itself is source to large reserves of hydrocarbons in the offshore areas of Saudi Arabia, Iran, India, and Western Australia. It is estimated that about 40% of the global offshore oil production comes from the Indian Ocean. The Indian government and select private oil companies and government bodies have been exploring for offshore petroleum and natural gas in the Arabian Sea and the Bay of Bengal, both of which have large reserves. International oil behemoths are off the northwestern coast of Australia, off the coast of Africa south of the Equator, and off the southwestern coast of Madagascar. It is worthy of note that India is the only country other than the countries of the Persian Gulf that produces commercial quantities of oil from offshore areas, with a large proportion of its total production coming from fields off the coast of Mumbai.[10] Australia's northwestern coast also produces some natural gas.

It is not just hydrocarbons, but other potentially valuable mineral resources, such as manganese, are found in abundance in the Indian Ocean region. Other minerals of potential commercial value are ilmenite (a mixture of iron and titanium oxide), tin, monazite (a rare earth), zircon, and chromite, all of which are found in near-shore sand bodies. Beach sands rich in heavy minerals, and offshore placer deposits are actively exploited by bordering countries, particularly India, Pakistan, South

---

9 Sakhuja V. (2003). 'Indian Ocean and the Safety of Sea Lines of Communications'. Institute for Defense Studies and Analyses, India., 18 July 2003. From www.idsa-india. org

10 http://www.britannica.com/EBchecked/topic/285876/Indian-Ocean/22775/Upwelling# toc 22780

Africa, Indonesia, Sri Lanka, and Thailand.[11]

Fishing Industry

Most of the Indian Ocean is within the tropical and temperate zones. The location, shallowness, tides and sunlight permeating into the waters enables the growth of numerous corals and other organisms capable of building, together with calcareous red algae, reefs and coral islands. These coralline structures shelter a thriving marine fauna consisting of sponges, worms, crabs, mollusks, sea urchins, brittle stars, starfish, and small but exceedingly brightly coloured reef fish.[12]

Tiny crustaceans that include more than 100 species of minute copepods form the bulk of fauna. The waters are richly populated by life forms ranging from small mollusks, jellyfish, and polyps, and other invertebrate animals ranging from single-celled radiolaria to large Portuguese man-of-war, the tentacles of which may reach a length of some 165 feet (50 metres). Squid thrive in large schools. Several species of flying fish, luminous anchovies, lantern fish, large and small tuna, sailfish, and various types of sharks have been the denizens of the deep. Sea turtles and large marine mammals, such as dugongs, toothed and baleen whales, dolphins, and seals also share the ocean with the fishes and crustaceans. The skies are ruled by the albatross and frigate birds. Several species of penguins populate the islands lying in the ocean's temperate zone and the Antarctic coast.[13]

People on an average obtain 16 percent of their animal protein from fish. As land-based food supplies reach their limits, fisheries will become even more vital to food supplies.[14] Despite great potential for commercial fishing, most of it is done by small-scale fishermen at shallow depths, while deep-sea resources, with the exception of tuna, remain poorly exploited.

The principal coastal species, such as shrimp, croakers, snappers,

---

11 http://en.wikipedia.org/wiki/Indian_Ocean#Trade

12 http://www.britannica.com/EBchecked/topic/285876/Indian-Ocean/22782/Biological-resources

13 http://www.britannica.com/EBchecked/topic/285876/Indian-Ocean/22782/Biological-resources

14 Anne Platt McGinn, Safeguarding the Health of the Oceans, Worldwatch paper 145, March 1999 p.20 http://worldwatch.org/worldwatchppr145Ocean health.pdf accessed July 18, 2005

skates, and grunts, are caught by littoral countries, while pelagic fish of higher value, including species of tuna and tuna-like species such as billfish that are found in tropical and subtropical waters, are exploited mostly by major fishing countries, such as Japan, South Korea and Russia. Shrimp is the most important commercial species for coastal countries. India accounts for the maximum catch. Lesser quantities of sardines, mackerel, and anchovies are also fished by the littoral states. As all the coastal nations lay sovereignty 'Exclusive Economic Zones' and the resources the zones contain, it has become possible for small states such as the Maldives to increase national income by 'selling' fishing rights in their zones to major fishing nations that have the capital and technology to exploit pelagic resources.[15]

Processed seafood is now a major export item of the littoral states. In addition, tourism has grown in importance on many of the islands.

Tourism Industry

Marine tourism is a major industry for all the Indian Ocean littoral states, especially for islands such as Mauritius, Madagascar, Comoros, Seychelles, Reunion, Zanzibar, Andaman & Nicobar, and Sri Lanka. The range of marine tourism includes scuba diving and snorkelling, wind surfing, fishing, observing marine life, all beach activities, sea kayaking, visits to fishing villages and lighthouses, maritime museums, sailing and motor yachting, maritime events, Arctic and Antarctic tourism, the cruise ship and ferry industry, and many more – all very dependent on a healthy marine environment.[16] Special coastal regions such as backwaters and mangroves contribute to ecotourism. Most of the coasts are covered with mangrove thickets with an animal life unique to the environment. These mangrove thickets stabilize the land along the water line, thus forming an important breeding and nursery ground for offshore species.

Militarization of the Indian Ocean

The Indian Ocean has been witness to military action in some form even since the days of the First World War. On the night of 22September 1914, the German light cruiser SMS Emden crept up to the port of the city of

15 http://www.britannica.com/EBchecked/topic/285876/Indian-Ocean/22782/Biological-resources

16 http://www.dlist-asclme.org/book/export/html/826

Madras (today Chennai) in South India and fired upon the city, specifically targeting the oil tanks near the port.[17] The Second World War brought a lot of action into this ocean. The Imperial Japanese Navy and Allied Navies conducted raids on supply ships and amphibious operations in Madagascar, Andamans and other islands.

During the Cold War, the militarization of this part of the world increased multiple folds. Western powers justified their presence in the Indian Ocean on the strength of traditional international maritime law.[18] The waters were the playing field for both the Super Powers in their cat-and-mouse game. Both the countries signed covert and overt military agreements with dominant states, such as Pakistan, Singapore, Malaysia, Australia, India and others, around the Indian Ocean region as a part of their global military alliance strategies. The growing militarization of these waters also stems from regional countries that maintain historic grievances, and even communal groups within these nations.

In the 1960s, when the United Kingdom vacated her Indian Ocean territories, The United States leased the tiny island of Diego Garcia. Though it began as a modest communications facility in 1973, the island is today a major US military base surveillance centre. The US military stores weapons here and uses the base for refuelling. The island is a critical link in the country's global network.

Today, militarization continues to expand due to the continuing importance of the Indian Ocean as a maritime trade route, as a source of natural resources, as a hub of many industrial activities and finally, as the region of tremendous economic growth. Ships of navies of all dominant seafaring nations frequent these waters. The Indian Ocean is today the operational zone of the Unites State's Fifth Fleet and Seventh Fleet that comprises of an Aircraft Carrier Battle Group (CVBG), an Amphibious Ready Group (ARG), surface combatants, submarines, maritime patrol and reconnaissance aircraft, and logistics ships.[19], [20] The US consists

---

17http://www.thehindu.com/news/cities/chennai/discovered-pictures-of-madras-after-emden-struck/article3804481.ece

18 VS Deshpande, "Indian Ocean as a Peace Zone Evolving the Legal Process", Indian Journal of International Law (New Delhi), vol. 14, No.2, April-June 1974, p166

19 http://www.globalsecurity.org/military/agency/navy/c5f.htm

20 http://www.globalsecurity.org/military/agency/navy/c7f.htm

of nuclear powered aircraft carriers (CVNs), nuclear powered ballistic powered submarines (SLBMs) armed with nuclear tipped warheads and nuclear powered attack submarines (SSNs).

The Russian navy also makes its presence felt in the ocean. Though it does not have a fleet stationed in these waters, its ships often visit ports in this ocean on friendly missions.[21]

Today, the Asian states of China and India are becoming economic giants with growing regional and global aspirations. To support their drive towards economic superstardom, they expand their influence their influence in and around the Indian Ocean region. To exercise their influence across the region and to enhance operational efficiency, China and India are establishing military and 'friendly' bases across the Indian Ocean. Not just that, both these states have also overtly stated their interest, rather the need, to 'nuclearize' their respective navies.

The People's Liberation Army Navy (PLAN) consists of nuclear powered ballistic missile submarines and nuclear powered attack submarines, such as[22]:

- Tang class (Type 096) - Rumoured to be in development for the PLAN

- Jin class (Type 094) - 3 in active service, 2 more under construction

- Xia class (Type 092) - 1 in active service

The Indian Navy had evinced interest in operating nuclear powered submarines since the 1980s. From 1988 to 1991, the Indian Navy operated 'INS Chakra' a Charlie-class nuclear powered submarine on lease from the Soviet Union. Since India went overtly went nuclear, its navy wanted to and built its modest nuclear arsenal, building and maintaining a fleet of nuclear powered submarines for delivery has always been a priority. This has today resulted in INS Arihant, India's first indigenously designed and built nuclear submarine. It also operates INS Chakra II, an Akula-class nuclear powered Hunter-Killer submarine on lease from Russia.[23]

---

21 http://news.xinhuanet.com/english/world/2013-09/18/c_132732854.htm

22http://en.wikipedia.org/wiki/People%27s_Liberation_Army_Navy_Submarine_Force#Nuclear-powered_ballistic_missile_submarines

23 http://www.ndtv.com/article/india/ins-chakra-top-10-must-know-facts-194179

Nuclearization of the Indian Ocean

While it may be important to deploy military strength across this region due to strategic and tactical requirements – as an effort on the war against global terrorism and to protect sea lanes against smuggling, human trafficking, gun running, and piracy, it also involves a growing number of nuclear powered naval vessels (surface and submarine) carrying nuclear weapons. This is a source of two major problems:

1. The presence of nuclear powered vessels ups the ante of adversaries, leading to deployment of more offensive platforms

2. A nuclear disaster in these waters will leave a catastrophic effect on the environment of the Indian Ocean region. It will definitely affect ocean based trade and industries such as fishery and marine tourism, thus affecting the economies of the littoral states, especially the islands and smaller states.

The second point is the primary concern of this article.

Nuclear Powered Naval Vessels

The age of nuclear powered vessels dawned during the 1950s. Admiral Hyman G. Rickover directed the design, development and production of nuclear marine propulsion plants in the 1940s. A prototype reactor was constructed and tested at the Naval Reactor Facility at the Idaho National Laboratory in 1953. The first nuclear-powered submarine, USS Nautilus, put to sea in 1955. The Soviets were not far behind. The Soviet Navy's first nuclear powered submarine was the November class K-3 "Leninskiy Komsomol", which was launched on July 4, 1958.

Since then, nuclear power has revolutionized the submarine, making it the true "underwater" vessel. It gave the submarine the ability to operate submerged at high speeds, comparable to those of surface vessels, for unlimited periods, dependent only on the endurance of its crew.[24] Surface ships such as aircraft carriers followed soon. Lloyd's Register shows about 200 nuclear reactors at sea, and that some 700 have been used at sea since the 1950s.[25]

---

24 "Nuclear Weapons at Sea". Bulletin of the Atomic Scientists: 48–49. September 1990

25   http://world-nuclear.org/info/Non-Power-Nuclear-Applications/Transport/Nuclear-Powered-Ships/

While the advantages of nuclear powered military vessels are widely popular thanks to the media, Hollywood and innumerable magazines, the potential dangers that nuclear power carries with it should not be overshadowed. History has shown is the potential dangers of a stricken nuclear powered ship. Military operations are a closely guarded secret. While national governments may selectively highlight a few positive outcomes from the use of military resources, negative issues are always kept under the tightest wrap.

List of Nuclear Accidents around the World

www.n-base.org.uk, the portal of N-Base Information Service, a UK based organization providing news and research on the UK nuclear industry, nuclear transports, waste production and management, and environmental discharges over the past 20 years, has listed 23 nuclear accidents from 1950 to 1993. The website states that as a result of the accidents involving US, Soviet, and Russian nuclear weapons or nuclear- armed ships and submarines "some 51 nuclear warheads were lost into sea. Also, seven nuclear reactors (5 Soviet and 2 US) from three Soviet and two US nuclear-powered submarines have been lost at sea due to accidents. Another 19 nuclear reactors from nuclear-powered vessels have been deliberately dumped at sea (18 Soviet and 1 US)."

It further emphasizes that the US Navy has "experienced" at least 380 nuclear weapons incidents – but the details are kept secret by the government. If this may have happened to the US and Russia, the question arises – wouldn't it have happened to other countries too? The site states, "The nuclear nations' operational arsenals contain over 21,000 nuclear weapons. Their militaries still retain hundreds of nuclear-armed launchers and nuclear-capable military units. The threat of a serious nuclear weapons accident has not disappeared with the end of the Cold War. This is particularly the case where the arms race remains the most active: at sea where nuclear-armed and nuclear-powered ballistic missile submarines still go on regular patrols at levels that have not changed much if at all from the height of the Cold War."[26] The experience of the US and the Soviet Union suggests not only are nuclear arsenals extraordinarily expensive, but they also come with serious safety, health, and environmental costs

Here is a list of accidents as provided in the website:

---

26 http://www.n-base.org.uk/public/report_links/air_sea_accidents.html

1. **11 April 1950**: Shortly after departing Kirtland Air Force Base (AFB) in New Mexico, a U.S. B-29 bomber carrying a nuclear bomb crashed into a mountain. The bomb was destroyed but its nuclear capsule with the fissile materials, which was also on board the aircraft, had not been inserted for safety reasons.

2. **10 March 1956**: A U.S. Air Force B-47 bomber carrying two capsules of nuclear materials for nuclear bombs, en route from MacDill AFB, Florida, to Europe, failed to meet its aerial refueling plane over the Mediterranean Sea. An extensive search failed to locate any traces of the missing aircraft or crew.

3. **27 July 1956**: During a routine deployment to England, a U.S. B-47 bomber skidded and slid off a runway at Lakenheath Royal Air Force (RAF) Base. The plane burst into flames and crashed into a nuclear bomb storage igloo in which there were three Mark 6 nuclear bombs. The bombs did not explode.

4. **18 August 1959**: A helicopter engine exploded on board the U.S. aircraft carrier USS Wasp (CVS-18) which was operating 250 miles off Norfolk, Virginia. As fires raged, the ship's crew prepared to flood the nuclear weapons magazine, but after more than two hours the fires were brought under control.

5. **4 June 1962**: A nuclear test device atop a U.S. Thor rocket booster fell into the Pacific Ocean near Johnston Island after the rocket had to be destroyed. The test was part of the U.S.'s first high altitude atmospheric nuclear test attempt.

6. **20 June 1962**: A second attempt to detonate a nuclear device in the atmosphere failed when a Thor booster was destroyed over Johnston Island. The nuclear device fell into the Pacific Ocean.

7. **5 December 1965**: While the U.S. aircraft carrier USS Ticonderoga (CVA-14) steamed en route from bombing operations off Vietnam to the U.S. Navy base at Yokosuka, Japan, an A-4E attack jet loaded with a B-43 thermonuclear bomb rolled off the Number 2 elevator, and sank in 16,000 feet of water. The aircraft carrier was positioned about 70 miles from the Ryuku Islands and about 200 miles east of Okinawa. The bomb, aircraft and pilot were not recovered.

8. **17 January 1966**: A collision occurred between a U.S. B-52 nuclear bomber and a KC-135 tanker aircraft while over the village of Palomares in southern Spain. The B-52 was on an airborne alert operation and carried four B-28 thermonuclear bombs. In the collision, the KC-135 exploded and caused the B-52 to break up, scattering wreckage over a 100 square mile area. One of the four nuclear bombs landed relatively intact, while the high explosives in two other bombs detonated upon impact with the ground scattering radioactive materials over the village and surrounding area. The fourth bomb fell into the sea and was recovered intact three months later after an extensive underwater search.

9. **21 January 1968**: A U.S. B-52G nuclear bomber crashed on the ice seven miles west of Thule Air Base in northern Greenland. The aircraft was on a airborne alert flight and carried four B-28 thermonuclear bombs. Upon impact with the ice the bomber exploded and all four nuclear bombs were destroyed, scattering radioactive materials over a large area.

10. **8-10 March 1968**: The K-219, a Soviet Golf II class (Project 629M) diesel-powered ballistic missile submarine armed with three nuclear SS-N-5 missiles, sank in the Pacific, about 750 miles northwest of the Island of Oahu, Hawaii. The submarine possibly also carried two nuclear torpedoes.

11. **27 May 1968**: The U.S. nuclear-powered submarine USS Scorpion (SSN-589) sank about 400 miles southwest of the Azores, killing all 99 men on board. The submarine was powered by one nuclear reactor and carried two nuclear-armed ASTOR torpedoes.

12. **12 April 1970**: The K-8, a Soviet November class (Project 627A) nuclear-powered attack submarine, sank in the Atlantic Ocean 300 miles northwest of Spain. The submarine was powered by two nuclear reactors and carried two nuclear torpedoes.

13. **29 November 1970**: A fire broke out in the stern of the U.S. Navy submarine tender USS Canopus (AS-34) while it was at the Holy Loch submarine base in Scotland. The tender carried several nuclear-armed missiles and two U.S. nuclear-powered ballistic missile submarines were moored alongside. It took four hours to

bring the fire under control and three men were killed.

14. **22 November 1975**: The U.S. aircraft carrier USS John F. Kennedy (CV-67) collided with the cruiser USS Belknap (CG-26) in rough seas at night during air exercises in the Mediterranean Sea off Sicily. The collision caused major fires and explosions, and the commander of Carrier Striking Force for the Sixth Fleet issued a "Broken Arrow" message -- at top secret communication about a nuclear weapons accident -- warning of a "high probability that nuclear weapons on the USS Belknap were involved in fire and explosions." Eventually, the nuclear weapons barely escaped destruction as the fire was contained just feet from the forward weapons magazine.

15. **16 April 1976**: The cruiser USS Albany (CG-10) experienced a nuclear weapons incident -- known as a "Dull Sword" -- when a TALOS anti-air missile's nuclear warhead was damaged.

16. **8 September 1977**: The K-171, a Soviet Delta I (Project 667B) nuclear-powered ballistic missile submarine, accidently jettisoned a nuclear warhead near Kamchatka in the Pacific Ocean after a build-up of pressure in a missile launch tube. After a search, the warhead was recovered.

17. **18-19 September 1980**: A fire and explosion in a U.S. Titan II missile silo near Little Rock, Arkansas, blew off the silo door and catapulted the missile's 9 megaton yield warhead into the air. It landed over a 1,000 feet from the silo, but it was only slightly damaged.

18. **9 April 1981**: The U.S. nuclear-powered ballistic missile submarine USS George Washington (SSBN-598) collided with a Japanese freighter in the East China Sea. The freighter sank and the submarine suffered slight damage to its sail. The submarine probably carried a total of 160 nuclear warheads on its 16 Poseidon C3 missiles.

19. **5 December 1981**: An A4-E Skyhawk attack jet of the aircraft carrier USS Ticonderoga, fell from the deck elevator and sank, with the pilot and one B43 thermonuclear bomb, into 16,000 feet of water. The ship was just 500 miles from mainland China. In

between the accident site and the Chinese mainland, however, lay miles of open ocean and one of the Pacific's most adamantly antinuclear nations, Japan.

20. **21 March 1984**: The U.S. aircraft carrier USS Kitty Hawk (CV-63) collided with a Soviet nuclear-powered Victor class (Project 671) attack submarine in the Sea of Japan. At the time of the collision, the USS Kitty Hawk is estimated to have carried several dozen nuclear weapons, and the submarine probably carried two nuclear torpedoes.

21. **6 October 1986**: The K-219, a Soviet Yankee class (Project 667A) nuclear-powered ballistic missile submarine armed with 16 SS-N-6 missiles (two warheads each) and probably also two nuclear torpedoes, sank 600 miles northeast of Bermuda. It was powered by two nuclear reactors and 34 nuclear warheads were estimated to be on board.

22. **7 April 1989**: The K-278 Komsomolets, the Soviet Mike class (Project 685) nuclear-powered attack submarine, sank off northern Norway following on board fires and explosions. The submarine was powered by one nuclear reactor and carried two nuclear torpedoes.

23. **27 September 1991**: A missile misfired aboard a Soviet Typhoon class (Project 941) nuclear-powered ballistic missile submarine in the White Sea during a training exercise. Fortunately, the submarine was able to return to base, but the accident could have sunk the submarine, along with its two nuclear reactors and nuclear-armed missiles and torpedoes.

24. **20 March 1993**: A Russian Delta III class (Project 667BDR) nuclear-powered ballistic missile submarine is struck by the U.S. nuclear-powered attack submarine USS Grayling (SSN-646) while operating in the Barents Sea close to the Kola Peninsula. The submarine suffered slight damage and was able to return to base, but the collision could have sunk the Delta submarine including its 16 SS-N-18 nuclear armed missiles.

There are many more such incidents that should be remembered, not just to give us a fright, but to drive home the point that nuclear power is a double-edged weapon and it comes at a cost.

According to David E. Kaplan, a staff writer at the Center for Investigative Reporting in San Francisco, and is editor of the Center's recent book, Nuclear California (CiRl Greenpeace, 1982)[27], a Soviet book titled 'Proyektirovanive Atomnykh Podvodnykh Lodok' ("Design of Nuclear Sub-marines") released in 1968 contained information on US nuclear submarine accidents. They cited ten serious incidents that the US navy denied - two of the accidents involved release of radiation in levels that "significantly exceeded permissible limits".[28]

One of naval history's most infamous disasters, the sinking of the submarine USS Thresher, was apparently due to an accident directly involving the submarine's nuclear reactor. According to the US Navy's official account, the submarine's reactor and fuel survived the immediate implosion of the ship and the corrosive action of seawater.

However, not all 'nuclear' related incidents have to be so dramatic to be environmentally catastrophic. Nuclear navies' most frequent type of accident are often the mistaken release of primary coolant, the pressurized water used to carry heat away from the reactor core, into the sea or river. In October-November 1975, the USS Proteus, a disabled submarine tender, discharged highly radioactive amounts of primary coolant water into Guam's Apra Harbour. In May 1968, Japanese scientists who were monitoring radiation in the sea water adjacent to the submarine USS Swordfish discovered levels up to twenty times higher than normal background. Their study led them to the conclusion that the high radiation levels were due to the discharge of coolant into the Harbour. Their study caused an international furore. The Japanese government warned the United States that nuclear ships could no longer call at Japanese ports unless safety was guaranteed.

This scarily long list of international nuclear accidents wouldn't be complete without mentioning the tragic loss of the Russian Oscar II class nuclear powered submarine Kursk, which sank on 12 August 2000 in the Barents Sea. However, the submarine's two nuclear reactors were adequately encased and mounted; they were automatically shut down and thus, prevented a nuclear meltdown or contamination.

---

27 http://oc.itgo.com/kitsap/nuclear/clymer.htm

28 Ibid

Admiral Hyman George Rickover, four-star admiral of the United States Navy who directed the original development of naval nuclear propulsion and controlled its operations for three decades as director of Naval Reactors, admitted that his nuclear plants are not foolproof. He said that the "whole reactor game hangs on a much more slender thread than most people are aware. All we have to have is one good accident in the United States and it might set the game back for a generation."[29]

Can we say that it is providence that has helped in keeping at bay a potential nuclear accident in our neighbourhood? We have been lucky this far, but with the growing number of naval traffic, can we continue to count our luck? The Indian Ocean region, as stated earlier, is a fragile zone populated by states that are now beginning to see economic progress. Any unforeseen nuclear incident in this region spells catastrophic impact on the littoral states and the environment. Till date, there have been not nuclear accidents in the Indian Ocean despite the presence of three nuclear states and the presence of many nuclear powered and armed naval combatants.

Environmental Issues in the Case of a Nuclear Disaster in the Indian Ocean Region

Despite robust processes, secure technologies and top most priority given to nuclear safety on nuclear powered military vessels, there is one factor that is not fool-proof: human fallibility. The influence of human error cannot be overstated, especially in naval forces that are constantly in the state of alert and are bombarded with information from a proliferation of sensors, all the while attempting to monitor a host of perceived "enemies." In his article titled 'Nuclear Subs: Environmental Hazard' in the Peace Magazine, author David Kraft states, "The only conclusion one can draw from the record is that accidents will happen, and no amount of engineering or mechanical fixes will eliminate the failures that accompany the operation of complex machinery. It is clear that being part of a nuclear navy does not exempt one from any of the laws, physical or behavioral, that govern other nautical pursuits."[30]

All the nuclear navies of the world, now including the Indian Navy, routinely operate warships and submarines with nuclear weapons around the world.

29 http://en.wikipedia.org/wiki/Admiral_Rickover

30 http://peacemagazine.org/archive/v05n3p18.htm

When an accident does happen, it would just a matter of time before contaminated hull and reactors get released into the surrounding marine environment. David's article states that The International London Dumping Convention of 1983 had outlawed the disposal of even low and intermediate levels of radioactive waste at sea due to their serious impact on marine ecology and fisheries. If this be the case, image the impact of high level radioactive wastes in large quantities, such as those contained in nuclear submarine reactors!

The Indian Ocean has strong currents and dynamic thermal layers. The rapid exchange of waters, across regions and across levels would easy spread any radioactive contamination from a submarine's wreck to the surface and quickly into the food chain.

The typical marine food chain starts with phytoplankton – the microscopic plants that account for as much photosynthesis in sea as plants on land. These micro-organisms absorb radioactive contaminants from the ocean. As the phytoplankton are eaten by larger zooplanktons, small fish, and larger marine animals, such as tuna, sharks, dolphins, whales and other members up the food chain, some of the contaminants end up in faecal pellets or other detrital particles that settle to the seafloor. These particles accumulate in sediments, and some radioisotopes contained within them may be remobilized back into the overlying waters through microbial and chemical processes.[31] Multiple research from around the world, especially one conducted in the Irish, Kara and Barents Seas, as well as in the Pacific Ocean, reveal that radioactive materials do move along with ocean currents and thus, do get deposited in marine sediments. They also move up the marine food cycle. Elizabeth Grossman, in her April 2011 article 'Radioactivity in the Ocean: Diluted, But Far from Harmless' states, "In the Irish Sea – where the British Nuclear Fuels plant at Sellafield in the northwestern United Kingdom released radioactive material over many decades, beginning in the 1950s – studies have found radioactive caesium and plutonium concentrating significantly in seals and porpoises that ate contaminated fish. Other studies have shown that radioactive material from Sellafield and from the nuclear reprocessing plant at Cap de la Hague in France have been transported to the North Atlantic and Arctic Oceans. A study published in 2003 found that a substantial part of the world's

---

31 http://www.whoi.edu/oceanus/feature/how-is-fukushimas-fallout-affecting-marine-life

radioactive contamination is in the marine environment."[32] This could have disastrous consequences for the small and large scale fishing industry of the Indian Ocean.

Let's take a look at tourism. The impact of a nuclear disaster at one end of the ocean may not directly impact tourism in regions at the other end. For example a radiation leakage in the western Indian Ocean may not affect tourism in Australia. However, it will make a dent in earnings. Military accidents of such nature are covered in deep secrecy. Their occurrence would, in all probability, not be disclosed. However the impact of radiation would be great and recourse, if at all any, would be minimal as the economies of most states are just beginning to develop.

There are other factors too that would play a major role in destruction of the industry. The Media is probably the most powerful. News of a major nuclear accident can cripple the tourism industry of any island nation as this specific industry is heavily dependent on its brand. The relatively new phenomenon of Social Media takes news to a different level – making it more personal and giving it an emotional appeal.

To top this, none of the Indian Ocean states either have a robust, proven nuclear disaster contingency plan for relief in its territorial waters or the technological prowess to assist in internal waters.

So how can the Indian Ocean states secure their neighbourhood? Is the Indian Ocean truly a 'Zone of Peace'? This is a serious question that all Indian Ocean member states have to ponder. The impact of a nuclear accident in the Indian Ocean will create multiple ripples across this pond – ripples that would hit growing economies adversely.

---

32 http://e360.yale.edu/feature/radioactivity_in_the_ocean_diluted_but_far_from_harm less/ 2391/

XVI

CONCLUSION

The traditional sense of security has given way to a far widening of the term. Previously only physical security of the state was the object of study. But now the entire focus has shifted to the level of the people and hence other issues like economy, food, social and environmental security have gained importance. Now security is for all and forever. Soldiers, tanks, bombs and missiles can no longer ensure complete security. A strong nation today needs a strong economy built on the foundation of an equitable resource base including soil, water, forest and all. Degradation or fall in the quality of the resource base will give rise to an unstable economy, fragile social fabric and weak political structure. Prolonged deprivation of particular sections can lead to disorder, insurrection within and between countries.

Thus the fact that environmental security would come to redefine our sense of safety and well being can not be over emphasised. The book looks specifically at the security aspect of environmental degradation using India as a case in point. Degradation or lowering of the quality of available resources is a serious issue. Due to exploitation and abuse of resources, water has become polluted often unusable. Precious water bodies have been filled to help urbanisation and expansion of cities. The tapping of drinkable water has lowered the water table and only the strict implementation of the rainwater harvesting technique has warded off severe water shortages in urban areas. The fertility and productivity of land has been affected due to the dumping of wastes, over use of pesticides and fertilisers and massive deforestation. Industrialisation has meant not only the production of new goods but also the generation of huge amounts of waste often dangerous to humans and other life around us. The chemicals and noxious gases that are the by products of factory processes mix with air, are let untreated, directly into waterways and even dumped on land. This has polluted the air we breathe causing health problems and also greatly affected our quality of life. Effluents from industries have a detrimental effect on aquatic life too. Leaching of land occurs often making it fallow. In the effort of meeting India's food demand more and more land is brought under cultivation destroying forests. It also has meant the excessive use of artificial fertilisers to speed up the growth cycles of crops and make them pest-resistant. Though we have attained self sufficiency in food production, our distribution network in woeful and hence many grow hungry despite bumper harvests. Much of India's forests have been cut down in the name of development of infrastructure like roads and railways. Depleted forests mean less rain, increased soil erosion and a cycle of destruction resulting in more and more loss. Resource scarcity will be a major challenge in the coming years and due to its impact on the everyday life of millions it could easily become a security issue.

The extensive havoc wreaked on the environment due to anthropological interference in the form of pollution, exploitation and over use can be felt from the drastic changes in weather patterns and resource availability all over the country. Thus, mitigating the effects of pollution through people's participation, increasing stakeholder awareness, enactment of strong laws and even stronger implementation procedures with regard to resource utilisation and undertaking a continuous search for better and sustainable alternatives to polluting or over exploited resources can alone improve the situation for countries like India.

The aspect of war, environment interface has been dealt with in depth. The process of planning and executing wars affects the environment. This is because of the use of ammunition that now has more and more fire power. Also, the environment impacts on war making and fighting. In fact, many wars have been fought throughout human history due to such effects on the environment. Lessons from global experiences could inform war preparedness of countries like India. India's strategic environment involves the continuous threat to fragile ecological areas like the Siachen glacier. The cold heights of the Siachen glaciers are being guarded all year through. This not only places a burden on the exchequer but has detrimental effect on the untouched surroundings. Removal of waste from these inaccessible areas is a daunting task. Accumulating waste is both a health and an environmental hazard.

Many of the problems that result in environmental degradation pervade the entire South Asian region calling for a common understanding and approach to these issues.

War as both the cause and effect of environmental degradation must be looked into more carefully. The targeting of economic assets and burning up of oil wells and disruption of water supplies are strategies of war but they continue to impact upon the environment much after the last gun has fallen silent in the battle field. Technology has proved to be both a boon and bane.

Terrorist attacks on installations like power plants, dams, or the use of chemical or biological weapons could also spell environmental disaster. Lessons, from the world over, need to be imbibed to frame stricter laws. However, there is a need to ensure effective implementation in the Indian context. The South Asian region could counter common problems with uniform legal measures. Greater attention needs to be focused on India's environment and problems tackled with caution to strengthen India's national security all around.

Securitising the environment is yet another area of interest. The phenomenon of climate change has been analysed deeply to highlight how scarcity and inequitable utilisation of available resources could lead to instability within the country and outside due to discontent and mass displacement of populace. The manner in which climate change affects defence preparedness has also been emphasised.

Two case studies presented as subsequent chapters seek to highlight the transborder effect of environmental degradation. The fishing industry has been severely affected due to marine pollution that has destroyed vital breeding areas like the coral reefs, and oil spills accidental or otherwise that have affected marine life. Loss of special ecological areas like mangroves and other developmental activities have also hampered fishing. It is hence suggested that a regional maritime law be enacted to deal with issues.

The political issue of occupation of Tibet by China has an environmental side too. This has been amply brought out in one of the chapters. The Tibetan mountains are the origin of most rivers of the South Asian region. The subjugation of the political aspirations of the Tibetan people has been compounded by systematic destruction of pristine ecological surroundings. In the name of development, China plans to develop a hydro electric project right near India's border and build roads that would forever destroy the Tibetan environment. This would not only severely degrade Tibet's environment but also endanger the livelihood of millions of South Asians. It might even result in conflict between India and China.

As a country with a large coastline India faces a daunting challenge by way of a polluted marine environment. As a sea faring economy, India needs to keep its waters safe and clean. Massive influx of population to coastal cities is not only burdening the land environment but also affecting the seas. The direct dumping of wastes into the sea has polluted the coasts. Industrialisation has also meant untreated effluents that are toxic to both human and marine life ending up in our waters. Fragile and unique marine ecosystems like coral reefs have been extensively depleted. Pollution has also affected the breeding patterns of several fish and other marine creatures. Release of ballast water from ships, accidental spillage of oil into the oceans and ship breaking is creating havoc with the marine environment. As India's energy dependency increases and trade improves, the importance of the sea lanes is set to accentuate. Therefore, special attention to restore coral reefs, prevent or at least treat effluents that are let into the sea and increase vigilance to monitor the movement of oil laden tankers and other ships with 'dangerous cargo' in Indian waters must assume increased urgency.

The non traditional area of environment has come under renewed focus because of the global trends of climate change and adverse human impact on our environment. With availability, quality and distribution of resources becoming contentious, environmental security of countries like India are important. Scarcity of resources most importantly water is already leading to tension within the country. If sharing of resources with other countries becomes problematic then it could escalate to a conflict. Protection and nurturing of the environment should thus be seen as a principal need not only for holistic development but also for India's national security objectives.

www.ingramcontent.com/pod-product-compliance
Lightning Source LLC
Chambersburg PA
CBHW071847270326
41929CB00013B/2128